THE
CHRISTIAN
FAITH

A LUTHERAN EXPOSITION

THE CHRISTIAN FAITH

Robert Kolb

A Lutheran Exposition

CONCORDIA PUBLISHING HOUSE • SAINT LOUIS

Concordia
Publishing House

Copyright © 1993 Concordia Publishing House
3558 S. Jefferson Avenue
St. Louis, MO 63118-3968

Unless otherwise indicated, Scripture quotations are taken from the HOLY BIBLE,
NEW INTERNATIONAL VERSION®. NIV®. Copyright © 1973, 1978, 1984 by Inter-
national Bible Society. Used by permission of Zondervan Publishing House.
All rights reserved.

Scripture references marked RSV are taken from the Revised Standard Version
of the Bible, copyrighted 1946, 1952, © 1971, 1973. Used by permission.

Scripture references marked KJV are taken from the King James or Authorized
Version of the Bible.

Manufactured in the United States of America

9 10 11 12 13 14 15 16 17 18   20 19 18 17 16 15 14 13 12 11

Contents

Chapter I
Our Faith and the Faith

"In the beginning was the Word" (John 1:1). "And God said, 'Let there be . . . ' " and all that exists came into being—by the power of his Word (Gen. 1:3, 6, 9, 11, 14, 20, 24). "How, then, can they call on the one they have not believed in? And how can they believe in the one of whom they have not heard? And how can they hear without someone preaching to them? . . . As it is written, 'How beautiful are the feet of those who bring good news!' " (Rom. 10:14–15).

God likes to talk. He began the world by talking it into existence. When his human creatures doubted his Word and fled from his presence, he came to call them back to himself (Gen. 3:9). To reclaim and restore his people, God has placed his power in human language: the good news that draws people to trust in him. His good news is the power he uses to bring people to salvation (Rom. 1:16). God's good news for his fallen human creatures restores them to that relationship within his grace and favor for which he designed them in Eden. This message of forgiveness and new life restores these fallen creatures to a full and perfect relationship with him— from his perspective. That righteousness is ours because we are made to grasp its word of promise in faith (Rom. 1:17).

We Live by Faith

This book is entitled *The Christian Faith*. We use the word *faith* in two different senses. *Faith* can refer to the object of our trust— what we believe in. *Faith* also refers to the human act of believing, of trusting, of placing our confidence in and depending on someone or something. Faith—in the second sense—is the very core of our being. It is our basic grasp on reality. If faith is misplaced, then all of life is skewed. If faith is misdirected toward one of God's creatures, rather than being directed toward our Creator himself, then life goes sour and spoils.

Faith—in the sense of the trust that provides the core orientation for our lives—is among the most important words in the human language. The contemporary Harvard psychologist Erik Erikson has affirmed what the biblical writers told God's people centuries ago. He has devised an eight-stage basis for analyzing human development, the course of human life. The first and fundamental stage of human existence (in the years between birth and age two), according to Erikson, revolves around trust or faith. This fundamental orientation largely determines the way in which individuals view the world. Learning to trust—or to mistrust—frees or binds us at all subsequent stages of our development. Learning to trust—or learning not to trust—the world around us determines much of our personality and the course of our life, Erikson insists.[1]

We trust first of all our mother and then our father, Erikson observes, because we are first of all children, infants, dependent creatures. Born into this world, we are at the mercy of those around us. They become objects on which we depend. How they perform as objects of our dependence determines how we view ourselves—and everyone and everything around us.

From those whom we trust we gain a sense of identity, security, and meaning. Without a sense of who we are, without a sense that we are safe and that we will continue to exist, without a sense that our lives have purpose and worth, we die. People wither when they have little or no sense of identity, security, and meaning. Being unsure about our identity, our security, and the meaning of our lives takes a tremendous physiological toll—to say nothing of the psychological damage such uncertainty inflicts upon us. We cannot survive without a sense of our ultimate identity, security, and meaning.

We Find Identity, Security, and Meaning in Our God(s)

In his explanation of the first commandment in the Large Catechism, Luther defines the word *g-o-d* in terms of trust: "A god is that to which we look for all good and in which we find refuge in every time of need. To have a god is nothing else than to trust and believe him with our whole heart. ... That to which your heart clings and entrusts itself is, I say, really your God."[2] According to

Luther everyone has a god, for everyone needs to depend ultimately on someone or something—or several persons and things for identity, security, and meaning. False gods abound. Trusting false gods is the root of all disruption in human life, that is, of all sin. But no one can exist for long without a god or two.

God has fashioned his human creatures to find some identity, security, and meaning in other persons and places than in himself. God has so structured human life that we find secondary levels of identity, security, and meaning in family members, in our work, in our accomplishments in the community, and in our service in our congregations. Behind such secondary sources of identity, security, and meaning, however, lies what ultimately gives us our "name," our sense of who we are. Behind these secondary sources of security and meaning lies what ultimately gives us haven from life's storms and what affirms that our persons and actions are ultimately worthwhile. That primary source of identity, security, and meaning is our god.

We can easily pervert what God has given us as secondary sources of identity, security, and meaning into gods. My wife is a wonderful gift of God. Much of my identity is wrapped up in being her husband. But I can become an idolater in my marriage. I can regard her as my ultimate source of identity. When I do so, I put us both in prison. I imprison her in my false set of expectations for her, which she cannot possibly meet. She is a fine wife; as a god she has her inadequacies. And I imprison myself in her inability to meet my expectations for a god. I inflict suffering on both of us through impossible expectations when I worship her instead of cherish her as a gift of God.

My occupation may become an idol in a similar fashion. Our jobs are gifts of God, avenues of service to other people and to the whole of his creation. We get some sense of identity from them. At a party, when we meet someone, we often identify ourselves by our occupation and place of employment. But when we cannot feel secure apart from knowing that we will never be fired, or when our life's sense of worth depends on getting a promotion or a raise, then we have turned God's good gift into an idol.

We all have many sources of identity, security, and meaning. We all have systems that offer some kind of promises for our lives from these sources, these gods. Systems of establishing our ultimate sense of identity, security, and meaning differ from idolater to idolater, but these systems all are objects of the trust that is at the very core of our beings. We put faith in our systems of establishing identity, security, and meaning, and these systems are called faith systems, belief systems. They can be called "the faith."

Faith Takes Form in the Word and Our Words

Faith rests upon someone or something. The Christian faith rests upon the person of our God, who has revealed himself as Jesus of Nazareth. Our faith rests upon who he is and upon what he has said to us. We have his revelation of who he is and his message for us in the Holy Scriptures. He gives our lives meaning and a sense of security. He has established our identities anew by planting his mark, the cross, on our heads and on our hearts. He gives this new existence reality as he sustains us with his Word of promise. He is the only source of our ultimate identity, security, and meaning.

Believers and Disciples

So we are people of faith, believers. This very term reminds us that we are dependent upon the object of faith. Some people distinguish the term *believer* from the term *disciple. Disciple* means simply "one who follows Christ and learns from him." The words in their biblical sense can be used interchangeably. Some contemporary Christians, however, try to distinguish those who excel at the performance of certain good works (disciples) from those who are "merely" church members (believers). This is not a biblical distinction. What we do as Christians is always secondary to, and a result of, who we are as children of God. Our actions flow from our attitude, an attitude of trust in Jesus Christ. To try to establish our ultimate identity upon what we do, rather than upon what God has done for us, always ends up in idolatry. We are first of all believers even as we follow Christ in our actions. There is nothing wrong with the term *disciple,* but disciples are first and foremost believers.

Believers are children of God. We do not create the objects of our faith. As earthly children our mothers are there—simply there— to be objects of faith. Our fathers pick us up so that we can learn to feel safe in their arms. Faith cannot exist unless its object elicits it. Thus, faith is not a good work over which we can exercise control. Faith is a gift from its object. It is also important to note that this trust is more than mere belief (as if there could be an indifferent acknowledgement of a God who loves us to death). Trust is more than intellectual assent. This trust grabs all of life; it permeates all decision-making for daily living.

God makes that happen by talking to us, even as our earthly parents shape our lives through their words. He speaks to us. He gives us his Word, a word of promise, and we respond with trust. We trust in him first of all because we hear him. He teaches us who he is and who we are and what his world is.

Doctrine: Its Content and Its Conveying

Teaching is a word like *faith*. It has two meanings. It is both the object, or content, that is taught, and it is the action of teaching. When I speak of my "teaching," I can be referring to what I want you to learn, or I can be referring to the way in which I convey what I want you to learn. As a matter of fact, you cannot have one without the other. Content and the conveying of content are inseparable. Good content will not be learned if it is poorly conveyed. The most skillful conveying of wrong content does no good.

The Latin word for teaching is *doctrina*. From it we get the word *doctrine*. Christian doctrine is simply the teaching of the Word of God. According to Luther and Philip Melanchthon, his colleague at the University of Wittenberg in the early sixteenth century, *doctrina* was a "verbal noun." That means that pure doctrine or true doctrine is not only the correct content of the Scripture, but it is that content conveyed effectively into the lives of the hearers of God's Word.[3] C. F. W. Walther, the first president of the Lutheran Church—Missouri Synod, said it this way in his theses on Law and Gospel: "Only he is a pure teacher who not only presents all articles of faith in accordance with Scripture but also correctly distinguishes between Law and Gospel."[4] Walther was saying that it is not enough to repeat biblical truths accurately. They must also be applied to the specific situation, to the specific needs, of our hearers. Proper biblical teaching bridges the gap between God's Word and the sinner who needs to hear it. This teaching aims not at mastery of information but at forming a friendship. This teaching of the biblical message intro-

11

duces two friends to each other: our God and another human creature. Teaching the content of Scripture forms relationships.

As a matter of fact, one of the Latin words for "priest" comes from two words that mean "bridge-builder." The priests of God, all believers, are called to be teachers of God's Word. They build the bridge between God, as he speaks his Word in Scripture, and the lives of those around them. God's priests connect one another to God and to each other.

For sixteenth-century Lutherans, *doctrine* was used generally in the singular. They seldom spoke of doctrines in the plural. There is one biblical teaching. The content of the Scripture is a unit. These Lutherans four hundred years ago recognized, however, that human creatures ask a variety of questions regarding the things of God. As believers formulate answers to these individual questions, they are using parts of the one doctrine, or teaching, of God in the Scriptures. We label these individual answers "doctrines." Luther and his contemporaries had two terms for what we call doctrines, in the plural. In writing confessions, such as the Augsburg Confession, these Lutherans divided biblical teaching into "articles of faith;" in writing textbooks on Christian teaching they divided the doctrine of the Scripture into "topics." The number of topics or articles of faith could vary from time to time, depending on what questions society raised for the church to answer. Certain topics are always going to be treated by believers as they teach the faith to others. Other topics may be given greater or lesser emphasis depending on the situation. Sixteenth-century Lutherans did not give extensive attention to the topic of Scripture in their confessions because all people in their Christian world agreed to a large extent on the nature of the Scriptures. They gave extensive attention to the topic of how the sinner becomes righteous in God's sight because there was substantial disagreement on that topic.

We might note that some theologians emphasize the distinction between proclamation, or *kērygma* in Greek, and teaching, or *didachē* in Greek. Within this distinction "doctrine" can be both proclaimed and taught. Proclamation confronts people with the Word of God and is aimed at inviting and drawing them into trusting God. It is God's direct address to us: "I am your God. You are my people." Teaching follows up with a broadening of understanding of what God is saying to us. It is third person discourse: it describes God and us. The distinction is important to recognize, but it is harder to draw precisely. Proclamation involves teaching, and teaching the Word of God can never be simply dry discussion and description of some object. Teaching the Word of God always grabs us at the heart. Teaching confronts and invites and draws us into trusting this word from our God.

The church formalizes the teaching or doctrine of Scripture in "dogmas." "Dogmas" may be formulated to convey what must be taught simply as a part of the ongoing life of the church. Often they are formulated because of the challenge to the biblical truth raised by those inside or outside the church who oppose Scriptural teaching. Those who raise such challenges inside the church are called "heretics," those who cause divisions among God's people. Heresy often begins as a well-intentioned attempt to bridge the gap between the biblical message and the culture. Such attempts become heretical when they abandon the message of the biblical writers to incorporate the deceptions of this world into the church's preaching. Believers are always faced with the temptation to do so as they try to make the teaching of Scripture clear to their own cultures. Therefore, the whole life of the teacher of the church must be a life of reexamination and repentance.

The Shape of Christian Teaching

Some people define biblical teaching as a series of topics. Like pearls on a string, these topics are all roughly of equal importance for them. If we conceive of doctrine in this way, we could say that losing any one pearl has about the same effect on the whole of biblical teaching as losing any other pearl. Some people could say that you dare not lose any pearl if you are to be dressed for the host of the heavenly banquet. Others could say that as long as you have a pearl or two left on the string, you are ready to be received at his table.

Others conceive of biblical teaching as a wheel, with a hub and spokes and a rim. They suggest that wheels cannot exist without hub and rim and some spokes, but other spokes may be broken without immobilizing the wheel.

Neither of these metaphors adequately describes the nature of biblical teaching. It is better to compare the doctrine of the Scripture

13

to a human body. The body of doctrine cannot exist if Christ the head is decapitated. It dies without the heart of our understanding of how we become right with God pumping away—although the heart, the doctrine of justification, may be partially diseased and still pump, it is true. This was evident in the medieval church, where preachers put a high but false premium on good works and still pointed people to Christ's saving blood. We see this in contemporary Christians who emphasize the contribution of our own personal decision in coming to Christ and still try to cultivate trust in his grace.

If an arm, the doctrine of Baptism, for example, is severed, the body may be able to survive. But it may hemorrhage and die. If the leg of the doctrine of the church becomes paralyzed, the body may survive, but it will be crippled at best, and it may fall down in a heap and crack the head, too.

So the question, "How much doctrine must be pure if one is to remain a Christian?" is simply a wrong kind of question. The whole of our conveying of biblical teaching needs to be accurate and on target—both because believers need to know what God wants us to know and because God's Word is true. Nonetheless, sinful doctrinal error does not always break our relationship with the Lord even though it makes it more tenuous.

North Americans often are accused of not being interested in what is true, only in "what works." Relativism regarding great truths is said to govern human thinking in our culture. This may seem to be true, but in fact people are indifferent to what is true and false only in those areas of life that do not seem important to them. When it comes to what matters most, everyone wants to know the truth. Whether it is how to fix the appliance or how to find peace in the heart, everyone longs to know what is right; everyone strives to learn the truth. When we form a relationship with another person, we want to know the truth about that person.

We teach the biblical message in order to create a relationship between God and our hearer. That relationship depends on expressing God's love in his Word. Our accuracy in our teaching can become a concern of self-justification; we may be striving to convey the biblical message accurately enough to earn God's love. That is wrong. On the other hand, we will always be properly concerned that our teaching accurately reflects what the biblical writers wrote, for therein lies God's Word of love for those around us. In teaching his Word faithfully, we will serve as faithful instruments in establishing the relationship of the loving Creator and the dependent creature who needs to know God's love and forgiveness. But this accuracy is never an end in itself. It is God's means of forming a relationship with his children.

Presuppositions Frame and Shape our Teaching

As we think about our own teaching of the specific topics of the biblical message, we need to recognize that we always teach these topics on the basis of certain presuppositions. We think within a conceptual framework. This conceptual framework or set of presuppositions guides the way in which we understand and apply specific topics. This conceptual framework expresses our basic view of reality. It shapes the way we establish what questions about life are important, what answers about reality we need to have.

Two examples may help explain. In the sixteenth century Lutherans fought over what we call "synergism," the concept that the human will must cooperate, or work together, with God's grace in converting the sinner into a believer. Both groups of Lutherans insisted that God saves sinners by his grace alone. One group, however, said that it only makes sense that when God gives his free gift, the human recipient must turn to pick it up. The warmth of the sun is free, they said, but you yourself have to decide to go out in the sun to receive that warmth. The other group believed that God bestows the gift of turning only to him. They taught that our wills are turned to him by his gracious directing, not by our own decision.

The two sides talked past each other for years because they did not address the matter at the level of presupposition or conceptual framework. The first group presumed that the adult sinner is also an adult in relationship to God. Adults must reach out to receive a gift that is offered. The other side believed that to enter the kingdom of God you must become like a tiny infant (Matt. 18:3). They taught that God lifts the one whom he is about to make his child into his own arms—because the sinner is dead in trespasses and sins.

The first group, presupposing an adult model for understanding the role of the human creature in conversion, employed a conceptual framework that did not affirm the absolute dependence of the creature upon the Creator. The latter group presupposed that sinners are dead in their ability to turn to God and that they must be like babies in conversion, which the Bible labels "new birth." These theologians began by presupposing that human beings are dependent creatures of God.

A second example: In the dispute over the real presence of Christ's body and blood in the Lord's Supper, Lutherans and Calvinists debated the definition of how Christ was present. Some of Calvin's followers were willing to concede that Christ was spiritually present in the Lord's Supper, but they rejected the Lutheran teaching that his human body and blood are also present in the bread and wine. Calvin had been influenced by the revival of the thought of ancient Greek philosophers, above all Plato. They believed that the material and the spiritual were opposite and could not be brought together. Calvin's followers presupposed that, in their phrase, "the finite (or material) is not capable of conveying the infinite (or spiritual)."

The Lutherans had been influenced to a greater degree by Hebrew thought, which divides the Creator from the created—whether material creation or spiritual creation—rather than the seen from the unseen. They therefore could believe that the Creator is able to use the material creation and the spiritual creation equally, as he was so minded. They did not believe it impossible at all for the infinite (the power of God) to use the finite (material elements) to convey God's forgiving power. Both Lutherans and Calvinists believed in the presence of Christ in the Sacrament of the Altar. Calvinists could not interpret the Words of Institution literally, however, because of their conceptual framework, their basic view of reality.

A conceptual framework is always influenced by the culture in which Christians live. But we must always strive to discipline our view of reality, which is inevitably in part a product of our culture, by the presuppositions the biblical writers have laid down for us. In the Scriptures alone we receive the bedrock of our view of reality. Whatever superstructure culture may bestow on us for viewing the world around us, beneath our culture's views of reality must lie the mind of Christ. What this means is that, within different cultural contexts, Christians may believe the world is flat or that it is round, but beneath such a view of reality must lie the biblical view that God created the universe and all that is in it. God's Word alone sets in place the fundamental relationships that make up our sense of reality: our views of the relationship between the human creature and God, and the relationships among human creatures themselves.

We Presume a Creator God

Lutheran theology presupposes that there is a Creator God and that we are creatures. You may say, "Well, of course; everyone believes that." But basic instincts cultivated by our contemporary North American culture deny that we are dependent creatures, totally dependent on the God who has created us. North Americans instinctively believe that freedom is their most important right and that freedom means that we can be whatever we want to be. The Bible insists that we presuppose that freedom is the ability to be what God wants us to be. Freedom is a gift, not a right, and a gift we have lost in its most significant dimensions through our sinfulness.

Lutheran theology presupposes that the spiritual is not superior to the material but that the Creator has made both the seen and unseen aspects of his creation good. We presuppose that both the spiritual elements and the material elements of our beings have been damaged by the rebellion of the human spirit, or heart, against our Creator (Gen. 6:5; Matt. 15:19).

Lutherans also presume that human creatures have rebelled against God and abandoned their relationship of trust with him. We presume that evil pervades all of human life. Again, we might be tempted to say, "Well, everyone believes that." As a matter of fact, many North Americans are extremely optimistic about human potential. Many of us believe that a little education will clear up a lot of bad action. Lutherans recognize that the attitudes that underlie actions are perverted by our sinfulness. We can take fully seriously the enormity of evil because we know that we have a Savior from every evil. We do not have to hide from the threat of evil outside or inside ourselves in some haven of self-deception, for we know that Christ has conquered evil. Therefore, we can confront the evils of this world without fear. We can even confront the problem of evil itself, the root question of why there is evil in the world, even though we know a logical answer will elude us.

17

We Presume Human Life Is Lived in Two Kinds of Relationships

A second set of presuppositions that guides Lutheran teaching is what Luther called the distinction of the two kinds of righteousness.[5] Luther emphasized that what makes life right—or whole or good—in relationship with God is not the same as what makes life right, whole, and good in relationship to other people. God's design for human life has two dimensions, two distinct kinds of relationship. Both are relationships of love. The first is the ultimate relationship, loving God with heart and soul and mind; the second—based on the first—is loving God's human creatures as we love ourselves (Matt. 22:37–40).

Our relationship to God is a relationship that originates in his love for us, his children. In this "vertical" relationship we remain his children, always dependent on him, always recipients of his love, always reacting to his love with the love for him that his love generates in us (1 John 4:7–12). God is the subject of our descriptions of this vertical relationship, even when we are acting. Our actions toward him are always responses to his love, which elicits our trust and love toward him. For sinners, our being right with God consists in what Christ has done for us. He is our righteousness. He is all that is right about us (1 Cor. 1:30).

In the "horizontal" relationship with other creatures of God, especially his human creatures, we adults function as adults, with responsibilities God has designed for us as those who represent him in meeting the needs of others, in showing his love to those around him. Here our righteousness consists in what we do for the neighbor, according to God's design for human living.

This righteousness in relationship to other creatures of God, a life spent profitably in good works, occurs not because we do the works on our own but because we do them on the basis of the righteousness God bestows on us as his children. Those who have fallen into sin cannot do good works, either in response to God or in response to the needs of other human creatures, in a God-pleasing way apart from the power of the Gospel.

Law and Gospel

Our use of Luther's distinction of the two kinds of righteousness is inextricably linked with two other governing principles for all of theology, which stand at the heart of his proclamation of the biblical message. The first is the distinction between Law and Gospel.[6] God's Law puts the burden on the human creature. Everything that calls for human action is Law. The Law is God's design for human life, and is in itself good. In our sinfulness we have brought its burden upon ourselves with crushing force. It becomes our enemy because we sin against it.

God's Gospel puts the burden on Christ. It is God's expression of love for us in every way in which he shows himself to be our good and gracious God, our loving Father, our Savior, our protecting and providing Lord. Above all, and in its most beautiful sense, however, the Gospel is God's love in Christ, in his self-sacrifice for us and in his gift of life through his own resurrection. This distinction of Law and Gospel guides our thinking as we use and teach all the topics that are discussed in subsequent parts of this book.

To apply this insight practically, we may regard the biblical answer to all questions regarding the significance of human life as, "Why do you want to know?" Until we recognize the agenda behind a question, we may give an answer that is technically correct but inappropriate and untrue for the situation in which the questioner is living. We must distinguish whether the question arises out of a false confidence in false gods or out of discouragement and despair over false gods. We must tune in on the specific needs the question expresses. For example, "Am I an elect child of God?" elicits the Gospel's promise for the despairing. The assurance of salvation that the answer to this question must give cannot be understood by someone who is seeking a license to sin. Therefore, in response to such a person, we presume that secure sinners cannot understand the Gospel. Thus, the conversation with the secure sinner focuses on the wrath of God. It does not offer a Gospel answer to the question as it stands. The proper distinction of Law and Gospel involves more than the repetition of Bible passages; it involves death and life.

Two Modes of God's Rule

Parallel to this distinction between Law and Gospel is Luther's distinction between God's two modes of rule, one for the vertical relationship and the other for the horizontal relationship.[7] God exercises his rule in the vertical realm through the Gospel, which creates new life. In the horizontal realm he exercises his rule through the Law and its structures as they form human deeds. The two realms have different goals as well as different methods of achieving these goals. Luther sketched the whole of the life of Christian discipleship through the use of this distinction between the two realms. Thus, it provides the conceptual framework for examining many of the topics of the chapters that follow.

We Presume the Theology of the Cross

Among the presuppositions that guide Lutheran theology is also a collection of biblical observations about God and the human creature that Luther labeled "the theology of the cross."[8]

God Hidden and God Revealed (in Hiddenness)

The first of the four points of the theology of the cross regards our teaching about God. Luther distinguished "the hidden God" from "the revealed God." The hidden God is God as he lies beyond human grasp, beyond human knowing. Thus if we describe God in his hiddenness, we present a God whom we do not know, instead we present God as we imagine him to be. These depictions present God as we wish that he were. He is, in the words of the nineteenth-century German philosopher, Ludwig Feuerbach, "God created in the image of man."[9] A picture of the hidden God, fashioned by human speculation, presents a God of glory, of power, of might. This is the opposite of the God whom we see on the cross; but God is hidden behind his own cloud of glory, and we cannot penetrate that cloud to see what he is really like. So our depiction of the hidden God is largely a reflection of our own feelings and fears.

Because fallen human creatures are so often angry at themselves for failing to meet their own expectations, the gods they fashion are usually gods of wrath. Because fallen human creatures so often find themselves unreliable, the gods they fashion are often capricious. Because human creatures want to make it on their own, the gods they fashion are usually gods who demand performance and accomplishment from sinful human creatures.

Some anthropologists label the "natural theology" of most peoples of this earth "primitive." It is animistic, placing divine power within created objects rather than in a Creator God. Such is the depiction of this hidden God that arises "naturally" from the sin-ridden human mind. The "natural theology" of most human thinking places the human creature in control. The ideas about God that occur to us "naturally," as sinners, deny him his rightful place in our lives.

The revealed God, on the other hand, is God as he presents himself to us, as Luther liked to say, in crib and cross—and in the crypt he left behind. The revealed God is the God who speaks to us, as the Word Made Flesh and in his inspired Scriptures. The revealed God is the God whose power is made perfect in weakness (2 Cor. 12:9), both ours and his. God's weakness in the cross of Christ is stronger than all human might and power. God's foolishness in the cross of Christ is wiser than all human wisdom (1 Cor. 1:18–2:9). It is true that God has revealed himself in the hiddenness of crib and cross and crypt. The last place human power and wisdom would look for God is in a manger, in diapers, or on a cross, on the way to the tomb. But precisely there our God reveals what he is really like. He reveals his unconditional and absolute love for fallen sinners.

Lutheran theology presupposes that God can be found only as the Revealed God, in the Scriptures, in the Word Made Flesh, in human language about this incarnate Word as it is preached and proclaimed, in sacramental forms at God's font and God's feast. Other descriptions of God tell us more about ourselves than about him. As Luther observed, "God will not deal with us except through his external Word and sacrament. Whatever is attributed to the Spirit apart from such Word and sacrament is of the devil."[10]

Such an understanding of God places him outside human control. He addresses us. He calls us. He invites us and draws us into his family. We can only respond. He came to ask Adam, "Where are you?" He has determined our rightful place. He declares what constitutes our righteousness. Some view "excessive" exaltation of God as a threat to our humanity. But recognizing God's place "above" us, as our Creator, does not deny our humanity. The revealed God reveals also what it is to be free as human creatures, to be the people God designed us to be (Col. 1:13–23). Therefore, Lutherans recognize throughout their interpretation of God's Word that we have

21

access to God and his nature only through his revelation of himself.

The Epistemology of Faith

The second point of the theology of the cross focuses on how we know this foolish and weak God. The Jews demanded signs, Paul reported. They wanted to have empirical proof. The Greeks demanded wisdom. They wanted a logical explanation (1 Cor. 1:18–2:16). Both Jews and Greeks wanted to know God on the basis of a process that human creatures control. They wanted to pin God down on their own terms. "Prove it" is still a common North American response to the Christian message. Our society wants empirical data; our society wants logical proof.

Our understanding of how God's Word functions depends in part on our understanding of how human learning functions. Epistemology is the study of how human creatures learn and know. God has provided us with several methods of learning, each appropriate for gaining knowledge in various areas of human life. Human creatures can also use each of these methods inappropriately, even sinfully.

Empirical Learning and Knowing. Most people in contemporary Western culture believe that the most valuable approach to gaining information lies in the empirical or experimental method, the "scientific" method of learning. This method relies first of all on the human senses' evaluation of data on the basis of a program of experimentation devised by the experimenter. The method presumes that knowledge can be proven by repeated testing. It claims an objectivity to its findings because they can be submitted to trial by others. Fellow scientists can then repeat the experiment to determine whether the original judgments, found in the original experiments, were correct. Objects that cannot be subjected to repeated experimentation lie outside the command of this approach to human knowledge.

This empirical epistemology puts the human creature in control of the process of gaining knowledge and thus in control of the knowledge gained from its experiments. I frame the rules for conducting the experiment. I perform the experiment. I interpret its results. I determine what truth it tells us.

People have always used experiments to gain knowledge, but

the much-vaunted authority of the experimental method in our culture dates back to the Scientific Revolution of the seventeenth century. The results of experimentation that this movement has produced—particularly in technology and medicine—have greatly enriched the human enjoyment of God's horizontal realm. This method of learning has greatly enhanced human ability to solve problems in the earthly realm and to extend many of God's temporal blessings for great portions of the world's population. Believers should recognize the countless blessings God has given his world through empirical research.

However, many in our culture tend to think that empirical or experimental testing offers the only path to truly reliable knowledge. They fail to recognize that the presuppositions of the researcher, the reliability of the instruments used in the experiment, and a host of external conditions may indeed influence the results of the experiment. Particularly at the level of presupposition or predisposition something akin to religious faith enters into the framing of this approach to knowing.

It must not be forgotten that those who pursue knowledge produced by empirical investigation do not view it as "fact" but rather as working theory. Therefore, the status of "theory" is not at all inferior, for the empiricist, to the status of "fact." This appraisal of knowledge in the horizontal realm is a healthy view. It can reflect the presumption that through God's gift of empirical testing human creatures never attain full mastery of God's creation, full knowledge of how it works.

Learning and Knowing through Reason. The second method of learning and knowing relies on human cognition and cogitation to gain the truth. Information and insight are gained through human reasoning, expressed in more sophisticated formal logical operations, such as syllogisms, or in the form of everyday common sense. Philosophers have disagreed on whether the basic principles of logical thinking arise out of the human mind naturally or whether they are grasped through human experience. In either case the presumption of this approach to human knowledge asserts that human powers of reasoning can understand the self and the world around us. Human logic can master the data that bombards from nature and human experience.

Much of Western culture has relied on the grand thoughts of

philosophers and the common thoughts of Everyone to solve problems and to push back frontiers of knowledge. Without rational knowledge life in the horizontal realm could not function. Human creatures enjoy this good gift of God and profit from its proper use. However, within Western culture different systems of logic have developed, and they do not all lead always to the same results. Between cultures gaps in logic open up. Not only do we lack agreement on some basic principles of logic, but we find that using the same principles, some of us come to different conclusions than others of us find. Presumption, presupposition, and predisposition all shape the way we use our minds and the conclusions to which they come.

Aesthetic Learning and Knowing. A third kind of knowledge gives human creatures access to the appreciation and enjoyment of the beauty of God's creation. Human reasoning and human emotion combine with sense perceptions to enrich our lives with the glories of color, shape, and form, of melody, harmony, and rhythm, of sights and sounds, of tastes, smells, and touches. Most people would agree that beauty is not merely a matter of individual taste. Most must also note that their own concept of beauty and their appreciation of its blessings do differ from the tastes of others in their own culture and certainly from the tastes of other cultures. This form of knowledge does not demand the same kind of "reliability" that the empirical and rational approaches to learning require. At the same time few would dismiss the deep significance this kind of knowledge has for daily life and the appreciation of our humanity and God's creation. Nonetheless, the raggedness of human knowing becomes apparent also in aesthetic knowledge.

Learning and Knowing from Authority. The fourth form of learning conveys information and insight through the voice of an authority. Most human learning and knowing has taken place through this method. Most human creatures have not had time to learn experimentally all that they need to know. Most have not taken the time to analyze rationally everything they need to know. We hope that our voices of authority have the truth, and we listen for the ring of truth in them. We review the conclusions of those voices of authority against the test of our own presuppositions. We nonetheless make a leap of faith to embrace the judgements of those who fix our appliances, manufacture and advertise a host of products for daily use, and plan our political and social policies. Far less often than we care to admit to ourselves do we pause for testing or rational evaluation.

God has so fashioned his human creatures that we can learn a great deal through experiment, through empirical ways of learning. We can also learn a great deal through the use of rational analysis, through human logic, and through aesthetic learning. We often must depend on the voices of authority for the information we need. In the horizontal realm each of these four ways of learning can be helpful and appropriate, in specific situations. In the vertical realm, however, the first three cannot lead us to truth. They always leave the human knower in control. When the epistemologies of human experiment, human rationality, or human aesthetic judgments try to define the origins and bounds of reality, they have gone beyond the limits of their competence. They go astray when they attempt to answer a different kind of question than the questions for which they were designed. We manage and manipulate the information we gain through our own experiments, our own logic, our own aesthetic sensitivities. Information about God must be learned through another means of learning. It must be heard from the voice of authority, the voice of God himself.

The theology of the cross teaches that neither the human eye nor the human mind controls our access to God. He controls that access, and he creates that access through his Word. He speaks, and the human ear listens. The human heart responds to his Word in faith. "By my own reason or strength I cannot believe in Jesus Christ, my Lord, or come to him."[11] God must step out of hiding. He must take the initiative. He does so with a promise. By its very nature a promise invites faith. The theology of the cross teaches that we can know God not through empirical proofs or logical reasoning, but only through faith. The faith the revealed God elicits from us through his Word relies on God's foolish and weak approach to us in the suffering and death of his Son.

Faith is not objective, dispassionate knowledge—the kind of knowledge the Enlightenment of the eighteenth century invented to assure objective, dispassionate human control. Faith is active; it is engaged with its object. It is knowledge that unites the one who trusts with its object. That is knowledge "in the biblical sense" (the euphemism for the intimate knowledge of husband and wife). Faith

25

embraces its object as a child clutches father or mother, as a bride embraces her bridegroom. Faith rests in knowledge of a word, which contradicts our existential logic for hanging onto life. Thus, this knowledge carries us out of the realms in which we retain a sense of control over our own destinies. Faith alone gives access to our God.

Thus, the faith of the believer does not rest upon anything else but Jesus. Neither signs of blessing nor signs of suffering will be taken as proof that the believer's relationship with God is functioning properly. Christians who point to their blessings as sure signs that God must love them are relying on a false basis for faith—just as much as are those who trust that God has to love them because they are suffering so much. Reliance upon our own feelings can betray us—feelings fluctuate—but God's promise to us does not. Signs of God's faithfulness to us will not rest in the good works we produce; God is faithful when we are not. Even the existence of our faith cannot be turned into a basis for our faith. When faith weakens, God remains strong in his love for us. Faith rests on Christ alone. Faith rests on his promise to be our only Lord.

Dying to Death, or Crucified with Christ

The third point of the theology of the cross focuses on what God did on the cross (1 Cor. 2:2). There he atoned for sin and swallowed death. There, in his own impotence and foolishness, he succeeded at the task of setting aside all that keeps us from him. There he succeeded at re-creating us in his own image. Luther called what happened on the cross "the joyous exchange." Life is restored to sinful human creatures, dead in trespasses and sins, only because God has exchanged our sinfulness for Christ's righteousness. We live only because Christ died with our sins on his back and buried them in his own tomb, the only place in the universe where our Heavenly Father no longer looks. We live because Christ shares with us the life he had the power to reclaim in his own resurrection.

In him, wrong is made right, and death is left behind for life, through God's peculiar way of doing things. The theology of the cross presupposes that the cross, death, is the path to life. The final result of this joyous exchange is that we who were buried and raised with Christ in Baptism (Rom. 6:3–11; Col. 2:11–15) are joint heirs

26

with him, even as we suffer with him, and will share glory with him (Rom. 8:17).

Thus, the theology of the cross spells out the death of all human pretension to merit, to winning life by human effort. It announces the death of human control over human destiny. This theology announces the death of sinners to sin and their resurrection to new life in Christ. It announces the death of death itself. This announcement liberates human creatures from the threat of death and thus bestows upon them genuine human freedom. Once sinners have seen the cross, there can be no more wallowing in guilt. Freedom is bestowed on us through God's own death, as the second person of the Trinity came to the cross, to save sinners, to restore their humanity.

Discipleship under the Cross

Fourth, the theology of the cross presupposes that the life of the believer, the life of discipleship—learning from and following after Christ—is a life under the cross (Matt. 16:24–26). Believers have their own crosses to "take up." Our crosses, however, do not save ourselves or save others. Instead, they convey the love of Christ to others in a sinful world of suffering. As we take up our crosses and follow our Lord (Matt. 16:24), we are living out life as it must be lived if the good and gracious will of our loving Heavenly Father is to triumph over evil. Only in this fashion has he succeeded in overcoming evil. Neither blessing nor cross determines whether we are in God's favor. Only his Word determines that—as it comes to us in Baptism and absolution, in preaching and the Lord's Supper, in our conversation with one another as fellow believers. We should not be surprised when our faith leads us into suffering for the sake of the neighbor. That is often the means the God of the cross uses to battle evil.

Life under the cross crucifies the habits of hell. The strong pruning hook of the Law combines with the believers' confidence in Christ's deadly death, and these believers find they have no need to use their hellish habits to defend themselves. Life under the cross gives rise to the habits of heaven. Faith perceives how God succeeds, in his own self-sacrifice and self-surrender, in his submission to human needs, his suffering, and his willing service.

27

Conclusion

So Lutherans keep in mind the four points of the theology of the cross as they teach any and all topics of biblical teaching. The theology of the cross creates the conceptual framework from which we understand who God is, how we relate to him in faith, how he has saved us through his own death, and how we live under the cross in our daily lives.

These presuppositions or elements of a Lutheran conceptual framework provide a kind of "grammar of faith," a series of guiding principles that affect the way in which we understand and apply all the topics we will discuss in this book. Each of these presuppositions recurs through each topic. When we treat the doctrine of God, we talk about the Hidden God under the theme "general revelation" and the Revealed God under the theme "special revelation." Two kinds of righteousness is a part of our treatment of justification by grace through faith in Christ as well as our consideration of the Law. This distinction is also a part of the conceptual framework of these two topics and every other in our theology.

No one comes to the text of Scriptures without a set of presuppositions, apart from experiences that have shaped a conceptual framework. Many come to the Bible without realizing what their presuppositions are and how their conceptual framework predetermines how they will read the text. We can now proceed into a review of the fundamental topics of the biblical message with some sense of how the way in which the Lutheran tradition's reading and understanding of the Scriptures has shaped its vision of their message.

Notes for Chapter I

1. Erik Erikson, *Childhood and Society* (New York: Norton, 1950); and *The Life Cycle Completed* (New York: Norton, 1982).
2. Large Catechism, Ten Commandments, 2, in *The Book of Concord,* trans. and ed. Theodore G. Tappert (Philadelphia: Fortress, 1959), 365.
3. Peter Fraenkel, "Revelation and Tradition: Notes on Some Aspects of Doctrinal Continuity in the Theology of Philip Melanchthon," *Studia Theologica* XIII (1959):97–133.
4. C. F. W. Walther, *Law and Gospel,* trans. Herbert J. A. Bouman (Saint Louis: Concordia, 1981), 26.

5. Martin Luther, *Lectures on Galatians, 1535, Chapters 1–4* Luther's Works, vol. 26 (Saint Louis: Concordia, 1963), 4–12; "Two Kinds of Righteousness, 1519," *Career of the Reformer: I,* Luther's Works, vol. 31 (Philadelphia: Fortress, 1957), 293–306.

6. Classic expositions of this distinction include C. F. W. Walther, *Law and Gospel* (see note 4 above); and Bo Giertz, *The Hammer of God,* trans. Clifford Ansgar Nelson (Minneapolis: Augsburg, 1973).

7. Gustaf Wingren, *Luther on Vocation,* trans. Carl C. Rasmussen (Philadelphia: Muhlenberg, 1957); and George W. Forell, *Faith Active in Love: An Investigation of the Principles Underlying Luther's Social Ethics* (Minneapolis: Augsburg, 1954).

8. Luther, "Heidelberg Disputation," *Career of the Reformer: I,* Luther's Works, vol. 31, 35–70.

9. Ludwig Feuerbach, *Das Wesen des Christentums* (1841), *The Essence of Christianity* (New York: Harper, 1957), 13–14, 22–43, 108.

10. Smalcald Articles III:VIII,10, *The Book of Concord,* 313.

11. Small Catechism, Creed, Article III, 6, ibid., 345.

Chapter II

God

During World War II, Father William Thomas Cummings claimed that "there are no atheists in foxholes." There are no atheists anywhere, if a "god" is that in which we put our ultimate trust. Everyone believes in someone or something to give life its ultimate sense of identity, security, and meaning. Human life depends—ultimately—on some kind of god or other.

Natural Revelation, or Glimpses of the Hidden God

God has left traces of his existence strewn all over his creation. Even those whose sin has deafened them to his call still catch a fleeting glimpse of him as they hurl themselves headlong from his presence. Sinners often try to abstract some nugget of truth from these glimpses. They try to construct a picture of God from the hints they sense in the creation all around them. These pictures reflect more of ourselves than of our God, as the theology of the cross reminds us.

Theologians label the traces and hints of God that fallen human creatures use to paint their own pictures of God "natural" or "general" revelation. None of these hints offers a complete view of God; sinners can only project the entirety of God from the small sense of him that fits their own disposition. For these two reasons the impressions of God that arise from "natural revelation" resemble the pictures of an elephant sketched by blindfolded people who each have hold of a different section of the elephantine anatomy. At best these abstractions are inadequate. At worst they deceive in a demonic way, for they set the sinners off in wrong directions as they try to seek or to please this hidden God.

Nature

God has left vestiges of himself in at least five places. Nature is the first. Paul pointed out that God has left the mark of his invisible nature, his eternal power and deity, in the things he has made (Rom. 1:20). God has left a witness to himself in the goodness with which he satisfies hearts with food and gladness, through rain and fruitful seasons (Acts 14:17). The argument that there must be a God because of the existence of creation is called the "cosmological" argument for his existence.

A related argument, also based on nature, is the "teleological" case for God. It argues that the "telos" of nature—the fact that it functions smoothly and moves towards its goal—proves that there must be a designer and creator for it all. Nature's inherent beauty and its sense of order and purpose proves the existence of its drafter, many would reason. To the eye of faith God's glory and presence are certainly reflected in the world around the believer as well as in the construction of the human creature (e.g., Is. 40:12, 21–26; Job 9:4–12; Ps. 139:13–16).

Today, in Western culture, many reject such reasoning. Our culture has developed explanations of nature's existence and order that do not point to a God for those schooled in the culture's belief systems. Godless explanations for an eternally self-recycling universe have existed in ancient and contemporary cultures, among the Greeks of old and the Chinese of today. Godless explanations of a constantly evolving universe prosper in the modern western world. Whatever nature is saying to humankind, it does not prevent some from indulging in what the Psalmist called the foolishness of denying that God exists (Ps. 14:1; 53:1).

History

Some argue that God can be seen as he guides and directs human history. The triumph of good and the punishment of evil in the annals of nations demonstrate that some divine person or force must be channeling human activity, they insist. This glimpse of God, or of God's work, has severe limitations. God is indeed lord of human history, but from any individual's personal perspective God is easily confused with human evil or human aspiration. Therefore, many people, particularly today, could conclude from history that if God is in charge, he has a mean streak in him. In this past century we have actually witnessed no increase in human villainy and turpitude; it only seems so because human hatreds and meanness have harnessed advanced technology to carry out their evil designs. But survivors of Nazi death camps and Cambodian killing fields, of Dresden, Hiroshima, or Baghdad, of civil wars from Biafara to Bangladesh, might well conclude that no God worthy of the name had been minding their store.

Conscience

Within the human creature lurks a longing for divine company as well. Paul pointed out that Gentiles, who knew nothing of Moses' law, still lived to a large extent according to God's plan for human life (Rom. 2:14). Conscience, the universal sense of right and wrong, points inevitably to the one who designed right and wrong for human creatures, the argument runs.

Anthropologists have produced something of a counterargument. They suggest that there are only two universal taboos, incest and cannibalism of kin; no universal definitions of right and wrong exist. However, a large part of the moral code of any culture is operative in most other cultures. The overlap of agreement among human cultures on how human creatures should behave is suggestive. However, to those who do not want to believe in a God who has shaped right and wrong for his human creatures, any agreement on right and wrong suggests no more than a commonality of human experience. Believers recognize that God has given them their sense of right and wrong for good human living. Unbelievers may doubt that part of God's goodness in manifold ways. They may reject the argument that conscience or morality proves that God must exist.

Furthermore, when conscience speaks, it usually tells us that we are guilty. We pay it little heed when it compliments us on making right choices. The "god" that conscience abstracts from its sense of morality is an angry god, who reaffirms our own anger with ourselves at failing once again to achieve good performance, or the good life. Conscience contains a hint of God, but this hint hardly serves as the basis for a friendly conversation.

Reason: the Ontological Argument

"But is it not simply *reasonable* to believe in God?" Different systems of reasoning have constructed different logical arguments for the existence of some kind of greater being. The ontological argument—the logical argument from existence itself—suggests that it is only common sense that there is someone or something greater than which nothing else is. That "greater than all else" must be God. Daily experience demonstrates time and time again that one thing is greater in some sense or another than other things. At the top of such a pyramid must sit God.

This argument will not convince those who do not believe that the order of existence is pyramid-shaped. Still others place strange conceptions at the top of the pyramid. Although it may be "reasonable" to believe in some kind of god, unassisted reason—believers will readily concede—cannot give us a glimpse of the true God.

Emotion: Encountering the Numinous

Finally, human emotion, it can be argued, betrays some sense of the divine. Early in the twentieth century the German theologian Rudolf Otto posited the sense of the "numinous" within the human creature. All people, he argued, have a nonrational and amoral conviction that someone or something greater than the merely human is out there, influencing their lives. This conviction forms the foundation of the human sense of the divine. Human creatures are "naturally" fascinated with the awe-inspiring powers that exercise control over their lives and "naturally" abase themselves before these powers, according to Otto.[1]

Human fears have shaped one set of pictures of the numinous. Human hopes have sketched another set, pictures of a God who helps and befriends the human creature. For most of human history hope has fashioned powerful gods to do its bidding. Under the influence of the Christian message some contemporary thinkers have tried to abstract a suffering god, resembling Christ on the cross, who joins vulnerable humankind in its suffering. God's omnipotence is sacrificed, in such a picture, in order to solve the problem of evil by placing God squarely and solely with his suffering people. This abstract sufferer reveals something of the hidden God but discounts what most humans, and all believers, have known about God. He remains omnipotent if he is to remain God.

The gods of human imagination and construction all break down. They reveal themselves sooner or later as, at best, only a small part of the picture of God that we long to see. These arguments are only temporarily convincing. Either our idea of God falls to pieces, or we fall to pieces under the inadequacy or the judgment of such a God.

Believers take pleasure in knowing that their God reveals himself in the majestic display of color in a sunset or a sun-illuminated canyon wall. They will acknowledge signs of his wrath and his mercy in the unfolding of human history. They will notice the effect of his creative hand in the operation of their own conscience, reason, and emotions. But they will also concede the severe limitations of making an argument on such bases to those who stand outside the faith. When unbelievers can be moved in the direction of knowing the true God through such arguments, believers will employ them. In general, however, they will cut the "small talk," talk of a God too small when captured in the limited descriptions of natural or general revelation. They will turn instead to God as he talks with fallen humankind. This God says, "I love you" from a cross and "I have life for you" from the mouth of a tomb.

Specific Revelation, or Listening to the Revealed God

The Word of God became flesh (John 1:14), so that he might tell us directly, "I have come that [you] may have life, and have it to the full" (John 10:10). This voice cuts through the abstractions of the constructed gods, fashioned in our own image out of the raw material of human premonitions and suspicions. From the cross this voice calls human creatures to die under God's wrath (Gal. 6:14); from the mouth of the tomb this voice breathes the forgiveness of sins upon fallen human creatures and raises them up once again to life (John 20:22–23). Only through this Jesus of Nazareth, crucified by his own people, raised by God from the dead, can salvation for fallen human creatures be found (Acts 4:10–12). When the constructs fashioned from the glimpses of the hidden God fall apart, sinners must be drawn to the Word of the Lord. Only then can they find the peace that God designed for them in Eden once again.

God's Mighty Acts and Their Interpretation

God does talk with his hands, but he handles things with his talk. The handiwork of his creation speaks only in muffled tones to sin-deafened ears, from creation in Genesis 1 through re-creation in John 1. While human beings have used many forms of discourse to describe reality, from philosophy to poetry, from metaphysics to fiction, God chose human history as the medium for his revelation of himself. He intervenes in human history, in mighty acts of judgment and liberation. God's people experienced his presence in Abraham's call from Ur and his journey to the promised land. They witnessed his judgment upon Egypt and his mercy toward Israel in the Exodus. They perceived his judgment upon them in the Exile and his mercy toward them in the Return. They acknowledged his intervention to save humankind in his own incarnation.

But the precise intention of those interventions would be subject to the whim of human speculation if the Holy Spirit had not moved prophetic voices to explain them (2 Peter 1:21). Contemporary observers might well have understood Pharaoh's debacle as the Egyptian gods' way of controlling their own territory and people. God's own interpreters were necessary to make it possible to understand what he was doing as he led his people out of Egypt. God likes to communicate with his people not through wind, earthquake, or fire, but in human language, in a still, small voice (1 Kings 19:11–13).

God's Talk and Its Written Form

God used the many and varied voices of the prophets to convey his message to his people (Heb. 1:1), and he finally spoke to the world through his Son (Heb. 1:1–2). His Word, his message for us, came in human flesh, as Jesus of Nazareth, who claimed all authority in heaven and earth because he is the author of life, the author of new life (Matt. 28:18). Human language lies at the heart of our existence. It marks us as the creatures we are, distinct in our own persons and cultures by the way we talk yet able to communicate across linguistic lines as we learn one another's languages. Human creatures may, indeed, have feelings too deep for words. They may enjoy music and other arts without being able to express verbally what they feel. But we talk, even to ourselves. Even as we think, we organize life verbally, in propositions with subjects and verbs implied if not stated—and certainly we relate our thoughts to others in words. The full enjoyment of our humanity depends on verbalization. God knew that. He designed his human creatures in that way. That is why he not only acted out his love in human history, he also explained his actions through the prophets. More than that, he spoke his love directly to his people through the voices of the prophets.

Those prophetic voices have been "made more certain" in the record of the Holy Scripture. This prophetic word enlightens human hearts and brings the dawning of the day to lives that lay in darkness (2 Peter 1:19–21) until the true light of the Word made flesh enlightened humankind (John 1:9). This Word, Jesus Christ, represents the culmination of all God's talk (Heb. 1:1–2). The nature and function of the Scriptures, as they give witness to God's love for us and address us with his saving love (2 Tim. 3:15–16), will be discussed in chapter XI.

God's revelation of himself—in human flesh and in his inspired Scriptures—addresses us directly. He not only talks about himself in the third person, he also talks to us in the words that we repeat from the Scriptures to one another, and he talks to us in the first person. He addresses us in the second person. He says, "You are my child." He proclaims, "I am your God." He gushes, "I love you. I forgive you all your sins." In his language, conveyed in his own incarnate person as Jesus of Nazareth, in the pages of the Bible, in the preaching and sharing of Christians with one another, such statements verbalize God's presence and power among us. In the words of his Gospel he has placed the power to save (Rom. 1:16).

Some Christians have reacted against an emphasis on the propositional, factual nature of the church's proclamation, wanting to emphasize instead its emotional side. Indeed, faith involves both the emotional embrace of God's promise as well as its content, expressed in propositions, in subjects and verbs. But God's promise—and his commands as well—cannot be conveyed apart from propositions, propositions that introduce the person of Jesus Christ to others and express his love for his people. These propositions, however, are not "mere" propositions. They are human words with

36

God's power in them. They do his work. They accomplish his purposes (Is. 55:11).

These human words are not encoded. They are not magical nonsense, apprehensible only by those who have the secret of how to decode them. They are just plain, ordinary human language, as Jesus of Nazareth was a plain, ordinary human creature. But these easily apprehensible words are not comprehensible to those who are not given the ability to trust them and understand them by the Holy Spirit. Although their meaning can be clearly ascertained by all, it cannot be accepted without the Holy Spirit's gift of trust. In John's gospel we are told that Thomas confessed that the crucified man in front of him had risen from the dead and was indeed "my Lord and my God" (John 20:28). The words are clear and easy to understand. They make no sense, however, unless our minds have been given the gift of comprehending God's gracious intervention in human history as Jesus of Nazareth. This lack of comprehension is in part a human problem; creatures will never be able to get their minds completely around their Creator. It is even more a problem of sin: sinners resist understanding the goodness of the God who intends to rescue them from their sin and restore them to his family.

God Addresses His Children

God's message for human creatures comes in the forms of Law and Gospel. His design for human life takes shape in commands. His gift of new life for human creatures is conveyed through his promise to be our God, his promise to regard and keep us as his children. Even those who have not been given the gift of faith can make rather accurate guesses about his design for human life. The Law speaks to fallen sinners through general revelation from any number of places in human experience. But God gives access to the Gospel, to his Fatherly and gracious intention for fallen sinners, only in the specific revelation of his incarnate Son, Jesus Christ, and in the inspired words of Scripture as they give testimony to his love in Christ—and in the words Christians use to convey this proclamation of his love to others.

The form of his specific revelation comes in an authoritative word of pronouncement. As noted previously,[2] God has given his human creatures several ways to learn how the horizontal sphere of human life operates. Modern-day Westerners prefer knowledge that comes through experiment, logic, or aesthetic appreciation. These ways of learning stand under human control.

Authoritative knowledge, however, does not stand under the control of the learner. When we learn from the voice of authority, there is no test but trust. If we acknowledge our status as creatures, then we must learn of the Creator from his voice, on the basis of his authority. Sinners prefer to do experiments or evaluate signs; they prefer to analyze rationally or evaluate wisdom. God speaks and elicits trust. Sinners regard his speaking as foolishness and weakness, but that is the form his authoritative voice takes as it conveys his power and wisdom to us (1 Cor. 1:18–2:16). That is the epistemology of faith.

God's specific revelation of himself comes in personal and in propositional form. He speaks to us on a human level, in a human creature like us and in the human language we understand and use for sustaining daily existence. He speaks nonetheless of his love, a subject higher than our ability to comprehend it fully, and so the mystery of his expression of his love will escape our final formulation. He tells us what we need to know—though not all that we would like to know—about himself. He speaks to save.

God Is a Person

God spoke to Moses and identified himself, "I am who I am" (Ex. 3:14). Interpreters of this name have proposed various explanations of what it means. God's identification of himself remains, after all of them, a mystery.

The ancient Jews modestly refused to let this Holy Name—"Yahweh" as they would have said it if they had said it—pass through unclean lips. They simply said, "The Lord," when they read his name in the Scripture. North Americans want to be on a first-name basis with everyone; they have begun to call him, for the first time in the history of the church, "Yahweh." He also goes by the name "Jesus, the Messiah." Unlike "Yahweh," this name is quite clear. It tells us that God has come in human flesh as the expected rescuer, the anointed Savior, of his people. He cannot describe his inner being to creatures, especially to creatures who have sinned. But he claimed a name. He wanted to be identified. He recalled for Moses the personal relationships he had had in the past with Abraham, Isaac, and Jacob (Ex. 3:6).

Some modern people want to believe that the ultimate power of the universe is not personal but rather a divine force. This denial of the personhood of God may spring from human discouragement with their own persons. If I have made a wreck of my own person and my own personal relationships, I will hope for something more in my deliverer than a "mere" person. Others believe that to ascribe personhood, on the human model, to God is to belittle him. Every human person seems too small to suffice as a god. God must be bigger than "mere" personhood. Ascribing him personhood is anthropomorphizing him: reducing him to human form.

Others shy away from acknowledging God's personhood, however, because they recognize that the personal is finally superior to the impersonal. They want to contend with a divine force rather than a divine person because they sense that this may even the odds between the human and the divine. Encapsulating the divine in the form of a "force" may tame its power. Yet, even when we do so, we are tempted to personalize the force as in the Star Wars movies: "May the Force be with you." Nature may replace God, but in so doing becomes our "Mother." Perhaps we strive against the depersonalization of God because we suspect that depersonalizing him depersonalizes us. Reducing him from person to force reduces us.

Of course, God reduced himself to human form in the person of Jesus of Nazareth. He is the original anthropomorphizer. It is not because we cast him in our own image that we think of him as a person. We are persons because he made us in his own image (Gen. 1:27; Col. 3:10). His person existed before our persons could be conceived.

Thus, he is the person who always was, is, and will be. He is the first and the last. Before and beside him there is no other God, no other origin and originator of all else that is (Is. 44:6; 45:5). He deserves ultimate trust since he designed and created human life (Gen. 1:27–2:25). He is the only reliable ultimate source of identity, security, and meaning for all his human creatures. He is God.

The Attributes of God

Perhaps because we cannot grasp his essence or circumscribe his being, we like to try to describe him. The seventeenth-century

Lutheran theologian Johann Andreas Quenstedt listed the attributes or characteristics of God: perfection, majesty, blessedness, unity, simplicity; he is spirit, invisible, faithful, good, independent of all else, eternal, immeasurable, omnipresent, immutable, and unable to be grasped by his creatures. He possesses life, immortality, the ultimate intellect, all knowledge and wisdom. He embodies will, freedom, kindness, love, grace, mercy, patience, holiness, righteousness, power, and truth.[3] Quenstedt and his contemporaries divided their lists of God's attributes into categories: those that describe God in terms not applicable to humans (eternal, infinite) and those that apply to humans in a lesser way (good, wise); those that speak of God in himself (eternal) and those that speak of him in relationship to his human creatures (gracious); those that describe him positively (good) and those that describe him negatively (immeasurable). Both the philosophical tradition of the West and the Scriptures had provided material for such lists and classifications.

The biblical writers described God largely in terms of his encounters with human creatures and often through titles that embraced certain characteristics. In the Old Testament God is frequently described as the king of his people, and the characteristics of the king are ascribed to him. God the King rules with power and glory forever; this king is praised for being faithful and gracious, for preserving and providing for his people and for hearing their cries (Ps. 145:11–20; cf. Psalms 93, 96, 97, 99). This king functions as judge, ruler, and Savior (Is. 33:22). He dwells in the midst of his people and replaces their fears and weaknesses with gladness and joy as he renews them in his love, as he removes disaster from them, brings them home, and restores their fortunes (Zeph. 3:15–20). God the King subdues other peoples and chooses his own people for himself (Psalm 47).

In the New Testament God is still acknowledged as king in ascriptions of praise (1 Tim. 1:17; 6:15; Rev. 15:3). His rule is frequently expressed in terms of his kingdom (Matt. 6:33). But Christ now directs prayer to the "Father" (Matt. 6:9; Luke 11:2) and calls the King "Father" (Matt. 13:43; 26:29). Paul came before God in prayer with the cry, "*Abba*, Father" (Rom. 8:15; Gal 4:6). Paul began most of his letters with acknowledgement of God as Father (Rom. 1:7; 1 Cor. 1:3; 2 Cor. 1:2; Gal. 1:3; Eph. 1:2; Phil. 1:2; Col. 1:2; 1 Thess. 1:1; 2 Thess. 1:2; 1 Tim. 1:2; 2 Tim. 1:2; Titus 1:4). Peter also called God "Father" (1 Peter 1:17). The Father is glorious (Eph. 1:17) and worthy of thanksgiving (Eph. 5:20). This Father has chosen and predestined his people to be his own family (1 Peter 1:2) and stands as their judge (1 Peter 1:17). This Father has qualified his people to share in the inheritance of the saints, has delivered them from the kingdom of darkness and transferred them into his own Son's kingdom (Col. 1:12–14). This Father embraces his children, loving them and giving them eternal encouragement and good hope through his grace (2 Thess. 2:16–17).

In the ancient Near East kings were described as "fathers" of their people. Both kings and fathers protected and provided for their subjects and children. The shift from "king" to "father" as a description of God may bring him nearer, as he came nearer in the revelation of his love in Jesus Christ. This shift did not alter the image of a loving and caring God.

The Trinity

The name *Father* and the characteristics that accompany it can apply to God as Trinity. But already in the New Testament the designation *Father* was also used to distinguish the first person of the Trinity from the second and third persons (Matt. 28:19; 2 Cor. 13:14). The term *Trinity* is, of course, not a biblical term. The formulation of the dogma of the Trinity in the fourth century, however, does reflect the earliest conviction of Christ's followers as they responded to his claim to be God. It reflects their faith in his assertion that the Holy Spirit is also God.

The New Testament Confession of Jesus Christ

Confessions of faith are formulated around the heart of the faith and around those parts of the faith under challenge. Among the earliest of Christian confessions was the simple formulation, "Jesus is Lord" (1 Cor. 12:3). That confession went to the heart of the matter. It affirmed the Lordship of Jesus against those who denied the possibility that this man could be God in human flesh. It is certain that Thomas' confession, that Jesus was "Lord" and "God," reflected the conviction of the disciples and their followers. They called Jesus "Lord" not as a matter of respect for a great man, but as a confession that he was God. They used the term *Lord* as Jews had customarily done, as a substitute for *Yahweh*. When Thomas called Jesus "my Lord and my God," he was using synonyms to emphasize his identification of the risen Lord as God in human flesh (John 20:28).

John the Evangelist expressed that same conviction when he confessed that this Word made flesh was "with God, and the Word was God" (John 1:1), and he reiterated that confession as he concluded his gospel by placing Thomas' confession near its completion (John 20:28). Oskar Skarsaune has shown that what caused the Jews—and later the pagans of the Greek society—to stumble was just this claim: God was appearing in human flesh. Jesus himself used Jewish traditions, which personalized characteristics of God to claim that he was God. Particularly the wisdom of God had been personalized, and when John called Jesus God's Word, he was reflecting this tradition. Jews believed in the complex nature of God's inner being. They did not believe that God could become flesh. They had not formulated a doctrine that would insist on three distinct persons, Father, Son, and Holy Spirit, within the Godhead. But such thinking was not offensive to them in the same way as was the claim that God had come in human flesh.[4]

Jesus himself most powerfully claimed to be God in human flesh by repeatedly claiming to be the "Son of Man." This title appeared with special significance in the one of Daniel's visions (Dan. 7:13–14), in which "one like a son of man" came to God from out of the clouds and was given the place of power and honor at God's right hand. Indeed, the Son of Man "was given dominion and glory and kingdom, that all peoples, nations, and languages should serve him; his dominion is an everlasting dominion, which shall not pass away, and his kingdom one that shall not be destroyed." For the Jews, only Yahweh could be described in the terms here ascribed to this "one like a son of man." Only Yahweh could hold dominion, glory, and rule. Only Yahweh could be served by all peoples, nations, and languages. Only Yahweh's rule would last forever. In this passage, which presents a person in human form with Yahweh's characteristics, God was edging his people toward the ability to conceive of God coming in human flesh. Some Jews in the intertestamental period got something of an inkling of what this suggestion really meant.[5] So did the Jewish leaders of Jesus' time. They were trying to convict him on a charge of treason, as a Messiah whom they regarded as a "Son of God," a special agent of God's rule (Matt. 26:63). He told them that that was hardly the half of it. He claimed to be the Son of Man and described himself in terms of Daniel 7, "seated at the right hand of Power, and coming on the clouds of heaven" (RSV). That was no longer treason, nor was it foolishness to the Sanhedrin. "He has spoken blasphemy," the high priest cried out. He had claimed to be God (Matt. 26:64–65). He claimed the same life-giving power as the Father and the same honor as the Father (John 5:21–23).

The Heretical Counterclaims

That claim was hard to believe. It was impossible to believe apart from the Holy Spirit's gift of faith (1 Cor. 12:3). It is little wonder that particularly Jews, who had always confessed that God was totally distinct from his creatures and was one, single Lord (Deut. 6:4), found it difficult to accept Jesus' claim to be the Son of Man, and thus the Lord God. In the succeeding three centuries people who wanted to follow Jesus but who also felt compelled to make sense of his claim to be God formulated a number of heretical solutions to the problem he posed with this claim.

Modalistic Monarchianism. One solution was provided by the "modalistic monarchians," who taught that the one ruler (Greek: *mon-arch*) or God appeared in three different modes, as Father, Son, and Holy Spirit, but did not consist of three distinct persons. Modalistic monarchians were also called Patripassians because they taught that the Father suffered, but in the mode of the Son.[6]

Denials of Christ's Divinity: Adoptionism and Subordinationism. Other heretics rejected the divinity of Christ. Some asserted that he was only a very good man whom God adopted as a special Son and gave special powers at his Baptism (adoptionism). Others claimed that he was a subdeity (subordinationism). The earliest adoptionists were probably the Jewish sect called the Ebionites, but in the Gentile world similar views were propagated, sometimes labeled "dynamic monarchianism" because this heresy claimed that the one ruler (*mon-arch*) had placed a special power (*dynamis*) upon the human Jesus.

Subordinationists tried to interpret the biblical message regarding Christ within the presuppositions or conceptual framework of the popular neoplatonic philosophy of the early Christian era. The conception of this widespread system of beliefs influenced the popular, multifaceted religious movement called Gnosticism, one of the chief rivals of early Christianity. In this world view the ultimate reality, pure spirit, had begun to break down, and the first emanation from its purity was called the Logos or Word. That Logos was not eternal, as was the ultimate spirit, and it represented a first stage in the degeneration of the purity, which alone could belong to the ultimate spirit.

A theologian from Alexandria, Arius (ca. 250–336), fell into subordinationism in trying to make it clear to people of his religious culture what it meant that Jesus Christ was the Word of God. He fit this term from John 1 into the conceptual framework of contemporary neoplatonic thought. He thus claimed that Christ was a creature of God, of a different substance or essence than God and thus not eternal. There had been "a time when he was not." He was subject to change. He was a being not so completely perfect as God himself.[7]

The Faith of Athanasius: Of One Substance with the Father

Arius' teaching encountered opposition, above all from Athanasius, the bishop of Alexandria (ca. 293–373). For most of the fourth century followers of the two fought with each other, notably at the Council of Nicea in 325. The Nicene Creed was begun there and completed about the time of the Council of Constantinople (381). This creed confessed the biblical teaching that Jesus Christ is God in human flesh. It did so in terms current in the theological debates of the time, influenced as they were by contemporary philosophical presuppositions. Above all, it used the formulation "of one [the same] substance" [Greek: *homoousious*] to identify Christ fully as God.

The Creed used John's mysterious term "only begotten" (John 1:14, 3:16 KJV) to affirm the eternal relationship between Father and Son in the one Godhead; the Son was "begotten of his Father before all worlds." He is God of God, light of light, true God of true God, and he was not created. He shares the same substance with the Father. There is no distinction between them in terms of their being

God. He created all things. The Nicene Creed affirmed in the language appropriate to its time what Christ had claimed of himself: He is God.[8]

Although disputes over the divinity of the Holy Spirit were less prominent, the church had to defend the biblical teaching in this regard as well. Christ himself had affirmed that the Holy Spirit is true God by warning against blaspheming him (Matt. 12:31). The Holy Spirit re-creates: he regenerates and renews the people of God as he brings them into new life (Titus 3:5). The equality of Father, Son, and Holy Spirit is affirmed by Christ's words (Matt. 28:19) and Paul's (2 Cor. 13:14).

The teaching of the church on the Trinity was summarized in a litany that assumed the status of a creed. Named for Saint Athanasius, whose teaching lay at its heart, it reflects later doctrinal developments regarding the relationship of the two natures, human and divine, in the person of Christ (see chapter VII). The Athanasian Creed was probably written in the fifth century. It confesses that God is one God, with three persons; the Godhead is not divided but the persons are not to be confused with one another. All three persons are uncreated, incomprehensible, eternal, and almighty, yet there are not three uncreated, incomprehensible, eternal, and almighty beings but only one. All three are God and Lord, but there are not three Lords or three Gods but only one.

Whether we encounter denials of this fundamental teaching of the Scripture in mainline Christianity or in sects such as the Jehovah's Witnesses, we must confront such denials with the simple biblical argument, the claim of Jesus Christ and his disciples that Jesus is indeed God come in human flesh. Every biblical expression of this confession that Jesus is God should be marshalled to combat such rejections of the heart of God's revelation of his love for fallen sinners. The ascriptions of titles indicating his divine nature, such as "Son of Man" in the sense of Daniel 7, "Word," and "Lord," should be coupled with affirmations from Jesus' own lips, such as "I and the Father are one" (John 10:30). It is also helpful to demonstrate that the Jews had no objections to a view of the complexity of God's inner person, and so the doctrine of the Trinity itself did not become an issue of controversy until it encountered rationalistic objections from Greek philosophy.[9]

The church has attempted to describe the distinction of one

person of the Godhead from another by using biblical terms to point to these distinctions without being able to comprehend or analyze the inner relationships of the Godhead. The church seized upon John's designation of Christ as "the only begotten Son" (John 3:16, 18 KJV) and upon Christ's description of the Holy Spirit as one who "proceeds from the Father" (John 15:26 RSV) to point to the inner distinctions within the Trinity. Particularly the latter refers in context to the relationship of the Spirit outside the Trinity, the mission to his people on which the Father sends the Spirit. It does not refer to the inner workings of the Godhead. But this biblical term is nonetheless useful in affirming that the persons of the Godhead are distinct from one another within the unity of the Godhead. The Father is neither begotten nor proceeding; the Son is begotten but not proceeding; the Spirit is not begotten but proceeding.

Although the ancient Jews did not try to analyze the inner relationships within God's being, they expressed their belief in his complexity by personalizing his wisdom, his Spirit, his Law or Word, and other characteristics. In the wake of his revelation as Father, Son, and Spirit, the church has confessed the inner relationships of the individual but inseparable persons of the Godhead with this language. However, we dare never forget that human wisdom cannot pierce the mystery of God's internal makeup or working. It can only confess the wonder of his being.[10]

The Filioque: "And from the Son"

Christians of the Eastern Orthodox confession have criticized the Western catholic tradition for asserting that the Holy Spirit proceeds from the Son (Latin: *filioque*) as well as from the Father because John 15:26 mentions only his proceeding from the Father. Western Christians have used the phrase "and the Son" in the Nicene Creed since the local Spanish Council of Toledo in 589. There the church was locked in a struggle with an occupying army of Germanic tribal invaders who were Arians. To affirm the full divinity of Christ the faithful believers of the native population confessed Christ's equality with the Father by adding this phrase to the Creed. Since the term in the Creed refers to the relationships among the three persons of the Trinity (and is only borrowed for this purpose from John 15:26), it may properly be used in this way. It affirms the full equality of each of the three persons within the Godhead.[11]

46

Conclusion

It has been said that the formulation of the dogma of the Trinity reduced the biblical message to Greek philosophical categories and abstracted its living vitality into foreign forms of thought. This is not so. Instead, in formulating trinitarian language, Athanasius and his followers built a bridge from the biblical message into the thought-world of their own day, effectively combatting attempts to subvert the biblical message into cultural forms that misrepresented it.

The dogma of the Trinity teaches us that God is one Lord and that he is three persons, distinct within the Godhead but eternally inseparable. This dogma enables us to confess and to teach that Jesus of Nazareth was God come in human flesh and that the Holy Spirit, true God, dwells in us and makes us God's temple.

Notes for Chapter II

1. Rudolf Otto, *The Idea of the Holy: An Inquiry into the Non-Rational Factor in the Idea of the Divine and Its Relation to the Rational,* trans. John W. Harvey (1917; New York: Oxford University Press, 1958).
2. On epistemology, see ch. I. above, pp. 7–29.
3. Johann Andreas Quenstedt, *Theologia Didactico-Polemica* (Wittenberg, 1685), I:284–85.
4. Oskar Skarsaune, *Incarnation: Myth or Fact,* trans. Trygve R. Skarsten (Saint Louis: Concordia, 1991).
5. Carsten Colpe, *"ho huios tou anthrōpou," Theological Dictionary of the New Testament,* vol. 8, ed. Gerhard Friedrich, trans. and ed. Geoffrey W. Bromiley (Grand Rapids: Eerdmans, 1972), 420–30.
6. J. N. D. Kelly, *Early Christian Doctrines* (New York: Harper & Row, 1960), 119–23; Jaroslav Pelikan, *The Christian Tradition: A History of the Development of Doctrine, 1: The Emergence of the Catholic Tradition (100–600)* (Chicago: The University of Chicago Press, 1971), 176–82.
7. Kelly, 223–51; Pelikan, 191–200. Cf. Skarsaune, 98–101.
8. Kelly, 252–69; Pelikan, 211–24. Cf. Skarsaune, 98–111.
9. See Skarsaune's argument throughout *Incarnation.*
10. J. N. D. Kelly, *Early Christian Creeds* (New York: McKay, 1960), 139–52; Kelly, *The Athanasian Creed* (New York: Harper & Row, 1964), 84–90; Pelikan, 211–25.
11. Kelley, *Early Christian Creeds,* 358–67. Pelikan, 212, 293; *2: The Spirit of Eastern Christendom (600–1700)* (Chicago: The University of Chicago Press, 1974), 183–98.

Chapter III

Creator and Creatures

I believe that God has created me and all that exists; that he has given me and still sustains my body and soul, all my limbs and senses, my reason and all the faculties of my mind, together with food and clothing, house and home, family and property; that he provides me daily and abundantly with all the necessities of life, protects me from all danger, and preserves me from all evil. All this he does out of his pure, fatherly, and divine goodness and mercy, without any merit or worthiness on my part. For all of this I am bound to thank, praise, serve, and obey him. This is most certainly true.[1]

The first article of the Creed is most certainly true. Yet it is precisely here where believers in North America fight their first and foremost battle with their culture.

Dependent on the Creator

As we hear in these words from Luther's Small Catechism, expressing our trust in God our Creator asserts our total dependence upon him. We depend on him for the daily material needs of earthly life, for protection from every danger, for preservation from all evil. Our faith that God is our Creator confesses that we earn not a thing for ourselves by what we do. All human life is totally a gift. It is significant that Luther teaches God's "pure, fatherly, and divine goodness and mercy, without any merit or worthiness on my part" at this place, not in regard to trusting in Christ for salvation in the second article. Rather, when we view life as our Creator shaped it in the first place, we see above all our dependence upon him.

North Americans want to believe that they stand on their own two feet. People in this culture insist that we are free to do what we can do, free to do as we please. The biblical faith confesses that we are dependent on God's goodness and mercy. The biblical faith confesses that we are bound to thank, praise, serve, and obey God. For us "to be free" means to be what he has made us to be—no more and certainly no less.

The biblical doctrine of creation describes the relationships God established as he fashioned his creation. He established himself as God and Lord of all his creation, also of his human creatures, whom he shaped in his own image (Gen. 1:26). He established the relationship of human creatures with each other in community and mutual support (Gen. 2:18). He established the relationship of human creatures to the rest of creation, a relationship of "dominion," that is, God-style support and service, love, care, and concern (Gen. 1:26–30). He established the peace and harmony within the individual human creature, which comes only from finding identity, security, and meaning in God alone. Finally, he established his entire creation as very good (Gen. 1:31).

C. S. Lewis observed that in the religions of this world a doctrine of creation "seems to be a surprisingly rare doctrine." Doctrines of creation are often expressed in "myths," that is, stories that are designed to confess the truth whether they are literally factual or not. Although there is some myth about creation in most primitive religions, these myths are, according to Lewis, "often religiously unimportant."[2] These religions acknowledge origins of some kind, but their stories of origins do not determine relationships for daily life. The core of daily life and self-consciousness does not depend on these creation myths. Unlike the biblical teaching regarding creation, such creation myths touch only the margin of human existence.

In contrast, the entire Scriptural message affirms God's preserving presence at the heart of daily life. This message rests upon the presuppositions (1) that God fashioned all the universe and every human creature himself (Gen. 1:1–31); (2) that God is mindful of his human creatures and has made us little less than himself (Ps. 8:5); (3) that he has given us dominion in relationship to the rest of creation, which is also the product of his creative hand (Gen. 1:26). As a result of this, his human creatures can only confess, "Yahweh, our Lord, how majestic is your name in all the earth!" (Ps. 8:3–8).

God Created All out of Nothing, and It Was Good

"By faith we understand that the world was created by the word of God, so that what is seen was made out of things which do not appear" (Heb. 11:3 RSV). Some believe it to be the height of rationality that a Creator created creation. For others throughout human history, creation has not been considered "creation," that is the product of a divine, creative agent. Some ancient philosophers believed in the eternality of matter. They posited one means of organizing this eternal "stuff" or another, by an external hand or an internal force. Others in the ancient world contradicted the biblical view of the goodness of the material creation by defining matter as a corruption of the good, eternal spiritual essence. Modern thinkers have persuaded many that the universe took shape out of a big bang or a very slowly evolving process, which took some preexisting something and pushed it in the direction of matter. Various cultures have thought that various views of the origins of the universe were rational. Through faith, the church has seen that God is Creator.

Creation out of Nothing

God did not have some preexisting matter at hand. Nothing is eternally coexistent with God. It is difficult to describe creation out of nothing (Latin: *ex nihilo*). The writer to the Hebrews asserts it as best he can. God fashioned what is seen out of that which did not have appearance (literally "that which was not a phenomenon" (Heb. 11:3). He is before all things (Col. 1:17). Before he formed the earth and the world, he existed (Ps. 90:2). At the beginning there was only God. Then he spoke, and creation came into existence (Gen. 1:1, John 1:1). "By the word of the Lord were the heavens made, their starry host by the breath of his mouth. . . . For he spoke, and it came to be; he commanded, and it stood firm" (Ps. 33:6, 9). The creation is his. He made it and us. He is the Lord.

The Goodness of Creation

The Lord labeled his creation "very good." On five of the six days of creation God observed that the product of his creative Word was good (Gen. 1:4, 10, 12, 18, 21, 25). At the end "God saw all that he had made, and it was very good" (Gen. 1:31).

Although Eden's gates are closed, God's "very good" still echoes, though sometimes faintly. Human experience with material things often discourages us from acknowledging that the material order is very good. We encounter the material in our own bodies, and we notice these bodies chiefly when they do not function well, when they are dying. We see the corruption of our own flesh, and we feel the temptation that surges through bodily desires. We encounter the things of this earth as they fall apart and disappoint us. We conclude that the created order is not good.

When we experience disappointment with God's material creation, we need to remember that it did not fall. It was fallen upon. The ground is cursed because God's human creation "ate from the tree about which I commanded you, 'You must not eat of it.' " Because of human defiance and deafness to God's voice, the ground is cursed (Gen. 3:17). The entire creaturely order has been groaning in travail together. But it will not be shucked off and thrown away, as the ancient Gnostics suggested it should be. Its anticipation will be met with the fulfillment of hope; it will be restored. It will be liberated from its bondage to decay along with the children of God (Rom. 8:19–23).

Thus, believers thank God for the entire material order, from their bodies to the farthest star. Believers praise God for the gift of his creation, for limitless possibilities of using it for good purposes, for expressing human love in manifold ways. Believers delight in God's limitless imagination. This creative imagination has designed human language and water and bread and wine as vehicles of his saving power. It has designed human sexuality and athletic ability and taste buds for the fulfillment of our humanity. Believers join the psalmist in acknowledging, "How many are your works, O Lord! In wisdom you made them all; the earth is full of your creatures. . . . I will sing to the Lord all my life; I will sing praise to my God as long as I live" (Ps. 104:24, 33).

At the same time believers do not regard the material creation in idolatrous fashion. In contemporary North American culture the abundance of material goods and the importance of human technology tempts us to rely too heavily on the material order for identity, security, and meaning. God has placed the material order around us to support human life as he planned it and to glorify himself. He did not fashion the created order so that humankind could exploit it for its own purposes or refashion it into an idol.

Christians therefore can affirm the materialists of this day in their judgment regarding the importance of the material. At the same time Christians contradict the materialists' belief that life depends upon having certain things of this earth. Those things enrich life; they do not establish, insure, or elevate it. To focus life on what God has made rather than on God blinds his human creatures to the fundamental reality that permits us to use the things of the earth rather than to be enslaved to them.

In Good Order

Chaos existed before God fashioned what is, in the midst of nothing (Gen. 1:2). God is a God of order. He does not proceed arbitrarily in his dealings with his human creatures. He has shaped human life and all the rest of creation with an inbuilt structure and design. Genesis 1 unfolds his creative acts by recounting what he brought into existence in orderly fashion on each of the six initial days that stand at the beginning of time. He wrought the universe with a sense of order, developing it from light and its separation from darkness all the way to the various forms of plant and animal life, finally climaxing in the creation of Adam and Eve.

Thus, believers trust that there is an underlying order to the world God made around them and for them. They believe that humankind is obligated to work to preserve this order and to combat abuses that would destroy this order. Believers are confident that God has given the gifts of human curiosity and human ingenuity in order to permit investigation and proper use of the created order. Such curiosity and ingenuity must always remain harnessed to the assignment God gives—to care for creation well and to love other human creatures effectively. Thus, believers use the gifts of curiosity and ingenuity and all the gifts in God's orderly creation in full consciousness of their nature as gifts from God.

He Made Us and Not We Ourselves

Human life begins and centers in God. There were no human beings until God created the human creature and blessed them—

52

no human souls, no human bodies, until the human creature became a living being by God's action (Gen. 1:27–28). God modeled us after his own image. God formed the human creature from the dust of the ground and breathed into this creature the breath of life (Gen. 2:7). Neither dust nor breath dare be forgotten. We are creatures of the breath of God. We stand in a symbiotic relationship with the rest of creation: From its dust we are fashioned; yet until we were here to till the ground, no plant of the field sprang up (Gen. 2:5). Nevertheless, God did not issue a license for human exploitation of nature. The whole created order belongs to God. Nature is designed to protect itself against human abuse. God stands in judgment over human misuse of his world and its resources.

The breath of God points to the vertical relationship that human creatures are designed to have with their Maker. The dust of the earth points to the horizontal relationships that human creatures are designed to have with the rest of his creation. What makes us right and human in relationship to God is our response of love and trust to the gift of life he gives without merit or worthiness in us, apart from any deeds we perform. What makes us right and human in relationship to the rest of creation is our proper performance of God's commands, our proper tilling of its ground, our proper care for its creatures.

God's design of the human creature gives us a reason to praise. He sparks awe and wonder in us because we see how "fearful and wonderful" he is. His image in us reflects his care and concern in creating our inmost being, in restoring us to a proper relationship with him, and in knitting together the body that emerged from our mother's womb (Ps. 139:13–18).

Biblical Anthropology: Dichotomous or Trichotomous?

God's human creatures have described their makeup as either dichotomous or trichotomous—two-part or three-part. Christ spoke of the destruction of body and soul (Matt. 10:28), incorporating all that is human in these two parts. The writer to the Hebrews divides the soul from the spirit, parallel to dividing joints and marrow in the body, suggesting that in the unseen part of the human creature there are two subdivisions (Heb. 4:12). Paul used this trichotomous description of the Thessalonians in his benediction upon them (1 Thess. 5:23). On the other hand, Mary's use of "soul" and "spirit" in the opening of her song of praise seems to make the two synonyms (Luke 1:46–47). Nowhere in Scripture does God clearly set forth his architectural plan for the human creature. The biblical writers worked with the cultural descriptions at hand in their societies. Therefore we need not lock ourselves into one description or the other.

Body and Soul

Because God is spirit (John 4:24), and thus unseen, and because our bodies do fail us in their mortality, we tend inevitably to think less of our bodies, particularly when they become uncomfortable. Christians know that their bodies are bound for resurrection (1 Cor. 15:42–44). The human body came from God's creative hand, out of the dust, fashioned with the nonphysical human components in the image of God for physical and nonphysical functions (Gen. 1:26–31; 2:7). God included that body in what he pronounced very good (Gen. 1:31). Therefore, God despises every kind of neglect or abuse of human bodies, of our own and of our neighbor's. He calls upon us to help and befriend our neighbor in every bodily need.

Whatever we may think of our physical components, we most easily designate the rest of what we are as "nonphysical." That fact demonstrates how much we are bound to our bodies. The body provides the orientation point for our thinking about ourselves. However, we think about ourselves as beings who include something other than the physical. We speak of people who do not think very well (or at least as we think) as "having lost their brain," but they still have a brain. We mean that it does not function as we think it should. We speak of people who do not feel what we would like them to feel as people "with no heart," though the mass of muscle in their chest cavity continues to beat. There is something nonphysical about us that is very important. Our minds and thoughts, our feelings or emotions, are as important for our sense of who we are as our bodies—perhaps more so.

Those unseen components are often lumped together and labeled "soul." The "soul" includes reasoning powers and the ability to feel; it includes will and conscience and personality. It includes

54

whatever makes the difference between a living body and a corpse; it embraces whatever it is that makes.us "alive." Untangible as all these things may be, they are real, and we are tempted to say that they are the real "us." Even if contemporary biophysicists are correct in their belief that all cognitive and emotional activity might be explained in terms of electrical charges tracing through human "grey matter," we refuse to be reduced to twitching ganglia hooked up to the central cerebrum and cerebellum.

Trust in the Creator Holds Life Together

Believers recognize that there is another "component part" to being human, even beyond body and soul. Body and the several components of soul (mind, reason, will, emotions, etc.), which we have described, remain functional—though not complete and whole—in the horizontal relationships of earthly life, even when sin reigns in our lives. To be fully what God made us to be, however, we must be in relationship to God as well. The trust that binds us to God takes place in the unseen functions of "brain" and "heart." That ability to trust God could be called a third part of humanity and labeled *spirit*. But it can be deceptive to place the vertical dimension of our humanity alongside the two component parts of humanity that can exist outside faith in God. Then it might be thought that faith is a "thing" (what medieval Christians called a "habit") that could be reinserted in the fallen human creature much in the fashion of an organ transplant.

Trust in God is not merely one more component part of our humanity. Trust is the relationship that grasps our whole being, body and soul—reason and will, mind and emotions. Trust fulfills our humanity by completing it with the vertical dimension of human living. Mistrust breaks that relationship. Unbelief misplaces that core orientation. Unbelief seeks ultimate identity, security, and meaning elsewhere, not in Yahweh. Our spirit is not just one more component part, like our bodies, our wills, our emotions, our reasoning (although *spirit* can indeed be used to describe these latter, too, in another sense). Our "spirit" instead arises from our whole being, drawn forth to embrace the God whose outstretched arms create the spirit of our trust, our love, our childlike fear of him who made us. *Trust* is a better word than *spirit* for the human end of the relationship with God.

Our spirit, our trust, rests in him. The Hebrew word *shalom* sums up what it means to rest in God. The usual translation of that word is "Peace," but it means far more than the cessation or absence of hostilities. The dictionary provides an array of definitions for shalom: completeness, welfare; unconcern, ease; prosperity; intact state, unmolested, unviolated; health; friendship, friendliness; salvation. The verbal form can mean "to be completed or finished," "to remain sound, uninjured;" "to make intact, complete, good."

In the Garden of Eden Adam and Eve did not so much "have peace," as a possession they had won for themselves, as they "were at peace." Their existence was wrapped in the blanket of harmony and settledness that God bestowed upon them as a gift. Such was their humanity. It was designed to be righteous, that is, in the right place, in the right relationship, first of all with their Creator. For them peace was having life all together, with all its elements in the right place. Peace was not rest, but it was restful. It was being confident that all was going well in the midst of every human activity. At the heart of this gift of peace stood, also for Adam and Eve, the favor and love of their God. For all their descendants peace is trusting that God presents us with the gift of his presence and preserves as his progeny.

In the Image of God

God is Creator, progenitor, father. He cares about us, and he loves us. He protects us and provides for us. He is the ultimate source of our identity, security, and meaning. He is God. He is the very center of our lives. It is impossible to marginalize him. He is either there, where he belongs, or he is absent, thrown out of our lives. He can find a place, space, in our lives only at their centers. He is Creator. That is what the doctrine of creation is all about.

We are creatures. Being a human creature is a wonderful gift. It is wonderful to be God's child, to be certain of his love and secure on his lap. God created us as part of his family, in his image (Gen. 1:26–27). Christians have interpreted what "in his own image" means in several ways. Some have defined it as human perfection, human holiness. Others have insisted that it is the human ability to

56

reason and to make decisions, elements of human nature that such people have usually defined as central to our humanity. Still others have believed that other human characteristics, such as our creativity and our desire to reproduce children of our own, must reflect God's image in some way. The image of God includes all these things. In our vertical relationship the image of God in the human creature was designed above all to reflect back to God the love and tender care God shows to us.

Exercising Dominion

In our horizontal relationship the image of God was designed above all to reflect to other creatures, particularly other human creatures, God's love, care, and concern for them. It is indeed wonderful to be God's child; it is also wonderful to have the adult responsibilities he has given his human creatures. These responsibilities are summed in the word *dominion* in Genesis 1 (vv. 26, 28 RSV). This word has been much misunderstood in Western culture because readers of the Scripture have translated this concept from biblical thought into worldly thought.

Dominion means "lordship." In the power structures of this fallen world lordship means power exercised for the sake of the powerful. It is true that King Louis XIV claimed not only to be the state himself but also to be "first servant" of the people of France. But in fact political structures set some people "in charge" not only to serve but also to be served. These power structures of this world are easily manipulated for selfish purposes, for the exploitation of others subject to them.

Dominion has a strikingly different meaning in the language of God. Gentile rulers lorded it over their people, but Christ taught the disciples that "it shall not be so among you" (Mark 10:43 RSV). Whoever is great among God's people will be servant to others; whoever wants to be first among them shall be their slave. The model is clear: Christ himself came not to be served but to serve and even to sacrifice his life as a ransom for his people (Mark 10:41–45).

God lords it *under,* not over, his creation. He is in charge, and he exercises proper authority. He exercises this control for the sake of his creatures, not for his own sake. So it is with the dominion that his people are to exercise. This dominion is designed to serve, to *lord* it in the sense of embodying the Lord's care and concern and love. This dominion exploits neither nature nor other human creatures for its own sake. It lords from below, supporting, uplifting, embracing—and guiding and directing as is appropriate.

In Genesis 1 God relates "dominion" specifically to nature, but believers recognize that they are called to deliver this same service of reflecting God's love and care to other human creatures as well. God observed immediately that it was not good for the man, Adam, to be alone (Gen. 2:18). He needed not a lord nor a servant but a helper (Gen. 2:18), one to stand next to him, in mutually supportive community. Human community is of the essence of this creature God has made in his own image. No one is an island. We are linked by far more than bells tolling at death. We are joined together in a common humanity by the God who has given us life, and with life responsibilities for one another.

For the exercise of the adult responsibilities of dominion in the horizontal realm of our lives, God structured situations of service. He designed human life to be lived in the places or situations of nurturing homes, providing occupations, cooperating societies, and worshiping congregations. In each of these situations God has given human creatures responsibilities—"response-abilities," the ability to respond to human need in God's image, as his "masks," behind whom he comes to provide and protect. Believers and unbelievers alike find life in these situations. In their responsibilities they find secondary sources of identity, security, and meaning. Unbelievers may view these responsibilities as opportunities or assignments, as delight or duty or dreary drudge. Believers recognize them as vocations, as callings from God to be his masks, to reflect his image in the incidental displays of love and concern that make daily life possible.

God's Claim on His Creation

The doctrine of creation establishes not only that God is creator and I am creature. It also establishes God's basis for evaluating me. His design, expressed in his law, asks whether I have loved him with my heart, soul, and mind, and have loved my neighbor as myself (Matt. 22:37–39). If I have not fulfilled my humanity in accordance with the design of the Creator, I have placed myself under judgment. Sin gets its very definition from the Law's design (1 Cor. 15:56). Furthermore, the doctrine of creation establishes the basis for my re-creation. I am created anew in the image of the Word who, as image of the invisible God, created all things and reconciles all things by making peace in the blood of the cross (Col. 1:15–20).

The doctrine of creation also establishes my own worth as a creature of God. It is blasphemy to blame mistakes on "being only human." God did not make junk. The problem with human living does not spring from our humanity. It springs from our abandoning our humanity, centered in God and lived in service to the rest of God's creatures. The human creature stands high in God's design for his universe (Ps. 8:3–8). To love ourselves more than we love God—to listen to our own voice rather than to God's—guts our humanity. To love ourselves in the way in which God loves us, as his children, confesses God's glory as our Maker and acknowledges our status as his creatures.

Furthermore, the doctrine of creation establishes the worth of all other human creatures. All prejudice, all enmity, all hatred is ruled out by the worth that God has placed on the life of every human brother and sister, even when they are living apart from him in unfaith. Total love, care, and concern for one another are ordained by God's placing us together with others in our common humanity, in the community of mutual support to which he has assigned each human being. He has called us to love one another as we love ourselves. His verdict, announced by his Son, that we are his loveable children prevents us from not loving ourselves and others as children of God.

Free to Be God's Children

The predominant contemporary views of human freedom present perhaps the most serious challenge to the North American believer's understanding of our status as children of God. Two views of human freedom—determinism and voluntarism—are abroad in this culture. These are contradictory, but in the thinking of many individuals, they are able to find an uneasy peace with each other.

Determinism

For the first time since the days of the early church, many in the culture around us have resigned themselves to a kind of determinism. Determinism places ultimate power for human decision-making outside the individual, setting the human creature at the mercy of something external. The powers and principalities of Paul's world (Rom. 8:38) have been replaced by genetic determinism or environmental coercion. People are being told—and thus often believe—that they are trapped by their genetic makeup. They cannot be what their genes have not programmed them to be. They are condemned to the illnesses or behavior patterns that their genes impose upon them.

On the other hand, people are told that their upbringing and home environment have patterned habits that are next to impossible to break. They are victims of a social and economic system that has effectively marginalized them from the chief benefits of society, and there is little they can do about it. The human being exists, in the view of the determinists, "beyond freedom and dignity."[3] Enhanced by "proofs" from the natural and social sciences, determinism seems to confirm much of human experience. Nonetheless, all the evidence that contemporary interpretations of the human condition amass for a deterministic view fails to convince us completely. Something in each victim of nature or nurture cries out against this judgment.

Voluntarism

The opposite of determinism is voluntarism. Voluntarism is the belief that the human will is free to exercise its choice on most if not all options before the individual. The belief in a free will, or free human choice, stands at the center of the North American value system today. It arises out of the conviction that each individual must take care of himself or herself. Voluntarism's roots go back in part to ancient Greek thinking. At the pinnacle of Greek philosophy, in the age of Socrates, Plato, and Aristotle, the figure of a Creator God had retreated over the horizon of religious thinking. The human being was left alone to decide and govern his fate. To think through the fundamental plan for human action in such an arena, it was necessary to posit a human will largely, if not totally, unencumbered by necessity, by outward force or condition. The Greeks built a successful society on the basis of this conviction. They found that encouraging at least the elite of society to act freely, according to rational standards, led to good government and benefits for the whole of the community.

During the age of the "Enlightenment," eighteenth-century Europeans came to similar conclusions. Disgusted at more than a century of wars disguised as religious strife, and increasingly self-confident because of technological and medical advances, they sought solutions for problems in the exercise of human rationality, executed in free choice. The Rationalist thinkers of this age reinforced the Greek heritage that defined the human being essentially as a freely willing, thinking, self-governing individual. (Brakes were placed on many of the worst implications of such a view by the strong sense of community that tradition and the necessities of a more primitive economy placed upon them.) This view was part of the theoretical basis of the American Revolution. The success of that Revolution and of the society it launched has only enhanced this view of humankind.

The concept of such a free will, working independently of its Creator and governing itself on the basis of its own rationality, cannot, of course, be found in the Scriptures. Human freedom, as described by the biblical writers, does not consist in the absence of any conditions, confines, or constrictions for human action and attitude. Genuine human freedom is a gift from God, to be used within his design for his purposes. This is not an imposition or a deprivation. It is the way God has made us. He has made me "free to be me," but free to be the "me" whom he designed and defined. He created us, and not we ourselves.

The Biblical Concept of Freedom

Freedom within God's design brings blessing and fulfillment to the human creature. God's gift of freedom liberates me, first of all, from everything that might threaten me. God's freedom permitted Adam and Eve to live without fear, safe and sure in his love. God's new gift of freedom in Christ bestows *freedom from every evil* that threatens fallen sinners: freedom from sin, guilt, death, and the condemnation of God's law. At the same time God's new gift of freedom in Christ restores our *freedom for service,* to God and to the rest of his creation. Living in shalom, in harmony and peace, with other human creatures and his nonhuman creation gives us the experience of true human freedom.

Bondage of the Will

Many label a third phenomenon "freedom," too. It is the freedom to exercise our wills against God. How God could permit such an evil to invade our humanity is not explained by Scripture and is not clear to human rationality.[4] Many have tried to reason that this exercise of the freedom to oppose God fulfills our humanity. The opposite is the case. In exercising our wills against God we destroy our trust in our Creator and thus lose the ability to fully enjoy his best gifts. We bind ourselves to a false source of identity, security, and meaning when we "freely" choose options that run counter to trust in God and to his plan for our lives. This bondage turns us away from God. We are no longer able to choose him, to turn freely to him. We cannot fear, love, and trust in him above all things because our wills will not function to make that choice. Revolt and rebellion are choices from which there is no turning back.

The alternatives for describing the possible shapes of human life are not exhausted by viewing the human creature as either a freely willing being or as a puppet, an automaton. The third alternative reflects the biblical reality: God made us neither to be independent beings who fulfill themselves in free choice exercised against God, nor to be puppets or automatons. He created us to be his children. The mystery of the relationship between Creator and human creatures is certainly not completely described with this definition of our creatureliness. Perhaps it is not adequately described for our curiosity. But such is Christ's definition of those whom he has come to restore to the Father's family (John 3:3–8; Matt. 18:3).

Sin has bound the human will to turn its back on God. Although we still experience the ability to make choices in the horizontal realm, we cannot turn to the true God. We seek substitutes for him without being able to turn to him. Only the Holy Spirit can turn us from false sources of identity, security, and meaning to find in him the one we can trust ultimately.

Freedom and Responsibility

This biblical view of the human creature does not, however, deny human responsibility. Instead of positing an individualistic human liberty as the essence of humanity, the biblical writers describe the human creature as able to respond. Our response takes place in relationships—response to God with trust and love, response to the rest of creation with responsible acts of love and care. In the Augsburg Confession Philip Melanchthon sorted out this paradox by teaching that human creatures are not free in "things above," in our vertical relationship to God, but are free in our horizontal relationships, in "things below."[5] Although, as we will see, this oversimplifies our human experience, it expresses the fact that in the vertical realm we are born and reborn as God's children. We have no more sovereignty of action or control over our relationship with him than infants have over their choice of parents, over their status as members of their parents' family. Melanchthon's definition also expresses the fact that God's law does hold us responsible for our own actions in regard to the rest of creation.

Even apart from biblical insights on the matter, human experience teaches vaguely something of this truth. Most people recognize, particularly at critical junctures in their lives, that they are unable to control the course of human events as completely as they would like. At the same time they enjoy the sense that their decisions do affect the direction of their own lives and often of the lives of others as well.

The paradox of the Creator's reality lies deeper than this easily resolvable tension within our experience. The Gospel assures us that our entire life lies safe in God's hand and that he is responsible for all in his created order; his Law demands responsible action from us at every turn. The paradox between these two statements will not be resolved but must remain, giving us peace on the one hand and calling us to account for our failures on the other.

Thus, the biblical view of human freedom and the human will does not fall neatly either into the category of determinism or into the category of voluntarism. The whole of human life lies in the hands of God, but he does not impersonally manipulate human fate in the manner of ancient projections of divine force or modern theories of genetic or environmental determination. Much of human life moves on the basis of human decisions, and we are convinced that our decisions do make a difference. But evidence accumulates quickly to echo the biblical view that we are not captains of our own fates nor masters of our own souls. The biblical view of God's loving care and fatherly responsibility for us lies alongside its view of our call to obedience and human responsibility, exercised by our own wills, in an uneasy tension.

Modern psychology does assist us in recognizing that the tension between free choice in things below and bound choice in things above is not the only distinction of importance for our analysis of sinful wills. Creaturely circumstances of various kinds limit the possibilities for choice in daily life. Not all people can be everything they want to be. Some will never have certain natural capabilities to perform certain acts or achieve certain accomplishments. Sin complicates the matter of choice not only in the vertical realm but also in the horizontal realm. In things below we often experience the visitation of the parents' sins upon the children (Ex. 20:5). Households twisted by sin teach sins to their offspring and thus cripple the will of the next generation. Such crippled wills are often not even capable of exercising free choice in things below. Many abused children, for example, seem to some extent bound to abuse their own children, for they have had ingrained into them a model for parenting that knows no other pattern of behavior than abuse. Such wills are bound in relationship to other human creatures, as well as in relationship to God.

Even if the will were completely free, freely chosen abusiveness would hardly be recognized as freedom. The very inhuman nature of the act would be seen by all as a form of bondage. So it is with every form of activity or attitude exercised against God. True human freedom lies only in acknowledging him as Creator and ourselves as creature. True human freedom enjoys being free from evil of every form, and it enjoys being free for service to God and others.

He is Creator, and we are his creatures, his children. His design for human life gives life as it can only be enjoyed. Therefore, the biblical teaching on creation challenges every way of thought that misleads people regarding the relationship between the Creator and his created order.

Challenges to the Biblical Teaching on Creation

Pantheism

The Scripture draws a sharp divide between the Creator and his creation. All biblical teaching rests on the presumption that God is indeed "wholly other" than what he has made. Pantheists deny that God and creation are fundamentally distinct and different. They equate God and creation. Some pantheists spiritualize creation and try to draw it, or its essence, into the nature of God. Materialist pantheists project some divine force into nature and equate nature and its individual elements with the ultimate in divine power.

Ancient Hinduism had pantheistic elements. The early modern philosopher Baruch Spinoza denied a personal divine being; he taught that the divine substance extends itself in the form of nature and creatures of all kinds. Some mystics within the church have taught that our goal as human beings is to unite with God's spirit, diminishing or eliminating the distinction between God and his human creatures. This belief denies God's uniqueness as Creator, and it denies the goodness of being God's human creature. The attempt to assert a participation in the divine nature for humanity destroys a biblical understanding both of who God is and of who we are. Any confusion of Creator and creation skews a proper understanding of their relationship.

Deism

In the Enlightenment some Western philosophers put distance as well as distinction between the Creator and his created order. Deists taught that there is indeed a Creator God but that he has lost interest to one extent or another in his creation. God removed himself from his creation and plays little or no role in its continuing development. Some Deists taught that God is totally absent from his world; he is like a clockmaker who, having created the clock, winds it up and leaves it ticking away on its own forever. Others taught that God exercises providence over his material world but has left the moral and spiritual order of things in human hands. Still others permitted him a role in the spiritual realm but denied that he had created a future life for humankind.

God has displayed his presence and asserted his concern and care for all of his creation. Human attempts to assert his absence from his creation may be based on what seems to be logical human judgment. Some of those judgments proceed from his seeming absence when evil seems to triumph. Others proceed from human self-confidence, on the basis of the ability of human reason and human ingenuity, to forge a better life. Evil's seeming triumph reflects the mystery of its very existence, and no adequate answer apart from God's love in the crucifixion of his own Son can be found. Human reason and human ingenuity reflect the genius of the Creator; both reason and ingenuity fail often enough to demonstrate that no lasting basis for human life can be found in them alone. Only God's presence in his creation sustains its operation and preserves the human community in the midst of all its woes. The Creator still preserves us.

Dualism

The mystery of evil does call into question the complete power of God over his creation. Therefore, some thinkers have from time to time suggested that two more or less equal divine powers must exist, and human beings must be victims of their continuing struggle, the struggle between good and evil. Different dualistic systems have described the final result of the struggle in differing ways. In some the struggle is eternal. In others good is supposed to win the final victory. In both approaches salvation is possible along the way as the forces of good win individual human creatures back from the evil force or god.

The most famous dualist is the shadowy third-century figure Manes or Manichaeus.[6] He taught that light and darkness, as eternal principles, are locked in conflict. His "Manichaean" doctrine found significant following in the period of the early church. Its echoes are still heard in the twentieth century in those searching for a logical explanation for the power of evil. Scripture teaches that God has asserted his own control of evil in the face of our perception of its seeming triumph. He claims his creation as his own even in the midst of its own defiance of him and its fall into evil. He remains Creator.

Gnosticism

Manes seems to have developed his views under the influence of a system of thought called Gnosticism.[7] So called because its followers believed that they had the secret "gnosis" (Greek for knowledge) of life, Gnosticism taught a dualism between spirit and matter. The varieties of this system of thought all rest upon the presupposition that the spiritual is good and matter is evil. The ultimate good was held to be impersonal spirit, existing as the unknowable Divine Being beyond the grasp of mortal humans. In some way or other this Divine Spirit generated or emanated separate spiritual beings, among them by some mischance a "Demiurge" or "Word" or creator. Through its agency creation came into being.

The entire material ordered was not viewed as good, however, by the Gnostics. It was evil, through and through, and it imprisoned sparks of the Divine Spirit, which had fallen down the ladder of generations or emanations to the worst possible situation, entrapment in a material body. Salvation was viewed as the liberation of the individual's soul or spirit from the material body. This would lead to progressive exaltation up the many levels of spiritual emanation. This exaltation would be completed in the loss of individuality, the absorption of the spark of soul that had once been individualized into the impersonal Divine Spirit at the other, highest, end of spiritual being.

Gnosticism deprecated both God's good material creation and human individuality. Saint Paul criticized both these errors by teaching the resurrection of the body (1 Cor. 15:42–44). God has fashioned each human creature through his continuing care of his creatures (Ps. 139:13; Job 31:15; Jer. 1:5), and he loves us as individuals. Our resurrection as individuals is assured; we shall live with him as individual human creatures. God's created, material order was made good. He continues to use it for the blessing of his people, in both the horizontal and vertical dimensions of human life.

Individualism and Materialism

In contemporary Western culture, however, both these good gifts of God, our individuality and the material order, have become idols themselves, sources of primary identity, security, and meaning for many people. These two errors demonstrate how God's gifts become perverted in the minds of fallen sinners. When people rest their lives upon their own rights rather than on God's plan of mutual dependence, they turn their backs on fellow creatures and on God himself. God created human beings not to be alone (Gen. 2:18) but for life in community and interdependence. I am not an "I"sland. I am a part of the mainland of God's humanity. Human worth cannot be found in reckless assertion of one's own individuality. Individuals find their true worth in the relationships that God designed for them with himself and with their fellow creatures.

Likewise, individuals do not enjoy their humanity when they try to depend on God's material blessings for their ultimate sense of well-being. God gave material gifts for his creatures to enjoy in mutual service, not as ends in themselves. They enjoy human living when they recognize these blessings as blessings and use them for the benefit of others as well as themselves.

Atheistic Evolution

Evolutionary dogma teaches that the material is primary and that the world came into being and operates without God. Evolutionary dogma must be distinguished from biological theories that use genetic or physical or chemical information in tracing changes within God's creation that fall under his normal management of this world.

The description of genetic change poses no challenge to the biblical teaching of creation. In the nineteenth-century battle against Charles Darwin's followers some Christians did try to defend the doctrine of creation by asserting an immutability of biological species. There are no biblical grounds to warrant such an assertion. God operates in his world through various mechanisms, which are part of his providential care. The biblical writers, inspired in their historical situation, had no knowledge of contemporary genetic theory, obviously. (Even Darwin did not; the discoveries of his contemporary, the Roman Catholic monk Gregor Mendel, which began modern genetics, were not published until after Darwin's death.) Genetic change and the development of new species may well be part of this plan of God. On the other hand, such theories may be surpassed by future scientific research and conceptualization. We do not need Scriptural precedent for the working tools of contemporary biologists in order to recognize, appreciate, and benefit from their work.

Some scientists label the theories that work with evolutionary change at the level of gene and chromosome "microevolution." When evolutionary thought is extended from a working tool for research to a framework for ascertaining and interpreting the meaning of life and of the universe, it becomes "macroevolution." "Macroevolution" is a dogma that rests upon leaps of faith like the dogmas of other systems of belief. Confusion between the two levels of usage behind the term "evolution" has led some Christians into focusing on the differences between evolutionary dogma and the biblical faith in unhelpful ways. Just as significant as this dogma's denial of the biblical account of the creation of the world is its faith in human powers to determine and define what reality is.

To understand the fundamental differences between the biblical teaching on creation and the evolutionist faith system, we return to epistemology, the manner in which human creatures learn and know. The faith system of contemporary evolutionary theory claims to establish its beliefs on the basis of the empirical, experimental, "scientific" method of learning. This method relies on the human senses' evaluation of data on the basis of a program of experimentation devised by the experimenter. The method presumes that knowledge can be proven by repeated testing. It claims an objectivity to its findings because they can be submitted to trial by others, who can find out by repeating the experiment that the original judgments found in the original experiments were correct. Objects that cannot be subjected to repeated testing lie outside the command of this approach to human knowledge.

Therefore, when the epistemology of human experiment tries to define the origins and bounds of reality, it has gone beyond the limits of its competence. It has gone astray when it attempts to answer a different kind of question than the questions for which it was designed. It exceeds the acknowledged limits of the scientific method set by those who use it, the scientific community, when it attempts to pierce the veil behind which lies the origin of all things and the ultimate control of the universe. When evolutionary dogma attempts to formulate a general theory of the beginnings of creation and its ultimate meaning, it goes beyond its own boundaries—it exceeds its own definition of the capabilities of its method. Origins are not subject to repeatable experiments, as empirical knowledge insists must be the case for it to be able to explain and confirm explanations. The guiding mechanisms for creation's engines lie beyond the grasp of experiment.

Evolutionary dogma cannot be truly scientific when it wanders into explanations that arise not from experiment but from leaps of faith beyond empirical testing. Evolutionary dogma cannot be truly scientific when it seizes upon faith statements from a voice of authority regarding issues on which there can be no experiment but only conjecture beyond the realm of empirical testing. The origin of the universe, since it cannot be repeated, must lie outside the realm of empirical explanation. The guiding principles that drive nature and human history must lie outside the realm of scientific analysis since they cannot be subjected to the instruments of empirical testing.

Christians confess that God lies beyond the instruments of human definition and control. By definition the ultimate power of the universe must lie beyond human control, unless that ultimate power is human definition and control. Because of this, truly theistic evolutionism is not possible. True "theism," that is, the faith in the God who reveals himself in crib and cross, must abandon the empirical epistemology of experiment when it listens to its God.

God tells us first that he created all that exists, not with a big bang but with a still, small voice that said, "Let there be." Whether that still, small voice loosed a big bang is beyond our knowing. If such a theory can add to the human good, it would be fine. But like all theories we establish to serve our needs in the horizontal realm, such a theory is at best tentative human knowledge.

Christians do well to distinguish and properly use the contrasting epistemologies that must govern knowledge of God and knowledge of his creation, also when they address the problem of evolutionary dogma in our society. The attempt to disprove evolution empirically is part of the way in which natural science proceeds according to its own rules. There are many more good empirical, scientific arguments against some fundamental presuppositions of evolutionary dogma than the establishment in the Western scientific community admits—although believers should not be blind to the inner logic of its dogma. Therefore, Christian biologists and philosophers may want to participate in the continuing testing of evolutionary theory through experimental argument. They should recognize, however, that conducting the defense of the biblical teaching of creation on the turf of empirical epistemology undercuts the biblical position.

Even if one could "disprove" evolution by empirical means, the source of that knowledge lies within human control. That disproof of evolution would still not accurately reflect how believers come to know God as Creator. Such an approach would put our knowledge of creation always at the mercy of the next theorist, who could use empirical terms to express a different dogma.

Believers also must recognize that their rejection of the system of dogma associated with the name of Charles Darwin must include rejection of "Social Darwinism" as well. The views that arose out of Darwin's concept of the "survival of the fittest" made a significant impact on social thought in Western culture. Racists and ruthless capitalists and imperialists used popularized Darwinism to propagate inhuman and antihuman views of humanity.[8] Social Darwinism issued a scientific license to many in the late nineteenth and early twentieth century for exploitation and oppression of others. The biblical doctrine of creation forbids such inhumane treatment of others.

Believers should also recognize that Darwin's interpretation of the natural world arose within the context of nineteenth-century Hegelianism and the broader currents of thought that embraced a doctrine of inevitable progress. Georg Wilhelm Friedrich Hegel (1770–1831), professor at the University of Berlin, codified the Enlightenment conviction that human history is moving in an inexorable drive "upwards"—toward an ever better, more perfect form of life. Even the age of the Enlightenment had experienced moments of discouragement in regard to this doctrine—the great Lisbon earthquake of 1755 killed 30,000–40,000 people and shook budding confidence among the Enlightened. Nonetheless, the technological and medical progress of the age encouraged high hopes for human progress.

The experiences of Mengele's medicine and the applications of technology employed by Adolf Hitler and Pol Pot have somewhat dampened enthusiasm for the doctrine of progress. But hope springs eternal, and most North Americans still want to believe in the inevitability of progress. A closer look at ancient or recent history permits no such illusions. Therefore, Christians should recognize that underneath Darwin's thought lies an untenable presupposition: that earthly life will inevitably and inexorably progressively improve, and do so on the basis of powers not defined as the power of Yahweh. From this presupposition some individual ideas of merit may proceed; for some aspects of God's creation microevolutionary explanations may be helpful. However, from such a presupposition will proceed a dogma that inevitably and inexorably opposes the biblical understanding of Creator and creature.

God remains the presupposition of his entire creation. He began it in the beginning, and he sustains and preserves it until that day on which he ends it. He is our Creator and we are his creatures. All human life proceeds from him. He is its starting point. All biblical teaching proceeds from the beginning, which lay in God's hand and Word. Not we ourselves, nor any other forces of the universe, but rather he has made us and all things, and he remains our caring Creator and loving Lord.

Notes for Chapter III

1. Martin Luther, Small Catechism, Creed, Article I, 2, *The Book of Concord*, trans. and ed. Theodore G. Tappert (Philadelphia: Fortress, 1959), 345.
2. C. S. Lewis, *Reflections on the Psalms* (New York: Harcourt Brace Jovanovich, 1958), 78.
3. In the words of B. F. Skinner, *Beyond Freedom and Dignity* (New York: Knopf, 1971).
4. See the discussion of theodicy in chapter IV below.
5. Augsburg Confession, Article XVIII, *The Book of Concord*, 39–40.
6. Jaroslav Pelikan, *The Christian Tradition, a History of the Development of Doctrine, 1: The Emergence of the Catholic Tradition (100–600)* (Chicago: The University of Chicago Press, 1971), 136–37.
7. Pelikan, 81–97; J. N. D. Kelly, *Early Christian Doctrines* (New York: Harper & Row, 1960), 22–28.
8. George L. Mosse, *The Culture of Western Europe: The Nineteenth and Twentieth Centuries, an Introduction* (Chicago: Rand McNally, 1961), 77–78, 200–205.

Chapter IV

God Provides

God claims that he has all life in his hands, and that he provides us with body and soul, limbs and senses, reason and faculties of mind, food and clothing, and everything else that we have and are. Our belief that God is daily and richly taking care of us provides a foundation for our entire life of trust. It provides the framework in which we praise our God in songs of the heart and deeds that touch the needs of others.

God Provides for His Own

God provides for all, for everyone and everything in his entire creation. He keeps it and us running. "In him all things hold together" (Col. 1:17). He upholds the universe by his word of power (Heb. 1:3). The God who made the world and everything in it, Paul told the Athenians, fashioned every human nation on the face of the earth. He has allotted them periods of time and geographical boundaries for their lives. Paul then used the words of the ancient poet Aratus, and perhaps also Epimenides, in confessing that in God we live and move and have our being and that our existence stems from him (Acts 17:24–28). He has promised to keep the seasons in their places (Gen. 8:22). God makes his sun rise on the evil as well as the good and sends the rain on the just and the unjust (Matt. 5:45). He preserves humankind and animal life (Ps. 36:6), and he provides for the interworking of all parts of his creation (Ps. 104:10–31).

God's people are particularly conscious of his role in their lives from conception and birth (Ps. 139:13, Job 31:15, Jer. 1:5) to death (Matt. 10:28–31). He who keeps inventory of the hairs on our heads (Matt. 10:30) holds his thinking, willing people in his own hand and plan (Ps. 37:24; Prov. 16:9). He keeps his people in his sight, delivering them from death and keeping them alive in famine (Ps. 33:13–

15, 18–19). Believers rest upon the assurance that God directs their lives for their good (Rom. 8:28). That does not mean that everything they experience is good. In an evil world believers suffer things that grieve God, too. But his hand directs good and evil in their lives toward good ends.

God Receives the Complaints of His Own

God's direction of life is not always clear to believers. Believers often encounter misfortune and suffer evil at the hand of other human creatures or at the mercy of nature. Some believers shy away from complaining to God about such suffering. Usually, such shyness is dishonest about our feelings. It also denies the depth of God's love for his human creatures. It is not wrong to cry out to God in anguish and to lay our suffering and sense of loss before his loving heart.

God did not create us to be angry with him, but we must recognize the difference between the cry of faith, "God, I am angry with you," and the cry of unbelief, "I am angry with God." The first shriek confesses God's lordship and our expectation of his goodness, even if in a negative way. It betrays sinful misapprehensions of how God is working in our lives, but it does not deny that we have only him to turn to in the evil hour. In response to such a shriek of pain and anger our heavenly Father is always ready to swoop up his children into his loving arms—even when they are throwing a temper tantrum—and cuddle them in his lap.

God's ancient people said, "The Lord has forsaken me, the Lord has forgotten me." In mock indignation God replied, "Can a mother forget the baby at her breast and have no compassion on the child she has borne?" Then he assured the Jews whose despair in the face of the devastation of Zion had overcome them, "Though she [your mother] may forget, I will not forget you! See, I have engraved you on the palms of my hands . . . Those who hope in me will not be disappointed" (Is. 49:14–16, 23). The maternal instinct of God our Father never fails.

Thus, even in anger and frustration over God's apparent absence or his mistaken direction of the course of our lives, we can boldly and confidently approach him as children approach a loving Father. Believers do experience days on which Job's words can give voice to their thoughts: "[God] throws me into the mud, and I am reduced to dust and ashes. I cry to you, O God, but you do not answer; I stand up, but you merely look at me. You turn on me ruthlessly; with the might of your hand you attack me" (Job 30:19–21). Finally, however, in the midst of all their suffering, God leads his people to confess with Job, "I know that you can do all things; no plan of yours can be thwarted" (Job 42:2). This confidence, shaken and battered as it might be, permits God's children to throw a fit at his feet, but it is also the handle by which he lifts us to his lap.

God Is Lord over Evil

God may seem to be absent because evil may seem to triumph. But God is lord over evil. When his people were suffering oppression in Egypt, he liberated them by smashing Pharaoh's tyranny. When the angels left their proper positions, he chained them in the darkness. When Sodom and Gomorrah indulged in immorality and unnatural lust, he punished them with fire (Jude 5–7).

God's control over evil is so complete that he could even claim it for his own purposes. He claimed responsibility for light and darkness, for "weal" and "woe" or "prosperity" and "disaster" (Is. 45:7). He could say, "Against this family I am devising evil, from which you cannot remove your necks" (Micah 2:3 RSV). He causes blindness and deafness even as he gives sight and hearing (Ex. 4:11). Amos could console his hearers by explaining, "Does evil befall a city unless the Lord has done it?" (Amos 3:6). None of these passages offers an explanation for the origin of evil. None of these passages can be easily dismissed by saying that what we view as evil—for instance, blindness—may not really be evil from God's point of view. The message of these passages points to a deeper truth. God is lord over evil. God has the whole world in his hands. God masters and moves all human history. Without piercing the mystery of evil these passages affirm God's lordship over everything, even evil.

Thus, when evil assumes control of people, God is not absent. He may be present in giving them over to their stubborn hearts (Ps. 81:11–12; cf. Acts 14:16; Rom. 1:24). This does not mean that he does not want them to be saved (1 Tim. 2:4). It means that he retains control of his creation.

God grieves over the evil that afflicts his people. God sets limits upon the evils that afflict them. These limits may not fall exactly where Job and his kin would prefer them to fall, but God does set limits (Job 1:12; 2:6). God never forgets his chosen people and is always sensitive to their limits (Matt. 24:22; 1 Cor. 10:13). He intervenes on their behalf and frustrates their enemies' plans (Ps. 33:10). He turns enemies into friends, a Saul into a Paul (Acts 9). Not always but often he takes the evil intentions of evil people and fools them; he brings good out of evil, as he did in Joseph's case (Gen. 50:20).

God is the loving Lord of his people. He answers their prayer that he keep them as the apple of his eye and hide them in the shadow of his wings (Ps. 17:8). He remains their Father and King.

God Preserves and Provides through the Created Order

God exercises his kingly, fatherly love by preserving and providing for his people. For instance, he feeds them. Sometimes he does that by sending manna (Ex. 16:14). Usually he provides food through his ordered system of provision (Gen. 1:19– 30, 9:3).

Nature Works According to God's Pattern

Nature works according to God's plan, under his direction, exhibiting a fairly regular set of natural causes or "laws." Human nourishment proceeds from, among other things, his governance of the weather (Job 36:26–33). The discipline of meteorology may not have mastered God's program for rain and lightning, but the patterns of weather are plain enough for squirrels and for farmers to give us reliable folklore. His plans regulate the course of seasons and days (Ps. 104:19–23). The "laws of nature" have been passed in the legislature of human observation and scientific analysis. Human investigators are always refining these laws. But God has written into the script for his creation a normal, regular, quite reliable pattern of action. This enables human creatures to use and manage creation— to exercise dominion under it.

Miracles

God cares for his creation through miracles as well. The word *miracle* may refer to any event in the physical world that deviates from the laws of nature that human investigators have formulated and that supersedes current knowledge of those laws.

Such miracles may proceed from God's power; they may reflect the power of Satan (Matt. 12:24). The word *miracle* may also be applied to any event that opens the eyes of human creatures to God. John recorded the "signs" Christ performed in order that his readers might believe that Jesus is the Messiah, God's Son, and that by believing they might have life in his name (John 20:31).

Some miracles provide for God's children; all of them invite faith. From the perspective of human analysis three types of miracles emerge. Some may defy explanation for all time; they actually transcend the way in which God normally works in his universe. Commercial production of quality wine from water lies beyond our imagination (John 2:1–11). Some miracles may be explained with advanced human knowledge. During the years of my university study the friend of a friend, we learned, had been miraculously cured of leukemia. A quarter of a century later I now suspect God used newly developed "miracle" drugs and the physicians who were experimenting with them in performing that miracle. The friend's remission still gave us cause for praise of God; it remains a miracle even when "explained." Third, some miracles may indeed have a scientific explanation. The Exodus was possible because God sent an east wind, and through its blowing all night long he drove back the sea (Ex. 14:21). But the circumstances and the timing of the Exodus remain a sign of God's providence no matter what the "scientific explanation" of paths across the water might be.

Believers must reject the claims of those who reject the possibilities of miracles because these people want to assure human control of God's universe. God retains control. He mocks us just at those moments when we believe we have mastered the technology to preserve life as we like it (Gen. 11:1–9). Believers must also avoid thinking that God is providing for us only when he works through miracles. He is utterly faithful in meeting the needs of his people, on his terms—not always on ours.

The Structures of Human Life Provide

God provides not only through the regular and irregular workings of the natural or physical world about us. He provides through the structures for human life that he has woven into the warp and woof of human society. His structure arises out of the four situations for human community—home, occupation, societal relationships (both the formal relationships of the political sphere and the informal of neighborly contact and associations for specific purposes), and congregational life. God provides through fellow human creatures, whom he uses as masks for his own presence and caregiving as he gives them roles or responsibilities to play. He provides as they function in fulfilling the responsibilities of spouse, parent, child; of supervisor or worker, of butcher, baker, and candlestickmaker; of legislator or bureaucrat, taxpayer or police, of neighbor or Little League coach; of worshiper and witness, of pastor, Sunday School teacher, or altar guild member.

God calls Christians to such responsibilities; he appoints all human beings to such tasks. Through the exercise of these "response-abilities" he meets the needs of others in an orderly way. Different societies organize the four situations differently and define the responsibilities of each situation in sometimes differing manners. God actively supports and governs his world through all his human masks whatever institutional forms their situations may take.

God Provides through Angels

If we weigh the biblical evidence, human creatures serve God as his primary means of meeting the needs of other human creatures. Nonetheless, the biblical writers occasionally noted the critical importance of God's angelic creatures in caring for his human creatures as well. The Scriptures give few details on the nature and none on the origin of the angels. Called "gods," assembled in God's council, in the Old Testament (e.g. Ps. 82:1; Ps. 138:1), they assumed the name "messenger" (Greek: *angel*) in the New Testament. In the intertestamental period Jews elaborated their description of the angels with elements from neighboring peoples. This does not alter the fact of the angels' existence. Because the angels do not subject themselves to human analysis and control, some have doubted their existence in the modern Western world. The angels do not depend on human belief in their existence to continue to provide God's care for his people.

God created the angels to praise and worship him (Is. 6:3). They serve as his messengers (Matt. 1:20; Luke 1:8–20, 26–38; 2:8–14; 24:1–8). They will assist the Lord in completing human history (Matt. 25:31; 1 Thess. 4:16). God has commissioned them to have charge of his people and guard us in all our ways. They bear us up on their hands and protect us from stumbling (Ps. 91:11–12). They confront the enemies of God's people, whether they be armies (2 Kings 19:35) or lions (Dan. 6:22) or jailers (Acts 5:17–21; 12:6–11). Around those who live in God's family his angel has thrown up a line of defense and rescues them from evil (Ps. 34:7).

Providence in the Face of Life's Tragedies

Evil abounds, even in the lives of those who live in God's family. The most piercing question believers and unbelievers scream into the ear of God or the dark of the night is "Why?" "Why is there evil in the world if God is good and almighty?" This is the ultimate of human questioning in a fallen world. Variations abound. In the realm of eternal salvation the question is phrased, "Why are some saved, and not others?" In the realm of daily life the question takes the form of demanding to know why my brother died young, why my company failed just before my pension was vested, why my attempts to win the right spouse always end in shame. "What did I do to deserve this?" we cry out as we notice that worse scoundrels than we are getting off scot-free. "Why is life so unfair?" we ask, but the concept of "fair" provides inadequate protection against the onslaught of evil.

Jesus' contemporaries posed the question to him more than once. His disciples wanted to know whether the man who had been born blind had brought his condition upon himself or whether his parents were at fault. It is not clear exactly what Jesus meant when he replied, "It was not that this man sinned, or his parents, but that the works of God might be made manifest in him" (John 9:2–3). The text does not make clear whether Jesus' "that" refers simply to the result of the situation or to its actual purpose. Jesus may have been refusing to indulge in speculation regarding the "why?" of the situation and simply commenting, "Whatever the cause, the result of his blindness is that God's work is to be made manifest here." However, to the Jewish mind, with its utter confidence in God's control of all things, Jesus may have been saying, "God had a purpose in this man's blindness: to give the opportunity to show forth what God is doing in me." We cannot tell from the text.

This same approach guided Jesus' address to two questions posed at another time by events around him. He cited two examples of the seemingly unfair way in which tragedy befalls people. Pilate's police had mingled the blood of some Galileans with their sacrifices. Jesus used this incident to meet the obvious question: "Do you think that these Galileans were worse sinners than all the other Galileans because they suffered this way?" "Or those eighteen who died when the tower in Siloam fell on them—do you think they were more guilty than all the others living in Jerusalem?" Jesus refused to answer the question. Instead, he used these incidents to call for repentance. He rejected the equation of such evils with a certain quantity of sin. Such a verdict stems from a false understanding of God's judgment. God's judgment is designed not first of all to punish but to call to repentance. "No," Jesus said. They were not the worst offenders; these Galileans had not sinned more than their fellow Galileans. Such questions missed the point. The only point that Jesus drew from these incidents was the need for personal repentance by all (Luke 13:1–5). He wanted the whole life of all his human creatures to be lived in being turned back to himself.

Theodicy

The question remains today: How can evil exist if God is truly good and completely powerful? No logical answer has ever been formulated to this most pressing of human questions. Efforts to solve the problem abound. The attempt to solve it is haughtily called *theodicy,* the justification of God. A German philosopher of the eighteenth century, Gotthold Ephraim Lessing, invented the term. The effort to vindicate God by explaining how he could ordain or permit natural and moral evil predates Lessing by millennia. But God refuses to permit his human creatures to justify him, to remodel him and refurbish his image, even in the face of evil.

Manichaeans tried to get God off the hook by inventing a counter-god and according it responsibility for evil. But a thoroughgoing dualism condemns the human creature to hopelessness in the face of the arbitrary struggle between two more-or-less equal forces of good and evil. There must be a more satisfying solution.

Evil Is Not an Illusion. Some have tried to deny the first of the three points of the dilemma: that evil exists. In the nineteenth century Mary Baker Eddy codified the hope that evil would prove to be an illusion into a religion, Christian Science. Much of Western culture since the Enlightenment has secretly hoped that she was right. The Enlightenment itself wished that evil had been somewhat overrated. Its rationalism hoped that human mastery of the world around us and human abilities to forge and force the good would triumph over evil. Holocaust and Hiroshima, the killing fields of Kampuchea, of Bangladesh and Biafra, have somewhat discouraged us. In spite of our experience in the twentieth century, however, even many Christians in North America hope to soft-pedal the human experiences of guilt and shame, of tragedy and tribulation and trouble, of despair, death, and damnation—and put on a happy face. AIDS and other diseases, crack and other drugs, random killing and other deaths all insist that we deny evil at our own peril. Denying evil makes fools of us all.

Is then God not good or not almighty? The poet Archibald MacLeish suggested in his play *J. B.* that God cannot be good if he is truly God (that is, all powerful), and he cannot be God (almighty) if he is good.[1]

God Is Almighty. The contradiction remains. Rabbi Harold Kushner is a good example of those who hang onto the hope that God is good and solve the problem of evil by conceding that God is not almighty. In his book *When Bad Things Happen to Good People*[2] Rabbi Kushner offers a two-fold "solution" to the question of theodicy. First, we may hope that God is evolving toward being almighty. Second, we must forgive and love God in spite of the fact that he does not come up to our standards for the good. Rabbi Kushner's is a thoroughly human god, truly a god created in our own image. Furthermore, he focuses only on the evils outside us, the evils over which we have no control. He avoids confronting the evil within. He proposes forgiving our limited, flawed god and re-maining—as far as is possible in the face of bad luck, sickness, and cruelty—in control.

God Is Good. The other possibility denies God's goodness. The drama *Amadeus* depicts the composer Salieri's struggle against evils directed at him from a god who had a mean streak in him. Salieri had pledged God his whole life if God would give him fame. God

81

went back on the bargain Salieri thought they had struck. The frivolous, impudent Mozart got the talent and recognition Salieri had wanted, as author Peter Schaffer weaves the script, and Salieri became bitter, despising God. (Who would not despise such a god!) Salieri's solution to the problem of evil placed all power in God's hands. But Salieri saw that power displayed in "the taunting of [an] unachievable, uncaring God."[3] Neither Kushner's god nor Salieri's satisfies. They satisfy neither the biblical description of God nor human longing and need.

The Biblical Approach to Theodicy

But why is there evil? The question remains unanswered and unanswerable from the vantage point of the fallen human creature. God does answer two other questions. He does tell us where evil is going. It is headed for its own tomb, led by our victorious Lord. He explored the way out of the tomb for us. He explored the tomb as the place where he will finally lay all evil to rest. Furthermore, God does tell us where evil puts us today. Evil puts us out of relationship with God. God comes to combat evil every day through the presence of his people. They turn back evil with their love for the vulnerable and suffering, for those who suffer bad luck, sickness, cruelty, or their own guilt and shame.

The Permissive Will of God. We may try to get God off the hook by distinguishing his absolute will from his permissive will. We know that God does not want or cause evil, so we presume that he permits it against his own will. This "solution" tries to pierce the veil of the Hidden God. It neither meets any basic kind of logical criterion for analysis, nor does it meet the need of the sufferer. It may persuade us emotionally to feel better about God, but Job did not find God's giving license for evil a great comfort. Neither do many others. Even when we have posited a permissive will of God, we have not answered the question of "why" he would permit evil even if he does not cause it. The dilemma remains.

Reward and Punishment as Explanation for Evil. The Scriptures offer several partial solutions to the problem of evil. Evil afflicts the guilty, for God visits iniquity upon those who perpetrate it (Ex. 34:7). God rewards good conduct and punishes sinful conduct. That is only just and fair. This answer has the strength of explaining a good deal of evil. We reap what we sow. We smoke, and we get lung cancer. We drive dangerously fast, and we have an automobile accident. God's Law keeps close track of us, and it dispenses its judgments.

This view helps us preserve a sense of order and regularity in the world about us. It preserves a sense of God's justice and fairness. But it does not explain "innocent victims." Too often it drives us to assess blame of some sort where none actually exists. Some smokers do not die young; some nonsmokers do. Some speeders never get caught, to say nothing of dying in an accident. Some pedestrians who never crossed against a light are struck and killed on their way to visit the sick or feed the hungry. Furthermore, this view focuses on human performance and human guilt. God's Law does that. We dare not so focus on human performance, however, lest we somehow suggest that creatures control their own fate. This approach to the problem of evil may bring some sufferers to repentance, but too often it will turn them in upon themselves, seeking a false explanation for suffering.[4]

Lament to God as a Reaction to Evil. At other times biblical writers turned to God in lament, as Habakkuk did when he cried out "How long, O Lord, must I call for help, but you do not listen?" (Hab. 1:2). Habakkuk looked to God for relief from suffering by calling down God's judgment against his enemies (Hab. 1:5–2:20). Jeremiah did the same: "Let my persecutors be put to shame, but keep me from shame; let them be terrified, but keep me from terror. Bring on them the day of disaster; destroy them with double destruction" (Jer. 17:18). Such expression of negative feelings—outright hatred for the foe—seems too impatient and too self-righteous. It puts the burden on God's back—and perhaps the blame on him for failure to deliver his people from their oppression. Yet it honestly vents the believer's frustrations and fears. It correctly calls judgment down upon evil. It expresses trust in God and thus puts the lonely lamenter in community, at least with God.[5]

The Suffering Servant. The model of the suffering servant of Isaiah (42:1–4; 49:1–7; 50:4–9; 52:13–53:11) suggests that suffering must be absorbed vicariously, that is, for others. However, those who take this model of thinking about suffering and transfer it from Christ to themselves may fall into self-righteousness in their suffering. Furthermore, on the individual level, suffering for others does not always deliver them from their suffering. Nonetheless, this model points to Christ's vicarious suffering for all human creatures caught in the trap of the ultimate evil, sin and its corollary, death (1 Cor. 15:54–57).[6]

Job's "Answer." The book of Job presents an impressive array of attempts to answer the question "Why?" None finally satisfies. Perhaps the greatest treatment of theodicy in human literature, this book finally challenges those who demand that God justify himself. "Shall a faultfinder contend with the Almighty?" God asks Job. "Will you even put me in the wrong? Will you condemn me that you may be justified?" (Job 40:2, 8 RSV). Job's final confession leaves the question unanswered. He can only acknowledge that God is God: "I know that you can do all things; and that no purpose of yours can be thwarted" (Job 42:2). He acknowledges his own unworthiness before God, "I despise myself and repent in dust and ashes" (Job 42:6). God remains God, and Job remains his child.[7]

God does not tell us where evil comes from in the first place. Philip Melanchthon summarized the biblical material by stating that "although God creates and preserves nature, the cause of sin is the will of the wicked, that is, of the devil and ungodly men. If not aided by God, the will of the wicked turns away from God."[8] But this answer stops short of the answer we demand in our misery. What lies behind or beyond our own perverted will and that of the devil? It would do us no good to know.

There are really only two possible answers. It is either our fault, or it is God's fault. Neither answer gets us out of our own mess. We need the answer to the questions about the present and future— where we are now with evil, and where we will be with it. Those questions God has answered in Christ, and that is enough. We need not and dare not chase after the Hidden God for answers to the question of the origin of evil. We can rest assured with the answers that the Revealed God has given us in the death and resurrection of his Son. We cannot justify God. God has justified us. He has justified our existence for eternity with him. That is all we need to know.

The doctrine of providence grabs hold of God. It climbs into his lap. "The doctrine of providence" is better said, "faith trusting a loving and providing God." The doctrine of providence leads us to reject faith as a good luck charm. Faith endures when evil seems to imply the absence of God. Faith clings to God's person and promise, even when no sign of blessing appears.

At the same time the doctrine of providence rejects fatalism: faith does not sing "que sera, sera" [Italian: whatever will be, will be]. Faith reaches out in confidence for the extended hand of God, even when it reaches blind. It rests assured that God's hand is there even when that hand is not evident.

That is enough to bring believers into chorus with Habakkuk. He began by rehearsing how human existence was severely threatened, how all had gone wrong (3:17–19):

> Though the fig tree does not bud,
>   and there are no grapes on the vines,
> though the olive crop fails,
>   and the fields produce no food,
> though there are no sheep in the pen
>   and no cattle in the stalls,
> [in other words, not much more could go wrong]
> yet I will rejoice in the Lord,
>   I will be joyful in God my Savior.
> The Sovereign Lord is my strength;
>   he makes my feet like the feet of a deer,
>   he enables me to go on the heights.

Or, as Paul said, "I have learned to be content whatever the circumstances. I know what it is to be in need, and I know what it is to have plenty. I have learned the secret of being content in any and every situation, whether well fed or hungry, whether living in plenty or in want. I can do everything through him who gives me strength (Phil. 4:11–13).

Only the Lord can ultimately preserve his people. He is, in fact, our last resort. It is good when faith finds him as our first resort. It then confesses that he had made us and still preserves us. It recognizes that—because of his providing love—it is our delight to thank and praise, to serve and obey him.

Notes for Chapter IV

1. Archibald MacLeish, *J. B.* (Boston: Houghton, Mifflin, 1958), 15.
2. Harold S. Kushner, *When Bad Things Happen to Good People* (New York: Avon, 1981).

3. Peter Schaffer, *Amadeus* (New York: Harper & Row, 1981), 150.

4. Daniel J. Simundson, *Faith under Fire: How the Bible Speaks to Us in Times of Suffering* (New York: Harper & Row, 1991), 17–41.

5. Ibid., 43–61.

6. Ibid., 63–79.

7. Ibid., 81–101.

8. Augsburg Confession, Article XIX, *The Book of Concord,* trans. and ed. Theodore G. Tappert (Philadelphia: Fortress, 1959), 40–41.

Chapter V
Sin and Evil

Although it is impossible for human thought to pierce and solve the mystery of evil, there can be no doubt that evil exists. Just a glance at what is going on in the world confirms what most people suspect on the basis of their own lives but do not want to admit. At some point or another everyone awakes from pleasant dreams with a fearful realization that something is wrong. Things have gone awry, plans have gone astray. Things are not right; we are not right with the world. The harmony and order and peace we would like has vanished. We are discontent with the way in which we shaped our identities. We are uncertain about how secure our lives may be. We are worried about how much life is worth and what it all means. We recognize that life has somehow missed the mark we would have liked it to hit. Life is out of sync, out of kilter. One Hebrew word for that is best translated "sin."

Evil Is Not to be Denied

Our dreams are often more or less on target. They tell us something of the potential for human life as God created it. Our sober assessments of our lives remind us that life has been fouled. Peace is elusive. The pursuit of happiness can become so consuming that the happiness never falls within our grasp. There is a big gap between hope and reality.

The reasons for that gap can be divided into two categories: the evil outside us and the evil inside us. Evil is everything that does not correspond to God's intention for his creation, for his human creatures. Evil exists because some of his personal creatures, angelic and human, turned their backs on him. Human creatures experience some evils over which they have no control—evils from the surging of natural forces not held within their bounds as God had originally planned, and evils from the grasping of other human creatures,

87

seeking to secure their own lives at the expense of others. Human creatures also experience some evils over which they do have control. These evils, for which we are personally responsible, we call sin. Most human creatures more readily recognize and acknowledge the former, external evils. More threatening to individual well-being and the harmony of our communities is sin.

Yet it is often hard for us to face the reality of either kind of evil as it disrupts the peace God designed for our lives. We often avoid facing the evil squarely. It is too much for us. Our security depends on our control, or at least on our knowing who has control. We can only be completely honest about evil when the threat is not too great—when either we or someone who stands by us can stave off the evil and provide victory over it.

After we have recognized the threat of evil from outside—from other people or from forces difficult for us to control—we also have to recognize its threat inside. The evil lurks within us, with a force that we also cannot always control. If we cannot control the evil within us, then what can we count on to give us a sense of peace, a sense of identity, security, and meaning with which to preserve our lives?

We have to deceive ourselves to preserve what we can of our life, of our identity, security, and meaning—unless we are living in the Truth, the one who is the way and the truth and the life (John 14:6). We human creatures have all learned well the delights of deceit from the father of lies and deceit, the devil, the deceiver (John 8:44). He is a murderer, and his lies, which become our lies, take our life away.

The Liar's Lie Infects Us All

The Scriptures trace the problem, the evil, back to the devil's murderous deceit, to be sure. The Scriptures make clear that God is good. He is not the cause nor origin of human sinfulness. He created his human creatures, along with the rest of his creation, good (Gen. 1:31). He takes no delight in wickedness. He abhors human sin (Ps. 5:4–6; Zech. 8:17). When Adam and Eve fled his presence, God too wondered why (Gen. 3:9–11).

Sin arises out of the devil's deceit (1 John 3:8; Rev. 12:9). The devil's fallen nature drives him to deceive (John 8:44), and since the fall in Eden he has practiced his deceit in leading human creatures astray from their life of trust in God (2 Cor. 11:3; 1 Peter 5:8–9). Satan (Hebrew: the accuser) is always questioning the goodness of God's human creatures and calling into question the propriety of their receiving his blessing (Job 1–2).

Scripture says nothing about the fall of the angels aside from mentioning it (Jude 6). The devil took many with him apparently, for there are many devils (Mark 5:9). "From the beginning" of human encounters with him the devil set out to take away the life that God had given the human creature, that is, to separate us from God (John 8:44). The devils recognize that they are engaged in a war to the death with God (Mark 1:23–24). But God is God; he has won. He has condemned them to "eternal chains in the nether gloom" (Jude 6 RSV), that "eternal fire prepared for the devil and his angels" (Matt. 25:41). Nonetheless, they continue to practice their limited but most formidable power in God's universe (Eph. 6:11–12; Acts 26:18). They assault human bodies (Luke 13:16; 2 Cor. 12:7), but above all Satan attempts to destroy the working of God's Word, the trust that forms the human side of the relationship between God and his human creatures. He does so by undermining human confidence in the truth of the Word (1 Tim. 4:1–4; Luke 8:12).

Judas' desire to betray Christ sprang from the devil's implantation of his evil plan into his heart (John 13:2). Yet the Scriptures never permit us to say, "The devil made me do it." The existence of evil poses big questions for us as we wrestle with how to put life right again. Where is evil taking us? Where has evil put us today? Where did evil come from? The Scriptures do not give us complete answers to that last question, but at least we know that the devil does not bear the blame and consequences of our sin. We do.

Doubt Calls God's Word into Question: The Original Sin

Adam and Eve were used to walking with God and chatting with him in the cool of the day. They were accustomed to being at his side. And then one day they fled from God and God missed them. They were in the wrong place, not the right place. The relationship was broken. Evil stems first of all from the broken relationship. The broken relationship is the origin and root of all sin. God created trust and love between himself and his creatures. Trust was broken, and peace fled when fear rushed into the heart of our lives (Gen. 3:10).

How did that happen? God had created everything by his Word. He spoke, and creatures came into being. Adam and Eve listened to God. They heard his call; they were used to talking with him. The relationship of the human creature with the Creator is at the core of what it means to be human. Everything that does not proceed from that relationship of trust in Yahweh misses the mark for our humanity (Rom. 14:23).

Satan came to challenge that Word of God. "Did God really say, . . ." the devil teased (Gen. 3:1). Eve began to play with God's Word. God had said in Genesis 2 (vv. 16–17), "You must not eat from the tree." Eve added in Genesis 3 (vv. 2–3), "You must not touch it." She tried to improve God's Word, perhaps in order to make certain that it could defend her in the way in which she wanted to be defended. She deceived herself into thinking she could take care of God's Word instead of relying simply on him to take care of her. Her attempt at mastery of the Word produced the devil's mastery of her. The devil's deceit led Eve, and Adam with her, to doubt and mistrust God. That was the original sin.

The root of all sin is human deafness to the Word of God. That inability to hear his expression of love corrodes our fundamental sense of identity as God's children, our fundamental sense of security in his hand, our fundamental sense of meaning as his people. Saying "no" or "not sure" to God's Word undercuts trust in him. From lack of trust—the need to secure life on our own terms—proceed all other sins. Breaking the first commandment inevitably leads to loving and trusting some other god. This lack of trust in Yahweh permits—necessitates—breaking each of the other commandments (Gen. 39:9). Thus, original sin, doubt, pervades daily human life.

Alternate Views of Original Sin

In their analysis of what went wrong with the human creature, Christians have come up with various answers. Eastern Orthodoxy teaches that the human creature was created incomplete though without sin, able "naturally" to "grow in divine life. Divine life is a gift, but also a task which is to be accomplished by a free human effort."[1] This view misses several important points. The "good" of Genesis 1 pronounced upon all creation posits a human creature truly good, in full relationship to God, without any need for further progress. The nature of sin is more radical than this view suggests. The broken relationship has destroyed the ability of the human creature to pursue the task of acquiring the divine gift of a full relationship with the Creator. The fallen creature is not so easily reparable or improved. The fallen creature has died in the sin of breaking away from the Author of life.

Traditional Roman Catholic theology also fails to focus adequately on the brokenness of the relationship. Original sin is defined as the "deprivation of sanctifying grace," which brings with it the necessity of submitting to suffering and death.[2] This quasi-quantifying of grace into a gift that God places in the believer focuses too much on what the creature *has* rather than where the creature *is* in relationship to God. The loss of God's grace stems from doubt of his Word, which has ruptured the relationship of his children with their Father.

Doubt Breaks the Trust

Some Christians overlook the fundamental fact that doubt broke the relationship of trust between creature and Creator. Often we think of the root of sin as disobedience, and we think of disobedience as doing something wrong. The problem goes much deeper than our actions. It goes down to the root of our attitudes toward life. The Hebrew word for obedience does not focus on what we do. The word in Hebrew for "hear" can also mean "obey." *Shama'*—hear. *Shama'*—obey. To hear God is to obey him. We do not obey because we are not listening. We doubt his Word. Sin is, at its root, being deaf to the Word of God, not trusting the Lord. "Everything that does not come from faith is sin" (Rom. 14:23).

Even in the most innocent of human creatures, tiny babies, original sin makes itself visible—in their sense of omnipotence, which demands and expects that all else will serve them; in their low frustration tolerance; in their sense of hurry and demand for immediate satisfaction.[3] Their mortality also reveals the curse. Babies die and death comes alone from sin (Rom. 6:23). Much confirms the psalmist's confession: from birth unrighteousness has plagued us; from conception sin has grasped us (Ps. 51:5).

Doubt Leads to Death

From the doubt of Adam and Eve has proceeded the doubt that deals death to every human creature. Judgment followed Adam's getting out of line, breaking his relationship with God. Death took control through him (Rom. 5:16–19; 1 Cor. 15:22). The church has called this fact "original sin." The doctrine of original sin has not been very popular among many Christians and has been an offense to those outside the faith. To inherit condemnation seems intolerable. We protest that we did not ask to be born this way, on the road to guilt, caught in mortality and evil. Our protest does not avail. Original sin is not a device biblical writers use to pin the blame for our sinfulness on Adam and Eve. The doctrine of original sin does not merely point out how unfair life is. Original sin is a teaching that reminds us of the impotence with which we are born. We have indeed inherited this state of despising the Author of Life, and thus true life itself. The doctrine of original sin impresses upon us that from Adam human creatures have lived under and experienced the curse—and tried to persuade themselves that they like it. This mortality, this determination to master our own lives apart from God, is not the original human condition. The doctrine of original sin repeats the curse; it also reminds us that our humanity was designed to do far better than this.

The doctrine of original sin offends us not only because it pins the rap on us without our being able to take control and do something about it. It offends not only because we stand under its curse together, as humanity linked to all its parts—Adam sinning for Eve, Eve for Adam, the both of them for all of us, and we for each other. It offends because Adam and Eve's doubt seems so inconceivable— and thus without excuse. Every human being would like to think that he or she would have done better at battle with the devil when the odds were even.[4]

Original Sin and the Bondage of the Will

The doctrine of original sin does contradict a concept of the freedom of the will, a desire to establish human autonomy and to define the human being as an independent, ultimately self-sufficient being.[5] The doctrine of original sin does point to God's being creator and thus judge of human performance. Yet, at the same time, although original sin is inherited, it does not remove responsibility from the sinful heir. Each individual has the "I" of self-will, the desire to control his or her own life.[6] " 'Will'is initially a future-tense action or verb ... The question is really not whether we 'have' free wills, but rather what we will do—what we are 'bound to' do—when we come up against God."[7] We all concur in Adam and Eve's doubt. Even when we claim freedom of the will, we will not choose God over alternative sources of ultimate identity, security, and meaning apart from his intervention into our lives.

Human creatures can muster the courage to admit how corrupt they are only when they know that God has intervened to save humankind from the corruption that has destroyed the vertical relationship with the Creator. Fallen, sinful eyes cannot pierce the mystery of human corruption, the destruction of the Edenic freedom from evil and for service. Our view of life, our understanding of how it functions, has been shortened and cut off. Even when we get a glimpse of its depth, the terror of its consequences blinds us. Jesus Christ has come as a second "Adam" to reverse the original Adam's desertion of Eden and to restore our humanity as God fashioned it for Eden. Only through this second Adam does the significance of the first Adam's folly and tragedy come clearly into our view and our grasp (Rom. 5:12–21).[8] The corruption or depravity is absolute or total in the vertical relationship. There sinners have lost it all. They cannot turn to God on their own. Their will automatically and instinctively chooses the alternative—any alternative—to their Creator, Yahweh.

This corruption or depravity has profoundly affected all horizontal relationships as well. The individual apart from God is the same individual whether acting in the vertical realm or the horizontal. Nonetheless, sinners can do outward acts for better or worse within the structures and strictures of the Law in its social and political aspects (civic righteousness). God's leash on the horizontal impact of human sinfulness often seems tragically and scandalously long. Fear and self-interest provide inadequate checks on the desire of sinners to secure their own lives on their own terms. Nobility of purpose can turn quietly into exploitation and cruelty. And yet people who do not worship Christ can often do better rather than worse. They can construct good governments and practice a fair amount of decency among each other. The need to use others to shore up their own sense of identity, security, and meaning rather than finding it serving God and neighbor causes them to trespass on the neighbor from time to time. But the corruption in horizontal relationships is limited—though it is always serious enough to prevent full enjoyment of life and often so serious as to institutionalize corruption, exploitation, and injustice. In contrast, Adam's and Eve's doubt totally and completely destroyed the relationship with God.

Some question whether Adam and Eve actually existed as historical beings. If they did not—if the fall into sin is not the historical revolt against God that Genesis 3 describes—then human sinfulness must stem from nature. The Creator must have built sin into the model of humanity. Sin would then be a necessary part of what it means to be human. Such a view destroys human responsibility and human hope.[9] Adam and Eve, creatures of God, stand at the beginning of human history. Their doubt, defiance, and denial of God permeate this history. We share Adam and Eve's doubt, defiance, and denial of God. We desire to be gods ourselves.

Falling Upward

Doubt turned immediately to denial that God is God. Here also, Adam and Eve's experience has become ours. Our doubt, too, defies his Lordship. Because, in the sinfulness in which we are born, we swept God from our lives, we had to desire to be like God (Gen. 3:5). We needed to supply ourselves with a new source of identity, security, and meaning. With God dethroned, we perceived a deficit in our lives, and we moved to fill it. We were dissatisfied with being "merely" human creatures, and so we tried to be more than mere creatures. In the process we became, instead, *less* than the perfect creatures God had fashioned in Eden. The fall into sin took place in an attempt to hurl oneself upward, not downward. Adam and Eve asserted their mastery over the Word, over God. They aspired to usurp God's place.[10]

Much of the Western church has equated original sin with pride. John Milton eloquently described the devil's fall in terms of pride.[11] Pride is certainly the cover we use. But the insecurity beneath human pride makes me wonder if sinful pride is not much like what the psychologist and philosopher Alfred Adler says about the superiority complex. Adler developed the concepts of superiority complex and inferiority complex. He argued, on the basis of his clinical experience, that there are no true superiority complexes. They all reveal an underlying inferiority complex. They arise from the need to compensate.[12] Sinful pride reveals only the vain attempt of the sinner to cover inadequacy and dissatisfaction. It indicates that we know more than we claim to admit about our true status and our real ability to control.

Defiance and denial divorce us from our God. This is no "friendly" divorce. We still listen to his call within our nature. But at best conscience and our sense of the numinous garble the message. God's Word comes now to accuse and condemn, to plague us as it pursues us, attempting to reclaim us. We run in the opposite direction, deserting God's presence, driven by fear and by pride.

Pride is only a nice try at reasserting our own ability to be god for ourselves. It does not work. Sooner or later we notice that we are not where we are supposed to be. In Psalm 51, David noted that and described our sinfulness with three different words. The first, *pesha'*, labels sin as "transgression, rebellion, revolt." We are trespassing where we ought not be, on God's turf. We have rebelled and revolted against him. The second word, *'awon,* means "iniquity." That means "not righteous," not in the right place, the right relationship, and thus practicing our humanity wrong. The heart of that false practice of our humanity lies in claiming false gods to secure our ultimate identity, security, and meaning. The third, *chata't,* means "missing the mark" or "missing the right point." It indicates that we have not aimed our lives properly. We are off the mark, off-target. We have found a place off-center for our lives, outside of the loving relationship that our Father designed for us.

But the gods we invent and claim—whether ourselves or other creatures fashioned by God—fail. Their power dissolves under the pressures of God's structure for human living. His created order cannot forever abide the assaults that human defiance launch against it. God's Law reveals the lies of our idolatries. God's Law points us again in the direction of Yahweh and thus labels as deception all reliance on false gods.

Dread Turns to Defensiveness
in Division and Disobedience

Our lies can drive the underlying fear out of our consciousness for a shorter or longer period of time. But finally what consciously or unconsciously shakes and moves our beings is the fear that Adam expressed. We do not have it "all together." We are naked in spite of our best efforts to clothe ourselves in our own accomplishments. Our desire to be God fails, and we are filled with dread, as was Adam (Gen. 3:10). Dread, the most powerful of sinful emotions, is there under the surface, always threatening to grab control. Only God's perfect love can drive it out (1 John 4:18). Without the intervention of God's love, dread twists our lives.

So we become defensive. We do not always recognize that sin exhibits itself in defensiveness. Sometimes that defensiveness takes form in hiding, fleeing from God's presence (Gen. 3:10) or running from the claims others have upon us, linked as we are in human community. Defensiveness can drive the sinner into the doldrums of apathy and withdrawal from human activities. At other times that defensiveness takes form in anger, abuse of others, and self-justification. The sinner knows that the best defense is a good offense, and so sinners are offensive. But we need to remember in dealing with sinners that their offensiveness arises out of the dread that is making them defensive.

This "defensive offensiveness" exhibits itself in division from one another. When the relationship with God—which gives us our ultimate sense of identity, security, and meaning—is broken, it is little wonder that we are also divided from our fellow human creatures. Only when we are confident that God is protecting and providing, can we open up our lives in that cruciform shape—arms outstretched to embrace and uphold others—the shape in which God made us.

Luther described sin as "being curved in upon ourselves," the self-enveloping fetal position, which is the opposite of the open, cruciform shape of life lived in Edenic peace. In sin we think that we cannot serve others because we doubt that we can depend on God for identity, security, and meaning. Now we think that we have to depend on God's creatures, at least in part, for our ultimate good and safety. They cannot be our gods, however; they will not serve.

We think that we need to use—manipulate, exploit—them instead of serve them. In so doing we always abuse them. So we grow angry, and we flee from them as well as from God. "That woman you put here with me" (Gen. 3:12), we say to God, recalling our division from him and at the same time trying to protect ourselves by hiding behind another human creature, using another human creature to secure our lives. It will not work.

Our broken relationship results also in disobedience to God's commands. Doubting his way of doing things, we do it our own way. This results in trespassing on the turf of others. We thus manipulate and exploit other people so that we can secure our own lives. This only encourages others to strike back, deepening the division through mutual disobedience. It seems to be impossible to break the circle of doing it wrong.

Despair Leads to Death, Death to Damnation

We bring upon ourselves a sense of despair because we cannot do it right. We cannot do it right because at the core of our beings we are not right, that is, we are not right with God. We have no peace. We are rest-less. We wear out. We die (Gen. 2:17, 3:19; Rom. 6:23). Doubt has produced a dread and defensiveness that lead us into division and disobedience. We call such sins "actual" sins—the actions that arise from the fundamental sinful attitude, which is the root of sin, the origin of sin in us, original sin.

Finally, the despair of being alone and doing it wrong brings to completion Satan's murderous lie. We die, and we are damned. From the original sin of doubt, with which we are born, the whole life of sin unfolds, and it keeps on unfolding until we die.

Division and Disobedience in Action

The church has employed several classifications that may help sinners understand the nature of the sins that plague daily human life. The fundamental distinction demarcates the original sin that destroys our trust in our Creator from all the acts of defensiveness that flow from that lack of trust. When we no longer "fear, love, and trust" in God above all things, we secure life by grabbing hold of other parts of God's creation. Instead of uplifting and upholding other human creatures and portions of nature, we grab hold and squeeze—for dear life. We abuse and manipulate God's creation. Only when trust in God gives us peace can we uphold and uplift, as he created us to do.

Actual Sins:
Vertical and Horizontal/Attitudes and Actions

These actual sins that our defensiveness exhibits may be analyzed in more detail if such analysis helps teach the doctrine of sin effectively. Original sin results in sins of thought, word, and deed. Those acts that exhibit our mistrust of God by abusing his name or his call to worship fall under the "first table" of the Ten Commandments, grouped there with the fundamental command to trust in him above all else. The "second table" of the Ten Commandments, commandments four through ten, treats acts that harm other human creatures in a variety of ways.

Another distinction can be made between the commandments that treat attitudes (one, and nine and ten—toward God in the case of the first commandment, toward other human creatures in nine and ten) and those that treat actions (two and three against God, four through eight against other human creatures). This distinction has been labeled the distinction between external sins of action and internal sins of attitude.

Sins of Commission and Sins of Omission. Still another distinction can be made between sins of commission and sins of omission. Sins of commission include those attitudes or actions that offend and harm directly. They break God's Law by doing the opposite of what it commands. Sins of omission break God's law by failing to do the positive it commands. They offend and harm in a passive or negative fashion.

Sins of commission are generally easier to identify. Sins of omission often have a much deeper impact on the relationship with God or the neighbor. Failing to "be there" with praise for God or for study of his Word only deepens the alienation between Creator and creature. Failing to be present with God's love or care for human neighbors deprives them of the support God intended them to have through human community.

Distinctions in Motivation for Sinning. The church has also distinguished sins in terms of motivation. Some sins we know we are committing; others are unknown, unwitting sins (Lev. 4:2). Our culture may blind us to the fact that certain actions are sinful. Holding another human being in legal bondage—slavery—almost inevitably leads to a variety of abuses that are ungodly. But cultural standards have obscured that fact from well-meaning Christian slave owners at times in the church's history, e.g. in ancient Rome or during the early history of the United States. Or we may do something that we would not mind having done to ourselves but would offend another person. In committing sins of which we are not aware we are exhibiting the deeply rooted and complex hold that sinfulness has upon the entire human being.

That pernicious and permeating hold upon our wills is also to be seen in the distinction between "voluntary" or planned sins and "involuntary" or unplanned sins. Paul complained of doing evil he wanted to avoid and failing to do the good he wanted to do (Rom. 7:15–19). This distinction does not lift responsibility from us; we experience the curse falling upon all our sins. Even when we protest that we did not plan to offend, offense is taken. When we felt trapped into doing what we "had to do," other people are still hurt. Even involuntary sins suffocate us.

Habitual Sins and Occasional Sins. The church has also distinguished occasional sins from habitual sins. Habitual sins are those that repeat themselves as part of our lifestyle; occasional sins are those we commit seldom, on specific occasions, or in specific situations. Again, each poses its own problems. But even the occasional sin reminds us of our sinful weakness and the need to be on guard and fighting against all temptations to depart from God's plan. Even habitual sins may be forgiven as we continue in the struggle against them. Their existence reminds us that the mystery of sin remains in the Christian life. Forgiveness does not always correct sinful habit. The struggle goes on. Believers must ask, "Why do you want to know?" as fellow believers ask about their relationship with God in the midst of their struggle against habitual sins. Only the Gospel can change such sinful habits, but defiant, secure sinners will not be able to hear the Gospel and must first be broken by the Law.

Individual Sins and Communal Sins. The struggle against sin continues for us as individuals and as members of larger groups. We distinguish those sins that we commit as individuals from those

99

we commit as members of society or of groups within society. Sharing blame with other members of the group, however, does not lift blame. We still feel responsible for sins with which we had nothing to do as individuals but from which we benefit. Our standard of living, possible only because some in Western society exploit other lands, places a burden upon us even though as individuals most of us have never consciously tried to exploit anyone from the Third World, we would claim. Indeed, contemporary white Americans did not personally hold slaves, and did not invent a system that systematically deprives racial and other minorities of justice. But they nonetheless suffer the consequences of this exploitation in a host of ways in which such exercise of racist injustice has twisted human relationships in this society. We suffer not only from our human solidarity in sin; we suffer as well from solidarity in sins committed by other members of groups of which we are a part. Such is the nature of human nature, as God made us in community.

Venial Sins and Mortal Sins. Some Christians have also distinguished sin into the categories of venial—the less serious, which are wrong but do not break the relationship with God—and mortal—the more serious, those that break the relationship with God. This distinction ignores the fact that each actual sin reveals the lack of trust beneath it. All sins are equal before God, for each betrays our corruption at the core, in our trust. Indeed, some sins are more serious to the neighbor than others. Most of us would rather be assaulted than murdered, for instance. God sympathizes with his human creatures as they suffer evil. He is not indifferent to the differences in what we suffer. But his heart is equally grieved by "small" and "big" sins. Each reaffirms our flight from him, our abandonment of our childlike stance before him.

Indeed, we may label the sinfulness that places us in the jaws of death as "mortal" (John 8:24; Rom. 8:13), for sin kills (Ezekiel 18, especially v. 4). But no particular actual sin offends God more or less than another. Failure to fear, love, and trust in God above all things—the original and underlying sin—separates us from the Author of Life.

The "Unforgivable Sin." Christ once referred to the "unforgivable" or "unpardonable" sin of blasphemy against the Holy Spirit (Matt. 12:31–32; Mark 3:29; Luke 12:10). He gave no details on what constituted this sin. Christians have speculated that it must be stubborn and unrelenting resistance to the Holy Spirit. The best response to questions concerning this sin is that the person who worries about committing it must not be. No profit can be found in pursuing speculation regarding this sin. Its mention should serve simply as a call to repentance and faith.

Evil in Its Several Forms

All these distinctions of sins reflect the human experience with the complexity of evil.[13] Individuals experience the breaking of God's plan for their lives in so many ways. When looking to the origin of the experience of evil, people find that some evils arise within themselves and some evils come from outside themselves. In the case of certain evils it is not always clear where the disruption began, and forces from outside combine with desires within to divert our actions from God's planned path.

Evils arise within when we plan to disobey God's Law and when we blunder into them, in what may be called involuntary sins. Evils arise from outside when nature or other human creatures assault. Some cults have suggested that we encounter evil only when we set ourselves up for it; they insist on total human control and responsibility. Believers experience the power of sin in a much more radical fashion. They recognize that the fallen universe can descend upon us without warning to disrupt our lives. They experience that fallen humans can descend upon us as they defend themselves, as they seek their own security at our expense.

Often, we encounter evils that do not sort out easily as either our fault or the fault of someone or something else. Through our own fault or the fault of others we may encounter other forms of evil. Some people experience in alcoholism and other substance addictions or kleptomania a bondage to a way of life that many in our culture would not label sin. Nonetheless, those plagued by these forms of bondage feel some sense of responsibility, some guilt, even when their bondage is labeled illness rather than sin. Homosexuality may be somewhat similar. The sinfulness of practicing sexuality in opposition to God's design may be denied, but in spite of the denial it remains a disruptive, rest-less way of life. Those bound by it blame it on their genes or their environment and claim they cannot change their orientation. Their bondage holds them fast, and it visits various plagues upon them even though "they cannot help it."

Evil corrodes human life today in other forms as well. Meaninglessness haunts people who believe that they are only going around once in life. They seek all the gusto they can. It is not always clear whether people deprive themselves of meaning or whether they are born into evil situations, in which others have obscured the meaning of life for them.

Others suffer evil in various forms of alienation or division from those who should be loving and supporting them. The divorce may have begun to set in because one or the other partner in the community failed to live responsibly. It usually moves towards its culmination between spouses, between parent and child, between employer and employee, between neighbors, with each side contributing to the division. Sinful defensiveness demands it.

The final and greatest evil comes from outside us, although we may hasten its coming, humanly speaking. That evil is death. Death speaks its "no" upon every human effort to defend life apart from its Creator.

Death is the big evil. Its mammoth grasp haunts us throughout our lives. Most evils are relatively small. The concept of the "banality of evil" reminds us that evil pounces upon us most often in cheap and tawdry forms. Hannah Arendt first used this term to describe the nature of the monstrous evil of the Holocaust.[14] She found that the perpetrators of the "final solution," the attempt to eliminate the whole Jewish people, were people altogether too normal in their appearance and outlook. A combination of opportunities and pressures led them into the possibility of practicing self-defense at mammoth cost to certain others. In their origins they were like the grocery store clerk next door, which means that they were like us. Evil at its insidious worst arises from the little advantages we take of our neighbor, the small compromises with the devil's lie, the almost unnoticeable sacrifices of conscience we make. It surprises us to realize how nice evil people can be. It surprises us how easily nice people do evil. We are surprised when we recognize how easily we ourselves have fallen into evil. Evil grasps from within and without, from all sides.

Reacting with Guilt and Impotence

As it dawns upon sinners that evil has struck again, they react in one of two basic ways. When we recognize that the evil has arisen from within, we feel guilty. When we feel overwhelmed or at least threatened by evil outside ourselves, we feel impotent.

Impotence

Impotence recognizes the loss of our own control of life. It recognizes that we have reason to be on the defensive. It may express itself in apathy and the fear of flight. It may express itself in rage, an angry yet often fearful attempt to regain control or at least to assert the sinner's power in some way. That assertion of power may often claim a third, uninvolved, person as its victim, particularly if the assault has come from someone difficult to challenge. The boss' putdown may be met by an act of revenge directed against spouse, child, or pet, because at home it is safer to demonstrate one's own pitiful power than to do so at work. The rage of impotence often drives us to foolish expressions of power, which may only damage us further. The fist slammed against the wall neither reclaims the position or opportunity that the supervisor has taken away, nor does it compensate for that loss. At best it vents the frustration of impotence. The impotence remains. Only the victory of God's power in Christ's resurrection can put all human impotence in the proper perspective, the perspective of the power of God's love.

Guilt

Guilt condemns from within. It may be the acknowledgment of God's standard; it may be the confession of failure to attain one's own standard. It poisons life, for it cuts away at our estimation of ourselves and of our God. Guilt judges the self; we put ourselves on trial against our own aspirations or demands. We find ourselves wanting. This judgment only reflects God's judgment. Even when we do not *feel* guilty, we are guilty before God. Guilt pronounces the verdict upon us. That is why most people try to avoid feelings of guilt. Guilt is the premonition of death. We may try to dodge our own self-accusation. For a time, guilt can lead to self-justification.

Unless we are utterly desperate, or unless we think we have a way out, we are inclined not to admit our guilt. But refusing to admit our guilt simply contains the pressure and makes it build.

We realize that in our sinful world guilt is not at all so simple a thing to identify. We sinners perceive ourselves both as victims of other people's sins and as perpetrators of our own misdeeds. We are both. In some instances, we are clearly one or the other. We become victims of other people's offenses as they career down the highways, as they play with the economic systems that determine our livelihood through insider trading or bank fraud or employment policies at the job. Or we perpetrate fist fights on the playground to demonstrate our self-sufficiency, or we cheat or gossip or lie to make a rival look bad and ourselves look good.

But in many instances the place where blame should fall is much more complicated. Child abusers, the experts say, often learned their pattern of raising children from their parents, who learned it from their parents. The driving need for some substance to support us— we call it substance abuse, but the real abuse is in what the substance does to us and to our loved ones—is something we blame on ourselves with deep shame and guilt. Yet the experts say that we cannot fully control those urges, as they admit they do not understand them either.

Labeling abuse of any kind an illness rather than a sin does nothing to alter the misery of both the perpetrator, who is also victim, and the victim whom he or she loves and yet hurts. The sins of the parents are being visited to the third and fourth generations of those who continue to live in defiance of the Lord (Deut. 5:9). And the sins of the parents and the children merge. The blame is laid at the heart of each individual in the chain, but there seems to be no free choice when patterns of sinful human interaction have been set before the child is two years old. Assessing blame may be helpful for victims, but assessing blame for the perpetrators may do no more than render them more conscious of their helplessness against ingrained habits from which the experts still have not found a sure and easy liberation. Assessing blame, in any case, simply pronounces the verdict: death.

Sinners must die. They must die forever in hell, or they must die in Baptism to be raised to new life in Christ. But sinners must die.

Notes for Chapter V

1. John Meyendorff, *Byzantine Theology: Historical Trends and Doctrinal Themes* (New York: Fordham University Press, 1979), 139, 143–46.
2. *Canons and Decrees of the Council of Trent,* trans. H. J. Schroeder (Saint Louis: Herder, 1941), 21–23.
3. John E. Keller, "The Realities of Original Sin in Clinical Pastoral Counseling," Third Concordia Academy, Wartburg Theological Seminary, Dubuque, Iowa, August 12, 1975.
4. Dietrich Bonhoeffer, *Creation and Fall: A Theological Interpretation of Genesis 1–3, Temptation* (New York: Macmillan, 1959), 104–5.
5. Gerhard O. Forde, *Theology Is for Proclamation* (Minneapolis: Fortress, 1990), 50.
6. Karl Menninger, *Whatever Became of Sin* (New York: Hawthorn, 1973), 13.
7. Forde, 43, cf. 42–47.
8. Ibid., 51. Smalcald Articles, III:I, 3, *The Book of Concord,* trans. and ed. Theodore G. Tappert (Philadelphia: Fortress, 1959), 302.
9. Forde, 51.
10. Ibid., 50.
11. John Milton, *Paradise Lost* (1667) (New York.: Norton, 1975), e.g. I.36, p. 7; XII.25, p. 264.
12. Alfred Adler, *Understanding Human Nature,* trans. Walter Beran Wolfe (Garden City, NY: Garden City Publishing, 1927), 72–80.
13. Robert Kolb, *Speaking the Gospel Today: A Theology for Evangelism* (Saint Louis: Concordia, 1984), 83–97.
14. Hannah Arendt, *Eichmann in Jerusalem: A Report on the Banality of Evil* (New York: Viking, 1964), 231.

Chapter VI

God's Law

Sinners must die, for the wages of sin is death (Rom. 6:23). How do we know that? God's design for human living tells us so; it tells us that "where there is no law there is no transgression," and that sin gets its power from the Law (Rom. 4:15; 1 Cor. 15:56). "The Law of God is good and wise, And sets his will before our eyes, Shows us the way of righteousness," the American Lutheran theologian Matthias Loy confessed in a hymn—and then added the sad fact of the matter, "And dooms to death when we transgress" (*Lutheran Worship* 329).

God's Law Is Good and Wise, But . . .

God designed human life to be good. His design or structure for life is a gift of his good will toward his human creatures. This structure, the Law, gives us the gift of living out his gift of life in joy and peace. Adam and Eve doubted God's Word, however, and as a result of that doubt they broke out of his structure for daily life. Because of this the Law, which once pointed them to good, pointed out their failure to live out God's design.

Within the Law's gentle boundaries the good human life was designed to be lived. These gentle boundaries have now become prison walls. Blinded to them as we often are, we slam ourselves against them, sometimes in a vain attempt to break out or to prove our own strength and self-sufficiency, sometimes without realizing it. In doing so we bruise and bloody the peace God gives, for the Law imposes upon us discouragement and dismay, disease and disillusionment, degradation and death.

Christ gave us a summary of what human life is to be all about in his description of the two kinds of righteousness: "Love the Lord your God with all your heart and with all your soul and with all your mind. This is the first and greatest commandment. And the second is like it: Love your neighbor as yourself" (Matt. 22:37–39). When we are not loving God as the ultimate source of our identity, security, and meaning, and when we are not loving others as well as we love ourselves, we are separated from the Author of Life. We are in death.

Doing what Christ has commanded does not give us life. Life gives us the ability to do those things. God's design for our lives is no more—or less—than a product of God's creative hand. He made it. The Creator could have made a different Law for us. He is Lord of his Law. It is only his instrument. It cannot give life. It can only describe life. God gives life. Even before the fall Adam and Eve lived by God's grace alone, not by virtue of their own performance of his prescriptions for the good human life. Each day in Eden was sustained by his gracious providing care. Human performance has never been able to secure human life.

So the Law's description of how life works can never perform the function of giving or restoring our life. The Law describes what life should be like, and therefore it assesses, analyzes, judges whether we are alive in God or dead in our flight from him. This assessment is its most important function for us sinners. The Law confronts us with our failure to be God's children. In doing so it pronounces judgment. It condemns. It kills.

Conscience

The channel through which God's Law speaks is called *conscience.* The Gentiles, Paul observed, did not have the Law of Moses written out for them as the Jews had. Nonetheless, they had a sense of what was right for human life. It was "written on their hearts," and it both accused and excused them as they made decisions for living (Rom. 2:14–16). This sense of God's presence and God's Law does not bestow a perfect knowledge of God—far from that (Rom. 1:21). Apart from Christ minds are darkened, hearts are hardened, sinners become callous and indulge in all sorts of evil practices (Eph. 4:17–19; Rom. 1:32).

As noted above,[1] some modern anthropologists have questioned whether any Law of God can really be read from the human heart. Moral standards differ significantly among cultures, they report. While this is true when investigators compare specific morals and mores, the large consensus on proper moral behavior among cultures suggests that all human creatures have not only an inborn sense that right and wrong exist but also some sense of the content of that Law.

Cultural and personal experience fill in the gaps. It is impossible to determine what instruction the human "heart" would give apart from cultural wisdom and experience, for all children grow up within the context of cultural moral instruction. That instruction, it should be noted, gathers the rational judgments of generations regarding what will make human life better or worse. From collective experience societies frame and adjust their own values and standards. All human culture is a continuing laboratory, a continuing experiment, on what shape human life ought to take. All these cultural experiments last a long time. Sometimes the experiment will continue over decades before a society concludes that it has made a false judgment on right and wrong regarding some area of human life.

Because of false cultural input, the conscience can err. Because of willful persuasion by the self that a wrong course of action might be right, the conscience can err. The conscience can also be dulled by various kinds of experiences. Human conscience does not always function as it ought since sin has blurred its vision. Its judgments are worthless in defining who God is. Nonetheless, its judgments regarding right and wrong in the horizontal dimension of human life are generally right enough to preserve life. Conscience produces civic righteousness, the right kind of action for maintaining society.

When believers are struggling to determine their own best course of action, they may experience struggles of conscience. Sometimes this will be due to blurred or false judgments offered by the cultural standards that govern the area of life under consideration. Sometimes it will arise from conflicts between two goods or between two evils, to determine which is preferable. Believers flee to Christ in the midst of such struggles. They plead for the Holy Spirit's guidance, but they take refuge in the forgiveness that Christ gives even when conscience errs.

The Use and the Uses of the Law

God's Law uses conscience as its agent in offering moral guidance to the human creature. Luther designated two "uses" of the

Law;[2] later Lutherans have spoken of three or more ways in which the Law functions in human life. Believers try to distinguish these "uses" or "functions" from each other as they speak God's Law to others, so that they may guide its use to particular ends.

Those who hear God's Law from the lips of believers may or may not receive the Law according to the use intended. God's Law contains God's power. That power, once loosed, is not easily controlled. A parent or teacher may intend to be curbing a child, but the child may not feel curbed. She may feel accused. We may think we have finally come across the opportunity to convince an unbelieving friend that he is a sinner and needs the Gospel, but he may hear that accusation as a threat, and he may only fall into line externally, without any internal conviction of his broken relationship with God. Or he may revolt with ferocity, not feeling the death sentence at all. We may be engaged in Christian instruction on right and wrong, but our hearers may be hearing the death sentence.

We have little control over how our Law is heard. And so we must always be sensitive to the effect our use of the Law—whatever its intent—is having on the person to whom we are addressing it. We dare never forget that whatever use we intend, the Law always accuses. At its friendliest, this guide dog is a domesticated wolf,[3] and we cannot predict when it will spring on us with its deadly accusation and reduce us to guilt once again.

The Law Curbs and Regulates the Horizontal Realm

In listing the uses of the Law Luther mentioned as its first function its ability to limit sin. It does so through its threats of punishment and its promises and offers of favor and well-being. The Law coerces us or entices us into proper external behavior. It keeps us in line, on the straight and narrow path, at least externally. This is the function with which sinners operate much more than the ultimately more important, "second," use of the Law, its theological use. The first, curbing function of the Law is also called the "political" use of the Law because it enables us to live together within the *polis,* the Greek word for city or community.

The political or coercive function of the Law keeps us in line by one of two methods. It entices us by offering rewards for good behavior. It scares us into compliance by threatening punishment for bad behavior. Not always but often the Law does entice or threaten us effectively, and we settle down to comply to it. Often we do so for our own sake, not for the sake of neighbor. But sometimes sinners catch a larger vision of life and come to act out of nobler motivations.[4] They come to believe that the welfare of the society compels selfless behavior. Never can the curbing force of the Law, however, turn sinners to faith and produce proper behavior performed simply for the sake of God.

We should not minimize the importance of this first use of the Law. It is very helpful and handy. Its force keeps calling self-willed sinners back to some sense of the original order that God designed for the good human life. It thus serves to preserve and protect recollections of Eden among us who have strayed far from its gate. In so doing, what God designed as the vehicle for human freedom has become his agent for compelling human responsibility. Thus, the Law makes my life tolerable in a sinful world. It counterbalances the self-centered, destructive urges that beset me in my sinful arrogance and ignorance. In this way it prevents me from doing some really stupid things to myself and other people. Furthermore, it prevents some really stupid people from doing evil things to me. God's Law befriends the victims of sinners. It protects sinners from themselves.

These people may not be good or nice to me for the right reasons. But they are civil to me. They may be hypocritical as they smile and help me. But their compliance—and mine—preserve order in our community. I would rather have my neighbor love me, for her love will assure that she will at least try to be a good and helpful neighbor over the long haul. However, if she hates me, but is afraid of the sheriff, and therefore does not try to hurt me, that is better than having no coercive force restraining her at all. I never want to be hypocritical myself. Hypocrisy, the product of the Law's coercive force, is one of the sinful lies that perverts my life. But it is not as bad if a neighbor who hates me is hypocritical and smiles. Bad motivation, but the action is much more pleasant than the violent alternative. Among sinners, hypocrisy makes the world go around.

Police use the coercive force of the Law to keep order in the part of society for which they are responsible. So do parents. So do teachers. That is part of their responsibility. They should not be afraid to face that responsibility and exercise it with a sense of joy in being God's agents for preserving what is better rather than permitting what is worse in a sinful world.

This "civic" righteousness that the "political" or "social" use of the Law produces is a good gift of God in the brokenness of our sin-ridden horizontal relationship. However, even at its best, it is also mischievous. It deceives us into thinking that our efforts in the horizontal dimension of life can affect the way we appear in the sight of God. That can result, as Luther noted in his Smalcald Articles,[5] in the Law's making the sinner more rebellious than compliant. Its threat of punishment can stir fires of resentment in the human heart. That resentment arises from our sinful desire to assert our own control and our own identity apart from God. Bowing to God's Law is the last thing we want to do as sinners. It's the "terrible twos" syndrome. We are not about to let God tell us what to do. The identity that we want to fashion for ourselves is at stake, and we sometimes do not surrender it when God wants to identify us as his children.

Worse yet, the curbing or political function of the Law can persuade sinners to confuse the two kinds of righteousness—and believe that human performance of good works can achieve righteousness in the vertical relationship, in God's sight. Such a plan is doomed to failure for two reasons. First, "there is not a righteous man on earth who does good and never sins" (Eccl. 7:20 RSV). Everybody has sinned and fallen short of the glory of God (Rom. 3:23). God demands perfection in human performance (Matt. 5:48). Furthermore, even apart from human sinfulness no human performance of the Law can make human creatures righteous before God. Goodness in his sight lies completely in his favorable disposition toward us. The Creator does not have to accept as his own anything that he has made. Even Adam and Eve found favor in his sight on the basis of his gracious disposition, not on the basis of their perfect performance of his Law.

The roots of all false religion lie in the confusion of compliance with God's Law and ultimate human righteousness. But the curbing force of the Law compels sinners to hope that their own performance will save them. The Law is "not a means whereby one could bargain with or vaunt oneself individually or collectively before God.

The Law is not a remedy for sin. Where it is so understood it only makes sin worse."[6]

Finally, the Law only evaluates sinners. God gave his people some hint of this in the way he phrased the key summary of his Law for them, in the Ten Commandments. He did not use the positive vocabulary of "should do" or "ought to perform." He used the negative vocabulary of "You shall not" in almost every case. The exceptions command worship of God and obedience to parents. The negative prohibition reminds those who hear the commands of their failure before it hints at their potential. It functions as mirror that reflects the state of our humanity, in our horizontal performance and in our response to God our Creator.

The Law Accuses and Crushes in the Vertical Realm

Luther called this function of the Law the theological use of the Law. He called it the Law's primary function because nothing could be more important for us sinners than to know that sin will not work. Christians often picture this use of the Law by describing it as the mirror that confronts us with the awful truth of how we look to fellow creatures and to our Creator. It shows our sinfulness. The creature was not designed to sin. The Law diagnoses what is going wrong with a life that cannot be brought together in a way that makes it feel like a perfect fit. It announces a verdict over fallen human performance: death.

The Law Reveals Human Sinfulness

The Law reflects our sinfulness: it teaches us that we are sinners (Rom. 3:20). Even Paul had to confess that his conscience had not sufficiently informed him of the full extent of his sinfulness. He had to encounter God's Law to appreciate fully how sinful even his covetous thoughts were. He had to confess, however, that all this did was to intensify his indulgence in coveting (Rom. 7:7–8). The Law reflects to us the picture of our brokenness, our perversion of our own humanity. Thus, however else we may encounter the Law— as a promise of better times to come in return for our adherence to it, or as helpful suggestions for improving life or as a threat not to get out of line—the Law remains our adversary. Its accusation is undaunted and consistent. It places the burden upon the human creature. As long as the human creature stands at the focus of discussion, the Law's burden will crush. Escape from its crushing condemnation comes only by shifting its burden to Christ.

The Law Reveals Evil Breaking Human Life

Second, the Law reflects as well the brokenness of the whole context of our human life. To label this primary use of the Law "accusing" limits our view of what the Law does as it points out our fallen condition. It reveals that we exist not only trapped in our own sin but also caught in the general evil around us. The Law squeezes and chokes sinners whenever they encounter the inadequacy of their own power to make life ultimately good. It suffocates us and makes us gasp for life's breath—that which God breathed into us in Eden—as it reflects the failure of our own mastery or control over the course of our lives.

Natural disasters and human devices confront us with our inadequacy and failure. Estrangement and alienation from those whom we ought to be loving—and being loved by—spell out clearly such inadequacy and failure. Meaningless moments, stretching into months, write out on the lonely walls of our existence that our own power is inadequate and that our own control has failed. We peek in the mirror of the Law whenever these inadequacies and failures command our attention. We see no pretty sight. We see life unraveling in the direction of death—sometimes at a rapid pace.

The Law Reveals God's Wrath

Third, the Law reflects God's wrath against our sin. God loves his human creatures so much that he cannot abide their falling outside the design for human life that he planned for them. Only within this design can his human creatures enjoy life fully. Only when they center life in him and fulfill their humanity as he fashioned it to be lived can they enjoy true peace. The father of all boils in anger when his children are being led astray and done to death, even when they are doing it to themselves. His jealousy (Ex. 20:5) reflects his love for us when we, caught in our sinfulness, cannot love him back because we have brought upon ourselves the terminal blindness and deafness of our doubt.

God wrote into his Law the curse that would safeguard his perfect plan for his human creatures (Gen. 2:17; Ex. 20:5; Deut. 27:26). Human experience recognizes that the curse works. We die (Ezek. 18:20; Rom. 6:23). Because God takes pleasure in his children's enjoyment of perfect peace, not of wickedness, he has no place for sinners in his presence. He destroys them (Ps. 5:4–6) and then raises them up to a new life in Christ. He reveals his anger against all ungodliness and unrighteousness (Rom 1:18, 2:5–9). Sins of every kind, at every "level of seriousness" in human eyes, offend God.

Human experience must acknowledge that false witness shall not go unpunished; liars will not escape (Prov. 19:5). God hates the pious works of those who exploit the poor and needy (Amos 5:10–27). God has prepared vengeance against abuses of human sexuality (1 Thess. 4:3–8). Those who display anger with others make themselves liable to judgment (Matt. 5:21–22). God requires a reckoning for those who take life (Gen. 9:5–6). The writer of Proverbs wishes upon those who transgress the fourth commandment a most horrible fate (Prov. 30:17). Above all, God's anger burns against every form of idolatry (Hosea 8:5; Amos 5:6). God loves his children too much not to be filled with wrath against that which takes them away from him.

The experience of this wrath in God's judgment upon his human creatures raises the question of our interpretation of his judgment functions. The expression and experience of his wrath remains problematic from the human standpoint on this side of his final Judgment Day. There his wrath will be expressed and experienced with crystal clarity (Matt. 25:41–46). Upon those who are not his children he will visit eternal punishment.

But human interpretation of evil and suffering short of Judgment Day confuses and fails us too often because of the irregularity of its visitation. We cannot make sense of evil as a "fair punishment" for specific sins. Some guilty individuals seem to escape such visitation, and some innocent individuals fall prey to the evils that seem to administer punishment to the sinner. Not all those who abuse their sexuality, either with homosexual or heterosexual sins, suffer AIDS—some do, and some do not. Furthermore, not all AIDS victims are guilty of the sins that have spread the plague so broadly among the population. Some fall victim to the virus because they have earlier fallen victim to some other ailment that has made a blood transfusion necessary. There seems to be "no justice." Therefore, when believers interpret the disease as an expression of God's wrath against specific sins and specific sinners, they focus on God, and unbelievers will get the impression that his wrath falls arbitrarily and that he must be an unjust God. Such a focus raises a question of theodicy, in which apart from faith, God cannot be justified.

For this reason some theologians have suggested that it is not God who directly visits such consequences upon sin. Rather his structure for human life, the Law, collides with the human pursuit of absolute freedom against this structure to produce the signs of his wrath. God placed his human creatures within his well-designed plan for human living. When they try to break out of this plan, and live out possibilities that God has not planned for this good human life, they crash and smash into God's good structure. God has written his displeasure with our deserting his plan for us into his structure for daily life. In a fallen and thus misshapen world some people are bruised by this collision with God's Law in different ways than others. Human intelligence remains sufficiently effective—even in its damaged fallen state—to avoid the consequences of trying to live outside God's structure for a long time, in some cases. Thus, the ways in which we suffer for breaking God's Law differ from individual to individual.

This reflects the reality of human experience. At the same time we dare never suggest that God is not angry with all human sin, whether he visits punishment directly and immediately upon it or not. Specific misfortune can seldom be attributed to specific sins. God may indeed use specific evils to call individuals to repentance, but no general theory of evil and punishment dare be formulated from such individual experiences. We often confuse the issue—and ourselves—when we attempt to correlate specific sins with specific ills or evils in an individual's life. However, the general correlation between sin and judgment does remind believers that God's wrath is real, even if its visitation can never be perceived as clearly or as regularly as we would like.

Thus, believers will ask, "why do you want to know?" when confronted with questions regarding the correlation of suffering and sin. When the agenda underlying the question for the individual asking focuses on God's intention toward humankind, the answer will give assurance of his gracious love for his fallen creatures. When the agenda focuses on human sinfulness, the answer gives aid to a spirit that seeks repentance, affirming God's displeasure at the sin that disrupts the lives of his beloved human creatures.

It is thus important to remember that the visitation of punishment should not be seen first of all as merely an assessment of blame but rather a call to repentance. Both to those on whom the tower of Siloam fell with their families and to all who heard of this disaster, their misfortune was a call to repentance (Luke 13:4). Christ rejects the proposition that their misfortune was a visitation upon them for particularly serious sins. He instead focuses on the need for repentance by all.

The Disruption of Human Life

Many forms of evil remind us not of individual sinfulness but of our common fragility and frailty in a world disrupted by sin. Attempts to tame the atom, for good and evil purposes, and attempts to increase food production, to feed the hungry, have both contributed to the spread of carcinogens in this world. Those who suffer cancer cannot be differentiated from those who do not on the basis of quantity or quality of individual sinfulness. In attempting to exercise responsibility and freedom, human creatures—even when trying to do their best—have fouled God's creation. It has turned back upon us, and it presses us in the trap that we fashioned as a means of improving life. At our best we fail at times. Such failures remind us that God is grieved by our efforts to control life on our own, even when we try to exercise dominion through atoms or fertilizers for the common good.

Thus, God's Law reflects God's discomfort and displeasure with our fallen and broken state. When sinners confront their own sinfulness or the fragile and frail nature of life in general, they recognize that God is angry about the situation. Some sinners will harden their hearts in defense against the Law's observation; others will despair in guilt. But the Law cannot tell us more than that things have gone wrong. The Gospel must follow the Law's diagnosis to bring the despairing sinner to the God whose wrath arises from his love.

To hear God's gracious word of Gospel sinners must recognize their need for the new life that the Gospel alone bestows. They must recognize that they are dead in their old way of life, living under their false systems for finding ultimate identity, security, and meaning. The primary force of the Law, its "second" or theological function, produces corpses.

Giving Witness to God's Law

It does not make sense to argue with a corpse. We may have to tell the corpse that he is dead. We may have to announce time and time again that she has no life apart from Christ. But we do not use the theological function of the Law effectively as a club. The coercive function of the Law works like a club. The theological function of the law works like a fine-tipped arrow, which pierces the heart. If the corpse simply will not listen to his own death sentence, then we gain little by belaboring the point. We wait for a more opportune moment to press home again the Law's accusation and condemnation, its death notice.

Satan's Use of the Law

Not only God but also Satan, the accuser, can use the Law in its condemning function.[7] Satan uses it with believers, and in his hand it becomes a weapon of deceit, to undermine the Gospel. He approaches believers who have had their sins forgiven, and he attempts to persuade them that their sins are not forgiven. When he uses the Law in this way, he is trying to drown out God's gracious voice and the gift of new life it gives.

Believers must resist this kind of accusation from the Law, for it takes away the comfort and power of the Gospel. Believers rightly hear the accusation of the Law, but they do not dwell on it or wallow in it. They are turned from its accusation to the Gospel, which becomes the complete focus for their lives. Depending on their emotional makeup and the kind of crisis of brokenness in which they find themselves, they may or may not "feel guilty" under its accusation. They simply acknowledge their guilt and flee from sin to the haven of the Gospel. Satan tries to interrupt that flight into the embrace of the Lord's forgiving arms by using the familiar notes of the Law's accusation as his siren song. The Gospel obliterates the lie into which the devil turns the Law when he condemns forgiven sinners.

The Instructive Use of the Law

Forgiven sinners, born anew through the Holy Spirit, liberated from the Law, do everything from a free and merry spirit—insofar as they are born anew. The Law functions to keep us in line and to accuse and condemn us whether we believe in Christ or not. But as believers encounter God's Law in daily life, they not only encounter it as an enticing or threatening curb and as an accusing and condemning mirror. We also turn to the Law for information regarding decisions we have to make as Christians. We need that information because our minds are not totally transformed into properly functioning human minds at conversion any more than our wills are transformed into absolutely trusting wills. Christians cannot always tell automatically how God would have us act in specific situations.

Some deny that there is a purely instructive use of the Law. They teach that the Law does guide Christian decision-making, but that it always does so as it curbs the mind and will, which remain tainted by disdain for God's plan and as it condemns such disdain. These theologians fear that an emphasis on the "third use of the Law," the use of the Law as a guide for the Christian, can become the central focus of Christian living. This distracts from the Gospel, from God's work and his love for us as his children. It focuses again on human performance even if the performance is understood as driven by the Holy Spirit. Therefore, these theologians reject any talk of a "third use" of the Law. They believe that it is more realistic to see that the Law remains ready to kill, even when we use it to aid in sorting out options for Christian action, when we need its information and input.

Others affirm a "third use" of the Law because they believe that believers do need information regarding God's will for their practice of the faith in daily life. Particularly in an age that lacks moral clarity in its cultural norms, they believe, Christians must emphasize the need for consultation with God's Law. The mind of the believer needs education to face the temptations of the world and its standards and the believer's own sinful inclinations.

Those who affirm and those who deny the propriety of using

118

the term "third use" of the Law are addressing two different agendas with their differing concerns. The central concern of each side deserves affirmation. Christians should do nothing to refocus the Christian life from God's gracious action in Jesus Christ. As he conveys Christ's benefits to us through his life-renewing Word, the Holy Spirit stands at the center of the believer's life. He produces the fruits of faith as a by-product of re-creating us as children of God. Yet, in the mystery of our existence as both righteous and sinful people of God, the struggle against temptation does not cease in this realm of existence. Christians need information for minds that are not always clear on what is right and wrong in a given situation. It is not only a matter of the believer's needing guidance in gaining insight into God's plan and structure for human life. The believer also needs the Law's condemning force to put sinful tendencies to death—on a daily basis. The Law cannot depart from the believer's life until sin does.

This "third use" of the Law also recognizes that believers do react toward the Law's curbing power in a different way, with different motivation, than do those who stand outside the faith. At times, in their sinfulness, believers will be curbed by the Law's threats or promises. At other times, however, the Gospel will be directing their wills and thoughts toward serving God. Then they search the Law for God's counsel, rejoicing in being able to please him through faith.

Christians reject antinomianism, the belief that believers can live without the Law. The Law is not the center of the believer's life; God's children do not focus their lives on their own obedience but rather on God's gracious favor toward them. Nonetheless, the Law continues to curb their sinful natures. The Law continues to expose their sinful desires. The Law provides information for their decision making as it curbs and lays bare. In this life believers who are righteous and sinful at the same time still need the Law. Just as firmly believers reject legalism, a dependence upon the Law and human performance of it for the assurance of God's grace. Legalists may claim to believe the Gospel, but their underlying security arises from their own ability to keep God's Law.

It has been suggested that the distinction between *law* and *command* may be a useful way of describing two differing functions of God's Law in daily Christian living. *Law* designates the oppressive functions of God's plan as it makes its condemning or curbing impact upon the believer's sinful will. *Command* designates the instructive function of that same plan, as God offers guidance for what the believer does—or will do, or should do, or ought to do.

We try to describe our actions according to God's plan with a variety of verbs. Some think that "ought to" or "should" sound too oppressive, that simply saying "the believer does" or "will do" is preferable. These latter terms try not to place a burden of expectation but simply describe the hoped-for reality of living out God's plan with the Holy Spirit's motivating power. The fact is, however, that any verb that describes what believers do or are supposed to do places the burden upon the believers. God's law wells up within any language that focuses on human performance. The Law—and for sinners, along with it, its accusation—remains inevitably and inextricably tied to any focus upon the human creature. Deciding what we are supposed to do will always suggest our failure to have done it and our struggle to try to do it.

There is a related problem involved in Christian decision making. The words of the Law given us in Scripture do not always tell us how to act, either. It tells us not to kill, but it does not tell us whether 55 or 85 miles per hour endanger the lives of those on the highways with us. It tells us not to commit adultery, but it leaves to us the evaluation of whether different styles of dancing promote adultery. It tells us not to steal, but it does not become specific on what a fair profit in a capitalist system really might be. It tells us to obey our parents and our government, but it does not tell us how to judge precisely when specific forms of obedience to parents or government cross the line and become disobedience to God (Acts 5:29). We are always compelled to make moral judgments.

We do need to remember, however, that the fundamental structure of God's design involves loving God absolutely and totally and loving our neighbors as ourselves. Amazingly, even believers often fail to recognize that the simple solution to vexing, puzzling questions about what we ought to be doing lies in what is commonly called the Golden Rule. Act as if someone else were doing the same thing to you in this situation (Matt. 7:12). The fact that this solution escapes our recollection so easily reminds us how thoroughly sin befuddles us.

Nonetheless, we dare never forget that the Law dogs the steps of believers and unbelievers alike throughout this life. It turns easily from guide dog to wolf. But against its devouring jaws stands Jesus Christ, God in human flesh, delivered into the Law's and death's jaws, so that he might give life to his chosen children.

Notes for Chapter VI

1. See chapter II, p. 32.
2. Smalcald Articles, III:II, 1–5, *The Book of Concord,* trans. and ed. Theodore G. Tappert (Philadelphia: Fortress, 1959), 303.
3. James Ame Nestingen, *The Faith We Hold: The Living Witness of Luther and the Augsburg Confession* (Minneapolis: Augsburg, 1983), 38–39.
4. Lawrence J. Kohlberg, e.g. *The Psychology of Moral Development: The Nature and Validity of Moral Stages* (San Francisco: Harper & Row, 1984). Cf. the evaluation by Gilbert C. Meilaender, *The Theory and Practice of Virtue* (Notre Dame: University of Notre Dame Press, 1984), 75–99.
5. Smalcald Articles III:II, 3, *The Book of Concord,* 303.
6. Gerhard O. Forde, *Theology Is for Proclamation* (Minneapolis: Augsburg Fortress, 1990), 76–77.
7. I am indebted to my colleague at Concordia College, Saint Paul, Stephen C. Stohlmann, for the following insights.

Chapter VII

The Person of Christ

The Jewish high priest, Caiaphas, posed the most critical and the most vital question in human history. The question was critical because it sets the person who asks it before the judgment of God. The question was vital because its answer gives life. Caiaphas asked Jesus of Nazareth to identify himself. "Tell us if you are the Christ, the Son of God!" he demanded to know (Matt. 26:63).

Jesus of Nazareth, Son of Man and Suffering Servant

Jesus himself had posed the same question to his disciples. "Who do people say the Son of Man is?" (Matt. 16:13). The disciples reported a number of rumors. Some thought that John the Baptist had come back from the dead as Jesus of Nazareth. Some said Elijah, or Jeremiah, or another prophet had returned to rescue Israel through the Word of the Lord. Jesus then posed the most important question for believers, the question that cuts to the core of our existence: Who do you say that the Son of Man is? Peter replied, "You are the Christ, the Son of the living God" (Matt. 16:16).

All Judea was waiting and longing for that Christ, the Son of David, God's special Son designated by royal anointing, who would rise up to rescue his people from Roman oppression. The Christ, or Messiah, was viewed by Jews as a human figure, a very special human Son of God (2 Sam. 7:14), who would have the power of God behind him and operate on the basis of the Word of God.[1] Jesus did not use the term for himself even though he did not deny that he was indeed God's specially designated heir of David. Instead, he called himself the Son of Man.[2]

In Palestine at our Lord's time everyone was anticipating the Messiah's return. But among those who looked to God for deliverance from Rome were also those who had picked up on a promise in one of the visions of the prophet Daniel. In Daniel 7:13–14 God showed Daniel a person called "one like a son of man." This Son of Man came to the throne of God and was given "authority, glory and sovereign power; all peoples, nations and men of every language worshiped him. His dominion is an everlasting dominion that will not pass away, and his kingdom is one that will never be destroyed." In the centuries leading up to our Lord's birth some Jews had nourished a hope that this Son of Man would come from God's throne to deliver them.[3] Note that this "one like a son of man" has the appearance of a human being, but he has the characteristics of God. Perhaps nowhere in the Old Testament's looking forward to the coming of God's deliverance is it clearer that this deliverance would be carried out by one who was human and yet had all the characteristics of God. To have God's characteristics, among the fiercely monotheistic Jews, was to be God, Yahweh himself. So it is no coincidence or whim that led Jesus to identify himself as the Son of Man.

He did so in his trial before Caiaphas. The leadership in Jerusalem was trying to get him on a charge of treason. They asked him to admit that he was the Messiah, so that they could take him to Pilate as a political revolutionary. When Caiaphas asked him to swear if he was the Christ, Jesus replied, in effect, "That is not the half of it. I am also the Son of Man, seated at the right hand of Power and coming on the clouds of heaven" (Matt. 26:64), the image the Jews had of the Son of Man on the basis of Daniel's vision. His identification of himself at the climax of his ministry only repeated what he had been saying about himself since he began to gather his disciples. When Nathanael confessed, "Rabbi, you are the Son of God; you are the King of Israel," Jesus promised greater things than those that had suggested to Nathanael that he was earthly heir of David. He promised that Nathanael would come to understand that this Jesus was the Son of Man, the fulfillment of Daniel's vision of one in human form who had all the characteristics of Yahweh (John 1:43–51). And if he looks like Yahweh, he must be God himself.

Jesus combined this title, Son of Man, which pointed to his divine characteristics, his being God, with the characteristics of another figure spoken of by a prophet, the suffering Servant of God, of whom Isaiah spoke in chapters 42, 49, 50, and above all in chapters 52 and 53. When Christ predicted his passion and death—and resurrection (e.g., Matt. 16:21; 17:22)—he combined the title "Son of Man" with the characteristics of the Suffering Servant. The one acquainted with grief, who bore the sins of many, was to be the Son of Man who had glory and dominion and rule.

Biblical Titles for Jesus Christ

"Messiah" and "Son of Man" and "Suffering Servant" are only three of many descriptions of the incarnate second person of the Holy Trinity that the Bible gives us. His contemporaries described him not in philosophical terms but rather in concrete images. He had presented himself to them with such portrayals. Some of his descriptions of himself take pictures from everyday life to tell something of who he is and what he does for his people—vine, bread of life, good shepherd, bridegroom. Others rely on those who had served God in the Old Testament—prophets, priests, the anointed kings—to supply the images on which Jesus based his description of what God come in human flesh would be for his people and do for them. Too often the church has narrowed its focus on Jesus Christ and not taken seriously the fullness of the biblical witness to him.

Theologians have organized what the Bible says about Jesus into different sets of categories. Oscar Cullmann used the categories of Jesus' preexistence as God, his earthly work during his lifetime, his present work for us today, and his future work at the end of time.[4] We could also use the categories that describe his work for us in another set of four ways: as the one who reveals who God is and what human life ought to be like, the one who is a sacrificial victim for his people, the one who conquers all his people's enemies, and the one who is a companion, guide, and helper in our daily lives.[5]

My Lord and My God

Jesus' own claim to be Son of Man makes it clear that he viewed himself as the one who fulfilled Daniel's vision of God's decisive intervention on behalf of his people (Dan. 7:13–14). There can be no doubt that by assuming this title he claimed to be Yahweh come in human form. Relatively seldom did Jesus' contemporaries call him "God" directly. Thomas did, when he encountered Christ come back from the dead. "My Lord and my God!" he confessed (John 20:28). In his confession he used two synonyms. The Jews had avoided letting the holy name *Yahweh,* which God revealed to Moses in the burning bush, pass between their unclean lips. So they substituted the word *Lord* when Yahweh's name appeared in the Scriptures. Thomas was using the Hebrew language's device of parallelism to emphasize that he recognized in this man Jesus God come in human flesh. Thus, the early church used words from Isaiah 45:23, which described the worship of Yahweh, to sing that "at the name of Jesus every knee should bow . . . and every tongue confess that Jesus Christ is Lord" (Phil. 2:10). The writer to the Hebrews (1:10–12) ascribed to Christ a description of Yahweh's creating power and his eternal nature found in Ps. 102:25–27.

The confession that "Jesus is Lord" spoke to Gentiles, too, because they used the title *Lord* to indicate that their emperor was divine. A divine emperor was but one of many gods, and so Jesus could not be considered *Lord* in exactly the same way in which Caesar Augustus was revered as Lord. But calling Jesus "Lord" told Gentile hearers, too, that this Jesus was divine. In what sense he was divine—that he is truly God, the Creator of all, had to be explained later.[6]

This confession that Jesus is Lord could be made only through the power of the Holy Spirit (1 Cor. 12:3). It was used to bring together Jesus' nature as God with his human mortality: the first preachers proclaimed that Jesus was both Messiah and Lord, and also the one who had been crucified (Acts 2:36; 1 Cor. 2:8) and then raised from the dead (Rom. 10:9). While, indeed, the term *lord* could refer to human masters and leaders, there can be no doubt that when Paul calls Christ "the Lord of glory," he is confessing that this man is God in human flesh (1 Cor. 2:8).

We often call Jesus *Lord* and *Savior.* We should never divide these words from each other, as if *Lord* refers to how Christ bosses us and *Savior* refers to how he rescued us. An ancient Near Eastern secular lord, or king, was first of all the protector and provider for his people. To be *Lord* meant also to save. And our Savior has saved us so that we can live as his children, in everlasting righteousness and innocence, serving him in joyful praise. His being our Savior means also that he is our Lord.

The Word Was God

The Evangelist John also confessed that Jesus was true God in human flesh through the use of the term *Word.*[7] John framed his entire gospel with his confession that God had come in human flesh. In his introduction he calls Jesus God's Word and God himself: "In the beginning was the Word, and the Word was with God, and the Word was God" (John 1:1). And John closes his book with Thomas's confession, "My Lord and my God" (20:28).

The Jews had always associated God and his Word very closely; the Word delivered God's power and served as his creative and preserving instrument (Genesis 1; Ps. 107:20, 147:18, Is. 55:11). They were scandalized, however, by John's attribution of this designation to the human Jesus. But John was explicit and thorough in his claim that Jesus of Nazareth, Word of God, had the attributes of God. He dealt with the mystery of the Trinity, using *Word* and *Son* to distinguish Jesus from the Father while still affirming that this Word and Son of God is truly God. Beginning Jesus' career as the re-creator of God's children (1:12–13), John set that career in the context of Genesis 1, echoing its "in the beginning." This Word made flesh was the true light who had glory "as of the only Son from the Father" (1:14 RSV). In the conclusion of this prologue to his gospel John again confessed, "No one has ever seen God; the only God,[8] who is in the bosom of the Father, he has made him known" (1:18 RSV).

The writer to the Hebrews repeated this concept of Jesus as God's Word come in human form as he opened his letter. God had spoken in many and various ways through the prophets. In the last days he spoke "by his Son, whom he appointed heir of all things, and through whom he made the universe" (Heb. 1:1–2). This Son of God was indeed the creative Word. He "reflects the glory of God and bears the very stamp of his nature" (v. 3 RSV). The Jews of Jesus' day believed that God's glory could assume a visible presence. They labeled this "dwelling" of God's presence among his people the *shekinah* (dwelling).[9] The writer to the Hebrews, struggling to express the revelation of God in human flesh, used this image as John did (1:14, 2:21, 4:20–26). According to Hebrews 1, Jesus not only brought God's presence into the world; he also was "upholding the universe by his word of power" (Heb. 1:3 RSV). Here again, the characteristics of God are attributed to "Jesus, the apostle and high priest whom we confess" (Heb 3:1), the human creature whom perhaps some of the original readers of the epistle had known as the rabbi from Nazareth. For these Jews, however, a rabbi with Yahweh's characteristics had to be Yahweh himself, distinguished perhaps from the Father by the designation "Son," but nonetheless God himself. All Hebrews acknowledged that "the Lord our God is one Lord" (Deut. 6:4 RSV).

God's Fullness in Human Form

Paul proclaimed the belief of contemporary believers: that they awaited "the blessed hope—the glorious appearing of our great God and Savior, Jesus Christ" (Titus 2:13). The church sang of Jesus as "in the form of God," which is being equal with God (Phil. 2:6 RSV).[10] Paul also used the concept of "image" to express the relationship of the human Jesus (whom many of his acquaintances had known) and the eternal God. As he used this term, "all the emphasis is on the equality of the [image] with the original."[11] Thus, Paul can affirm that Christ is the image of God, who has shone as a light into human hearts to give the light of the knowledge of the glory of God (2 Cor. 4:4). The Messiah Jesus "is the image of the invisible God." "In him all things were created . . . all things were created through him and for him. He is before all things, and in him all things hold together. . . . In him all the fulness of God was pleased to dwell" (Col. 1:15–19 RSV). Indeed, the Messiah, Jesus, the Lord is the one in whom "all the fullness of the Deity lives in bodily form." He is the one who bestows fullness of life upon his people, and he is the one who holds all power and authority (Col. 2:6, 9–10).

Paul also taught that this bodily indwelling of God in human flesh came about when God sent forth his Son to be born of a woman and born under the Law (Gal. 4:4), as one who had emptied himself and taken the form of a servant, born in human likeness, humbled in human form even to the point of dying on the cross (Phil. 2:7–8). In Galatians 4 Paul may reflect a changing usage of the term "Son of God" to designate much more than Messiahship. "Son of God" was becoming an affirmation that Jesus was truly God. Hebrews 1 and 2 also suggest that this term was moving beyond its usage as a designation for a specially chosen human being, whom God had made his own agent for special messianic purposes. The church came to see that the Messiah was to be God in human flesh. Isaiah's prophecy had been given its fullest meaning when the angel told Joseph that Mary would have a son called Jesus, to fulfill the prophet's words, " 'Behold, a virgin shall conceive and bear a son, and his name shall be called Emmanuel' (which means God with us)" (Matt. 1:20–23 RSV). The power of the Most High overshadowed Mary, and without a husband she gave birth to a child whom the angel called "God's Son"—in more than a Messianic sense—because the Holy Spirit had come upon her (Luke 1:31–35).

The Virgin Birth

The doctrine of the virgin birth certainly affirms the *virgin* nature of Mary. Jesus, her son, was born in a unique and unexplainable fashion. He was God's own Son as a human creature. We have no idea how the power of the Holy Spirit worked in his conception. This man, born of the virgin, is true God.

It must also be noted that the doctrine of the virgin birth also affirms the *birth* of our God. God has come in human flesh, in the greatest of the mysteries of our salvation. Throughout the history of the church faithful and not-so-faithful teachers of the biblical message have struggled with the mystery. It defies human explanation; it will not be captured within the grasp of human rationality. In the course of the struggle with the mystery the church has forged its dogmas of the Trinity and Christology.

The Dogma of God in Human Flesh

During the first three centuries the world around the church asked it many questions regarding this Jesus Christ, and Christians formulated many answers. Some of those answers were not based as much on God's Word as they were based on cultural presuppositions. Thus, as the church combated heresy from within and outright attack from without, it formulated a confession and definition of who Jesus is and what he has done in terms that were understandable in the Greek and Roman world into which the church had spread. The Greeks and Romans did not know Daniel 7; they did not know that calling Jesus the Son of Man was a confession that he is Yahweh in human flesh.

In confessing who Jesus is, the church met two challenges: the denial that Jesus is truly human and the denial that Jesus is truly God.

Docetism: The Denial of the Humanity of Jesus Christ

Those who denied that he is truly human are called Docetists, from the Greek word *dokeō,* which means "to seem."[12] They claimed Jesus only seemed or looked human. It seems to make sense that God would not be caught dead in human flesh, particularly from the perspective of spiritualists, such as the Gnostics, who believed that the material creation was at best inferior and at worst downright evil. Even Christians who were influenced by such cultural presuppositions were convinced that God could not come in human flesh. They could not understand how the infinite Divine Being could be so closely linked with the material and created order as Paul and John had claimed. So they said that God's appearances as Jesus were not those of a human creature. He only seemed human, as would a ghost or phantom.

In these days also, some people within Christian denominations are embarrassed by the idea that any God worthy of the name would show up in human form. They want to speculate about a hidden god rather than confess the God who has revealed himself in crib and cross and crypt. They say that Jesus Christ was a great human being, an important prophet, but that the truly divine in Jesus was his message, his idea of God's love.[13] Others may so emphasize Jesus as a divine miracle worker that they shortchange his humanity by focusing on his divine status and power to the practical exclusion of his human nature. They prefer to ignore the crib and cross as they glory in the God who looks like us but cannot be, if, at the same time—according to their presuppositions—he is really so much more. The infinite God, however, did assume the finite flesh of his human creatures to accomplish their salvation.

Indeed, Jesus of Nazareth, our fully human brother, is more. He is the second person of the Trinity. In the first years of the church an opposite, yet often parallel, opinion to the Docetist opinion arose among some Christians who could not believe that God could become human. They denied that Jesus was truly God—and in so doing denied that God had become a human creature.

Adoptionism and Subordinationism:
The Denial of the Divinity of Jesus Christ

Adoptionism. In the early church two modes of denying Christ's divinity appeared. Among the earliest of those who denied that Christ was Lord and God were certain Jewish Christians in Palestine, called Ebionites. They employed the first of the two modes and fall into the classification of adoptionists. Adoptionists believe that Jesus was such a good human creature, who kept God's Law so perfectly, that God adopted him as his most special Son. Jesus remained only human, but he exhibited God's will so perfectly he may even deserve some kind of veneration. In the Gentile world Paul of Samosata and others taught a similar doctrine, which was labeled dynamic monarchianism. It taught the unity of God as the monarch (one ruler), who had placed a special power (*dynamis* in Greek) upon the human Jesus, the power of an impersonal holy spirit of God.[14] Some mainline Protestants today believe that the human Jesus was no more than God's specially adopted Son, who gives us a model of the perfect life and inspires us to live it.

Subordinationism. Also in the early church some denied that Jesus was truly God in a heresy we label subordinationism. Such people believed that Christ was indeed more than human but that he was not fully God. They believed that he was a subordinate deity. Arius, a priest in Alexandria in the early fourth century, best exhibits subordinationism. In trying to convey to people in Alexandria who Jesus Christ really was, Arius transferred the language of Saint John, who had called Jesus the Word (John 1:1–18) into the context of popular pagan religious life. In some popular philosophies and cults of the day, influenced by later Platonic thinking, the "Word" was the first departure from the unity of the Ultimate Spirit. With the Word's separation from the Ultimate Spirit came the breakdown of that ultimate unity of spirit, which these cults regarded as salvation. The Word therefore was not perfect. But it was the beginning of the process of creation, and so Arius thought that this comparison was what John had in mind in his first chapter. Therefore, using a biblical term to express a pagan idea, Arius taught that Jesus Christ was a subordinate divine being, imperfect and not fully God, not eternal as was the Ultimate Spirit, even though close to that god.

Today we find it harder to construct a world of semi-gods and demi-gods. Therefore, it is harder for our contemporaries to make sense of subordinationism. Nonetheless, there have been North American Christian theologians in the past century who have tried to suggest such an idea. In their view, while Jesus Christ could not be God himself, he certainly could be more than human, somewhere in between fully God and merely a man.

Chalcedonian Christology

Arius vs. Athanasius. The church dealt with Arius' denial that Jesus is true God in the Council of Nicea in A.D. 325. There, under the leadership of Athanasius, the bishop of Alexandria, it chose the contemporary philosophical language of "nature" or "substance" to express the biblical confession that Jesus of Nazareth was God come in human flesh. Such language, though not used by the biblical writers, made it clear to Christians of the fourth century and all subsequent centuries that Jesus is Yahweh (1 Cor. 12:3). In the creed the church began to formulate in 325 (completing it in the 380s) it acknowledged that Jesus is "of one substance with the Father." This term, *homo-ousios* (Greek: "of the same substance"), was reinforced with other anti-Arian statements. Jesus Christ is not subordinate, and thus he is eternal. He was "begotten of his Father before all worlds, God of God, Light of Light, very God of very God, begotten [that mysterious term that designates only the distinction between Father and Son within the Trinity], not made . . . by whom all things were made." With this confession the church established its belief that Jesus was truly God, that his nature was divine.[15]

Apollinaris. By A.D. 381 the church had to meet another challenge to its understanding of who Christ is, that of a theologian named Apollinaris. Apollinaris tried so hard to explain how Jesus was truly God that he fell off the edge in the other direction. He denied that Jesus was fully and completely human. He said that the human creature is composed of body, soul, and spirit, and he taught that Jesus had a human body and soul but that his spirit was the eternal Word, the second person of the Trinity. The church said no, at a council at Constantinople in 381; Jesus has a fully human nature as well as a divine nature. He is completely human—and completely divine.[16]

Nestorius. The church also had to define how the human na-

131

ture and the divine nature were related to each other because the culture around them forced Christians to reconsider again and again whether God and the human could come together in the way in which the Bible says they do. By the year 431 the church was confronted with the teaching of disciples of a theologian named Nestorius. They taught that there was no real connection between the two natures of Christ, that they lay along side each other as two boards bound together. At a council in Ephesus in 431 the church said no. The two natures are so closely brought together that we can say that Mary is the Mother of God, *theotokos* in Greek. Nestorius was willing to call Mary the Mother of Christ, but not the Mother of God. We confess with Paul that Jesus, the Son of God, the second person of the Trinity, was born of a woman and, like all other human creatures, was born under the Law (Gal. 4:4).[17]

Eutyches. As so often happens, in reaction against Nestorius, another theologian named Eutyches, went too far in the opposite direction. He claimed that as the human and divine came together in the incarnation, the divine nature, being so superior to the human, swallowed up the human. His followers are called Monophysites, or one nature-ists. The Coptic churches of Egypt and Ethiopia remain monophysite to this day. In 451 at Chalcedon a council of the church rejected Eutyches' view. It taught that the divine and human natures are so united in the one person of Jesus Christ that they are inseparable, but always distinct. Although the human does not become divine nor the divine human, they share characteristics.[18]

The Personal or Hypostatic Union. The relationship that the Council of Chalcedon defined between the two natures within the one person of Jesus Christ, the second person of the Holy Trinity, is called the "personal" or "hypostatic" union. In the words of the Athanasian Creed "although he be God and Man, yet he is not two, but one Christ: One, not by conversion of the Godhead into flesh, but by taking the manhood into God; one altogether, not by confusion of Substance, but by unity of person." The union of God and human creature in Jesus Christ thus brings together the nature of God and the nature of humanity in this one, single person. This union does not blend or obliterate one nature or the other. The two remain fully and inseparably united, even if the two natures remain ever distinct, ever the nature of God or of humanity itself.

Nestorius had taught that Christ's divine and human natures are both distinguishable from each other and must remain quite separable, even in this personal union. Eutychus had taught that the two natures are not only inseparable but ultimately indistinguishable. The Council of Chalcedon confessed that the two natures are inseparable but remain distinct from each other.

The Communication of Attributes or the Sharing of Characteristics. In the mystery of this personal union the two natures function together as one person. In so doing each nature shares its characteristics with the other. This sharing of characteristics between the two natures is called the communication of attributes. We cannot talk about the characteristics of the human nature without including the divine since the two natures are inseparable.[19]

Lutheran theologians of the sixteenth and seventeenth centuries tried to define the sharing of characteristics through the formulation of three principles. The first principle, the principle of properties (or characteristics or attributes) [Latin: *genus idiomaticum*] stated that "such properties as are peculiar to the divine or human nature are truly and really ascribed to the entire person of Christ, designated by either nature or by both natures." Thus, when Paul stated that they had crucified the Lord of glory (1 Cor. 2:8) or Peter reminded his hearers that they had killed the Author of Life (Acts 3:15), they were speaking of the human characteristic of mortality but designating Jesus with divine titles or names. In the original words of the hymn "O Darkest Woe," written by the seventeenth-century Lutheran hymn writer Johannes Rist (1607–67), we can even say, "O woe and dread, our God is dead." God cannot die, and yet in the personal union of God and the human creature Jesus Christ, the second person of the Trinity was there on the cross, dying for us.

The second principle, the principle of majesty [Latin: *genus majestaticum*], teaches that the second person of the Trinity shares with his human nature all his divine characteristics for common possession, use, and designation within the one person of Christ.

The third principle, the principle of the actions of office [Latin: *genus apotelesmaticum*], teaches that in his actions each nature within Christ performed what is peculiar to itself, with the participation of the other. The mystery of this personal union of God and man will always remain a mystery. We can only confess it.

Lutherans regard the sharing of the characteristics of the two natures as an important insight into God's coming into human flesh. We use it to help us confess how the human body and blood of Jesus Christ can be present in a mysterious way in the bread and wine of the Lord's Supper. His body and blood share with the divine nature that characteristic of being able to be present wherever, whenever, and in whatever form God wills. It is also of great comfort to us to know that he who shares our human nature is sitting in the councils of the Trinity. God not only knows our human experience through his divine omniscience but also through the human experience of the second person of the Trinity.

In this human creature, Jesus of Nazareth, the fullness of God was pleased to dwell. That is who he is: fully God and fully human. His person interests fallen human creatures not because of its uniqueness, however. Instead, he commands our attention because through him God reconciles all to himself, restoring the peace of Eden, of humanity as he created it, through the blood shed by this God-man on the cross (Col. 1:19–20).

Notes for Chapter VII

1. Georg Fohrer and Eduard Lohse, *"huios," Theological Dictionary of the New Testament,* vol 8, ed. Gerhard Friedrich, trans. and ed. Geoffrey W. Bromiley (Grand Rapids: Eerdmans, 1972), 347–53, 360–62; Oscar Cullmann, *The Christology of the New Testament,* trans. Shirley C. Guthrie and Charles A. M. Hall (Philadelphia: Westminster, 1963), 270–305.
2. Carsten Colpe, *"ho huios tou anthrōpou," Theological Dictionary of the New Testament,* vol. 8, 400–77.
3. Ibid., 420–30.
4. Cullmann, 1–10.
5. Robert Kolb, *Speaking the Gospel Today: A Theology for Evangelism* (Saint Louis: Concordia, 1984), 98–128.
6. Werner Foerster and Gottfried Quell, *"kurios," Theological Dictionary of the New Testament,* vol. 3, ed. Gerhard Kittel, trans. and ed. Geoffrey W. Bromiley (Grand Rapids: Eerdmans, 1965), 1039–95; Cullmann, 195–237.
7. Gerhard Kittel, *"Jesus Christ the logos tou theou," Theological Dictionary of the New Testament,* vol. 4, ed. Gerhard Kittel, trans. and ed. Geoffrey W. Bromiley (Grand Rapids: Eerdman, 1967), 124–36; Cullmann, 249–69.
8. Textual variants indicate that one must choose between "the only-begotten Son" and "the only-begotten God" at this point. On the principle of choosing the more difficult reading, the latter translation is correct.
9. Horace D. Hummel, *The Word Becoming Flesh: An Introduction to the Origin,*

Purpose, and Meaning of the Old Testament (Saint Louis: Concordia, 1979), 78–79.

10. Johannes Behm, *"morphē," Theological Dictionary of the New Testament,* vol. 4, 750–52.

11. Gerhard Kittel, *"eikon," Theological Dictionary of the New Testament,* vol. 2, trans. and ed. Geoffrey W. Bromiley (Grand Rapids: Eerdmans, 1964), 395.

12. J. N. D. Kelly, *Early Christian Doctrines* (New York: Harper & Row, 1960), 140–42; Jaroslav Pelikan, *The Christian Tradition: A History of the Development of Doctrine, 1: The Emergence of the Catholic Tradition (100–600)* (Chicago: The University of Chicago Press, 1971), 89, 173–74.

13. Dietrich Bonhoeffer, *Christ the Center,* trans. John Bowden (New York: Harper & Row, 1960), 78–85.

14. Kelly, 115–19; Pelikan, 175–76.

15. Kelly, 223–69.

16. Ibid., 289–301; Pelikan, 228, 239–40, 248.

17. Kelly, 310–30; Pelikan, 231–33, 242, 245, 251–56.

18. Kelly, 330–43; Pelikan, 262–75.

19. J. N. D. Kelly, *The Athanasian Creed* (New York: Harper & Row, 1964), 91–108; Pelikan, 263–66. Cf. The Formula of Concord, Article VIII, The Person of Christ, *The Book of Concord,,* trans. and ed. Theodore G. Tappert (Philadelphia: Fortress, 1959), 486–92, 591–610.

Chapter VIII
The Work of Christ

Jesus Christ has reconciled us to God through the blood of the cross. That is the heart of our faith, the core of our existence. God has become a human creature so that he might straighten out our relationship with him once again. He has entered into our existence so that he might restore us to living as his children. The church has described how God has given us righteousness in his sight once again in a number of ways.

Humiliation and Exaltation

The church has analyzed Christ's work in the two stages or states of humiliation and exaltation. In what was probably an early Christian hymn Paul's contemporaries sang of Christ Jesus (Phil. 2:6–11),

> "Who, being in very nature God,
>   did not consider equality with God something to be grasped,
> but made himself nothing,
>   taking the very nature of a servant,
>   being made in human likeness.
> And being found in appearance as a man,
>   he humbled himself
>   and became obedient to death—
>   even death on a cross!"

The humiliation of his obedience unto death, however, set the stage for his exaltation:

> "Therefore God exalted him to the highest place
>   and gave him the name that is above every name,
> that at the name of Jesus every knee should bow,
>   in heaven and on earth and under the earth,
> and every tongue confess that Jesus Christ is Lord,
>   to the glory of God the Father."

This confession regarding the course of Christ's earthly life from incarnation through his return to heavenly glory affirms that Jesus joined fallen humanity under the curse of death. As an analytical tool, his humiliation does not consist of his becoming human, for he remains truly human after the state of humiliation ended in his death. He humbled himself unto death: his humiliation consisted of being regarded as worthy of death, of becoming sin (see 2 Cor. 5:21) as he assumed the sinfulness of fallen creatures. In presenting Christ's humiliation, the church has included all that led to the cross, as confessed in the Creed, from his conception and birth through his suffering, death, and burial. (It is important to note that, strictly speaking, only his assumption of human sinfulness, not his incarnation, is genuine humiliation.)

Christ's exaltation embraces the course of his triumph over all the enemies of his people. Although some sixteenth-century Lutherans believed that he completed his sufferings in the descent into hell, most Lutherans have taught that he "preached to the spirits in prison" as a mark of his victory over evil (1 Peter 3:19–20).[1] The exaltation took place in his resurrection, in his ascension, in his sitting at the right hand of the Father. His exaltation will be exhibited further in his return to judge all human creatures. This exaltation reveals that he is the Lord and invites the praise of his name, the name above all other names (Phil. 2:9–10). In tracing his humiliation and exaltation we note how God entered fully into the evil and sin that assault us, and how he disposed of all that threatens his people through his own death and resurrection.

Titles for Christ

In the Middle Ages theologians such as Thomas Aquinas used a three-fold designation of Christ's "offices" as a summary of his work in behalf of sinners. John Calvin picked up this three-fold summary of "prophet, priest, and king" to outline his treatment of Christ's work in his *Institutes of the Christian Religion*.[2] Luther used each of these biblical designations of Jesus Christ individually, and later Lutherans also used the organizational principle of the three-fold office to summarize the work of Christ. The title *prophet* embodies Christ's role as the one who reveals God to his people. The title *priest* presents his work as the victim who takes the place of sinners under the Law, sin, guilt, and death. The title *king* embraces his victory over every evil that plagues his people. To these three categories into which we might organize what Christ has done for us, we can add a fourth: his activities as our companion, helper, and guide in daily life.

Christ the Revealer

"No one has ever seen God; the only Son, who is in the bosom of the Father, he has made him known" (John 1:18 RSV). Jesus claimed for himself the status of an Old Testament spokesman for God, a prophet, that is, one who "forth-tells" the Word of the Lord (whether he uses "foretelling" or prediction in that proclamation or not). Only God's chosen prophets had been able to speak the Word of the Lord with the confident, "I tell you the truth," and "truly, I say to you." The rabbis of Jesus' time could say, "The prophets have said of old," but they could not say, "Truly, I say to you . . . " (Matt. 5:18, 26; 6:2, 5). With this affirmation of his own words Jesus was announcing that what he said revealed God's Word and will in a way that Israel had not experienced since the last of the Old Testament prophets, Malachi.

Prophet. The Jews of his day were longing for the Prophet of the Day of the Lord, the one whom God had promised to Moses (Deut. 18:15–18). God had promised to complete his prophetic revelation of himself on his Great Day (Joel 2:28–32). Some who heard Jesus recognized that he was indeed the prophet upon whom the Spirit of the Lord rested (Luke 4:16–21), one like an Old Testament prophet or perhaps the long-awaited Elijah (Mark 6:15), the promised eschatological prophet (John 6:14). His contemporaries heard from his own lips and recognized that the Father had sent Jesus on a special assignment of proclamation and revelation (John 4:34; 5:30; 6:38; 9:4; Luke 4:18; Rom. 8:3). They heard in his words a special kind of authority (Matt. 7:29; John 7:46).[3]

Son of Man. His revelation repeatedly emphasized that he was the Son of Man, the human form who possessed all of Yahweh's characteristics. His disciples confessed that he was Lord and God. John spoke of his revelatory activity with the designation "the Word become flesh" (John 1:14). In him people experienced the image of God, the presence of God's glory. The titles that biblical writers used to demonstrate that Jesus of Nazareth was God come in human flesh present him in his activities as the revealer of what God is really like.[4]

Light. Other titles also present him as God's revealer. Particularly those titles that use the concept of "light" focus on Christ's showing his people both who God is and what true humanity is. He enlightens us regarding our vertical relationship with our Creator and our horizontal relationship with others, for he bestows on us the gift of God's righteousness at the same time he gives us the supreme example for the righteousness of human interaction. He lights up the lives of his people (John 1:4) and opens the eyes of the blind (Matt. 11:5). He both lights up the pathway through life (Matt. 4:15–16; Is. 9:1–2) and is the pathway on which truth and life are found (John 14:6). Christ's light challenges the darkness that threatens his people and chases it away (John 1:5; 8:12; 12:46).[5]

Jesus as Medium and Message. Jesus Christ communicates the presence of God into the midst of a fallen world. He served as God's prophet, the medium whereby God conveyed his message to his people. A well-designed medium God fashioned in him! He translated the message of his ultimate love for his defiant creatures into human form and flesh. This medium, Jesus of Nazareth, is also the message itself. For God was in Christ reconciling the world to himself (2 Cor. 5:19) by the blood of his cross (Col. 1:20). He demonstrated his love for us in that while we were still sinners, Christ died for us (Rom. 5:8).

This message is a message of foolishness and weakness from the standpoint of fallen human creatures. God chose what is foolish and weak in the world's eyes to shame the wise and the strong (1 Cor. 1:18–30). The crucifixion of the Lord of glory (1 Cor. 2:8) reveals both the ultimate love of God and the foolishness and impotence of this world's attempts at mastery. Sinners tried to put Christ away, in the grave, but he came back to end their existence as sinners. He came back to give them new life (Rom. 6:3–11). Thus, as Christ repeats who God is to us in his own person, he pronounces the end of all fallen human endeavors to secure life on our own terms. In his recounting of God's love for us he shatters every hope we have apart from him.

Theologians have called God's revelation of himself in Jesus Christ a "revelation under the form of opposites." His ultimate power is "revealed" in the hiddenness of the weakness of the cross; his ultimate wisdom is "revealed" in the hiddenness of the foolishness of the crib. God did not send Christ to open the door into the presence of God and let fallen human creatures peer into the ultimate majesty of our Creator. God sent Christ through that door, shutting it behind him, to "reveal" what God is like and who he is for us on our level and in our terms. These terms contradict what we imagine God to be like.

In God's "self-disclosure" life springs forth from death. His sinlessness is displayed in his conviction for the worst of sins, blasphemy (Matt. 26:65). His omnipotence reveals itself in weakness. His wisdom takes form in the ultimate foolishness of the cross (1 Cor. 1:18–2:8). His love is exhibited under the form of the wrath of a Father forsaking his Son on the cross (Mark 15:34). His presence moves into our lives through that ultimate forsakenness. His justice and righteousness triumph in the moment of ultimate injustice. The Author of Life dies (Acts 3:15).[6] Precisely at the most fragile and frail point of his humanity Christ reveals the ultimate expression of who God is and how he acts toward us. Such is the revelation of our God.

During the state of his humiliation Christ directly exercised his prophetic office, in his proclamation of God's Word and in his living out of God's love. Now, as the exalted prophet, he continues his ministry of proclamation through those who trust in him, as they spread the message of his love.

Christ the Vicar and Victim

God sent his Son, born of a woman, born under the Law, to redeem those who live under the Law and make them his family (Gal. 4:4–5). Jesus Christ takes our place (serves as our vicar) in the presence of every enemy that threatens the lives of his people, guilt and the accusation of the Law, the devil and death itself. He became the victim of all that assaults us, and as the stand-in for us, he received the full brunt of the Law's condemnation and death's icy chill.

The Suffering Servant. The figure of the suffering servant of Isaiah 42, 49, 50, and 52–53 offers the ultimate depiction of self-sacrificing love. Jesus consciously chose the pattern of the servant's being "handed over" and being killed—and then rising—as the framework for understanding his own suffering and death (Matt. 16:21; 17:22; 20:17–19). In the fourth Servant Song (Is. 52:13–53:12) the servant's substitionary suffering stands at the center of his activity even though there is reference to what would occur in Christ's resurrection: the servant was to "see his offspring" and "prolong his days" (53:10). But the servant—despised and rejected, a man of sorrows and acquainted with grief, despised, stricken, smitten by God, and afflicted—was above all wounded for our transgressions and bruised for our iniquities. Upon him was the chastisement that made us whole, and with his stripes we are healed. The Lord laid upon him the iniquity of us all. He bore the sin of many and made intercessions for the transgressors. How and why the servant bore the sins of others is not explained; the fact that he interceded for transgressors with his body is absolutely clear.[7]

Reflecting this prophetic pattern for dealing with the sins of others, Jesus emptied himself, took the form of a servant, and humbled himself, to the point of obediently going to the cross (Phil. 2:6–8). He came to serve and to be a ransom given in place of those sinners (Mark 10:45). He challenged death as he died in place of those who were still hostile to him (Rom. 5:6–8). Twice in his epistles, Paul may have referred to Is. 53:10, "he makes himself an offering for sin" (RSV). Rom. 8:3 may be translated "sending his own Son in the likeness of sinful flesh and as an offering for sin, he condemned sin in the flesh, in order that the just requirement of the Law might be fulfilled in us, who walk not according to the flesh but according to the Spirit." 2 Cor. 5:21 may be translated, "For our sake God made Christ to be an offering for sin, though he knew no sin, so that in him we might become the righteousness of God." In any case, Jesus Christ came to take human sinfulness upon himself and to destroy it as he carried it in the place of sinners and on their behalf.

High Priest. The concept of sacrifice for sin is connected with the image of Christ as priest or high priest. The practice of sacrifice to appease or coerce gods of one kind or another lies deeply imbedded in various religious systems. Sacrifices performed in the right manner could entice or compel favors from the divine and set aside the wrath of the gods in most of these systems. The Jews did not conceive of sacrifice as the ultimate religious meritorious work or as a magical means whereby they could bring Yahweh to do what they wanted him to do. They received their sacrificial system as a gift from him, as a means through which he reconciled them to himself (Heb. 10:1–10). God himself had arranged and performed the expiation, that which takes away sin from his children, by becoming the propitiation, that which sets aside his own wrath, for them (1 John 2:2; Rom. 3:25). It remains a mystery how God can both give himself over as sacrifice and ransom and at the same time remain in charge of making the sacrifice. This mystery is expressed in his being the priest who offers himself for the people and remains forever as their mediator.[8]

The writer to the Hebrews used this image of the priest extensively. He described Jesus as the human high priest designated to make expiation for the sins of the people (2:17). Yet he was without sin himself (4:15; 7:26–28), and so he could complete the final, ultimate, all-sufficient sacrifice for sin (9:26; 10:10). He built the bridge that mediating priests build by becoming the sacrifice himself (9:12–14, 28). As both priest and victim, he purified his people's consciences through the sprinkling of his own blood (9:13–14). As the Lamb of God, without spot or blemish, he freed his people from the futile ways inherited from their fathers, so that they might be given the gift of trust in God (1 Peter 1:1–2, 18–21; Rev. 1:5–6).

Sacrificed on the cross in his humiliation, this Lamb of God has been raised to triumph over every enemy of his people. At God's throne he continues in his exaltation to serve as mediator, or bridge-builder. He continues to be a priest forever, after the model of the king-priest, Melchizedek, the mysterious figure who appeared with the name "King of Righteousness" to Abraham but was performing priestly duties (Heb. 6:20–7:19; cf. Gen. 14:17–20). He now lives to make intercession for those whom he draws near to God (Heb. 7:25). Only he who gave himself as a ransom for all is able to mediate between God and his human creatures (1 Tim. 2:5). He serves as advocate—defense attorney—or mediator for sinners (1 John 2:1). There he continues to argue against the accusations that spring from Satan's brief against us. The Lamb whose blood conquers Satan casts away the accusations of his people's accuser (Rev. 12:1–12).[9]

To the images of Jesus Christ as suffering servant and priest Paul added a further description of his substitutionary role. Jesus took upon himself the curse placed upon all those who do not obey God's Law. He became a curse for us (Gal. 3:10–14). He became sin for us (2 Cor. 5:21). Luther found this "the most joyous of all doctrines and the one that contains the most comfort." He commented on Galatians 3:13:

> It teaches that we have the indescribable and inestimable mercy and love of God. When the merciful Father saw that we were being oppressed through the Law, that we were being held under a curse, and that we could not be liberated from it by anything, He sent His Son into the world, heaped all the sins of all men upon Him, and said to Him: "Be Peter the denier; Paul the persecutor, blasphemer, and assaulter; David the adulterer; the sinner who ate the apple in Paradise; the thief on the cross. In short, be the person of all men, the one who has committed the sins of all men. And see to it that you pay and make satisfaction for them."[10]

Luther continues with the Law's judgment upon Christ: "I find him a sinner, who takes upon himself the sins of all men. I do not see any other sins than those in him. Therefore let him die on the cross!" The Law, Luther reports, attacks and kills Christ, thereby purging the whole world of its sins and liberating all from death and every evil. In this attack on Christ a "wondrous duel" has taken place, between the fury of the powerful, cruel tyrant, sin, and the righteousness of Christ. Christ won. He conquered, killed, and buried the curse by assuming it for sinners.[11]

Christ the Victor

In this duel with sin Christ not only appeared as victim. He also appeared as victor. He is the one who was put to death for the trespasses of sinners, but he is also the one who was raised to give them righteousness (Rom. 4:25).

King or Messiah. In his humiliation he ruled as king from a cross, with a crown of thorns and the broken scepter of a reed. He did so as a king who functioned differently than sinful, human kings (John 18:33–37). His central concern was the truth, which he both proclaimed and embodied (John 14:6). Thus, in this way he led the subjects of his kingdom through death into the exaltation of the royal triumph of the resurrection.

Theologians have sometimes divided Jesus' rule and role as king into three categories. His "kingdom of power" comprehends his rule over all parts of the universe, including his providential care of human creatures on a daily basis and his final triumph over the principalities and powers that oppose him. His "kingdom of grace" embraces his exercise of kingly rule over his own people on this earth, as he sovereignly forgives their sins and protects them as his children. The "kingdom of glory" is his rule of his people beyond the confines of this earth, around his heavenly throne. These kingdoms do not exist as three separate agencies in Christ's kingly rule. They simply represent a human attempt to understand how Christ's loving care embraces all that he has created. For he is king of all.

As the Messiah, the Son of David, Jesus assumed rule over God's people. That rule embraced their liberation from their enemies, the foremost messianic role. But he did execute that rule in his own way, exercising his dominion from below, as the royal servant of his people (Mark 10:45).[12]

Savior. Jesus' own name meant "savior" (Matt. 1:21). Therefore, the concept of his saving intervention in the lives of sinners was expressed primarily in the term *Messiah,* the one expected as the Savior of God's people. The title *Savior* occurs relatively seldom alongside the name *Jesus,* which embraces it already. The angels defined Jesus' role as Savior, both to Joseph (Matt. 1:21) and to the shepherds (Luke 2:11). This Savior, born in David's city, was Christ the Lord—Messiah, yet Yahweh himself (cf. Peter's confession in Acts 2:36)—come to save his people from their sins.

The title *savior* was frequently employed by the so-called mystery cults of the early Christian era. They forged saviors who would help adherents escape from the evils of the material body with its impurities and from mortality. Paul confronted these false saviors directly when he proclaimed the coming of the "Savior from [heaven], the Lord Jesus Christ, who, by the power that enables him to bring everything under his control, will transform our lowly bodies so that they will be like his glorious body" (Phil. 3:20–21). "Our Savior, Christ Jesus, ... has destroyed death and has brought life and immortality to light through the gospel" (2 Tim. 1:10). "Our great God and Savior, Jesus Christ, who gave himself for us to redeem us from all wickedness and to purify for himself a people that are his very own, eager to do what is good" (Titus 2:13–14). Believers anticipate the return of such a Savior so that he can complete the victory he won in his resurrection.[13]

Victor over Death. In his resurrection Christ disarmed all the foes of his people and at the same time canceled the bill of indictment lodged against those whom he came to forgive. His people had been dead in trespasses and far from God's family, but God made them alive through the death and the resurrection of Christ (Col. 2:11–15). As the Word who had made all things in the beginning, the promised Messiah, Jesus, the Christ, entered into death in order to triumph over it and reclaim life for sinners caught in its clutches (John 1:4; 1 John 1:2; John 11:25–27). He entered first into death in our behalf (Heb. 6:20), so that he might be the firstfruits of death in his own resurrection (1 Cor. 15:20). As the Second Adam, he retraced Adam's steps into death, so that he might lead Adam and all his heirs out of death (Rom. 5:12–17; 1 Cor. 15:20–23).

Christ's resurrection liberates his people from their sins and thus from death (1 Cor. 15:54–57). His resurrection causes them to be "steadfast, immovable, always abounding in the work of the Lord" (1 Cor. 15:58 RSV), for they know that what they are doing has meaning and purpose in the Lord. As he bestows the fruits of his resurrection upon his people through their Baptisms, they walk in newness of life. They consider themselves dead to sin and alive to God in Christ Jesus. Therefore, they do not let sin rule in their mortal bodies. They yield themselves to God as people who have been brought from death to life, recognizing that all parts of their lives have been given new life in order to be God's instruments of righteousness (Rom. 6:4, 11–14). Having been raised with Christ in their Baptisms, having their lives hidden away with him through their baptismal deaths, believers seek Christ's will. They set their minds on things above. They look forward to appearing with him in glory when he, who is their life, comes again (Col. 2:12; 3:1–4).

Christ the Victor has come back from the grave to deliver to his Father the complete rule over all his creation once again. He put all God's enemies under his feet and subjected all things to God as a result of his resurrection (1 Cor. 15:24–28). He has promised his royal return as the Son of Man, who comes from the clouds to exercise God's dominion (Matt. 24:27–44; 25:31–46).

Ever since the Enlightenment, people have raised objections to the possibility of bodily resurrection. The church has had to affirm

Christ's resurrection and the resurrection of his people against claims that such miracles do not happen. The resurrection of the Lord and of his people are, it must be noted, inseparably connected. You cannot have one without the other, Paul argued (1 Cor. 15:12–19). Since the resurrection of the crucified Lord of glory was a unique event, it cannot be tested in ways in which believers could produce empirical proof. Since the resurrection of the dead occurs on the Last Day, tests cannot be run on this phenomenon, either. Therefore, the church must simply confess the resurrection of the dead—of the dead Lord and of his dead children—against such objections.

Contempt for the material order in various philosophical traditions, both in Eastern and Western religions, has tended to diminish the prominence of the proclamation of Christ's bodily victory over sin and death in his resurrection, even within the church. The Resurrection of the Body—Christ's and his people's—stands at the center point of the faith the church confesses (1 Cor. 15:3–5). Death and resurrection is the central theme of its confession of the Lord who became the Messiah, the royal deliverer, of his people by appearing in flesh and blood, in crib and cross, and out of his crypt.

Christ as Companion, Helper, and Guide. As our providing and protecting king Christ extends his rule into our daily lives. His rule exhibits itself in various ways, often incomplete and broken from our perspective as evil inundates us. Yet he has assured us of his presence and power in our lives throughout our earthly life (Matt. 28:18–20). His healing and feeding during his lifetime on earth demonstrate his concern for his people's bodily sustenance and health (Matt. 4:23–24; 14:13–21). Above all, his presence sustains the vertical relationship he creates and maintains with his people.

This relationship he described in countless images in the New Testament. The intimate union of the believer and the Lord is depicted in terms of the relationship of bride and bridegroom (Matt. 9:14–15; Mark 2:18–20; Luke 5:33–35; 2 Cor. 11:2; Eph. 5:22–23; Rev. 19:7; 21:9). This image echoes what Hosea's marriage to the prostitute Gomer (Hos. 1:2–3) presented: God is faithful to his people even when they are unfaithful. Christ joins sinners to himself, shares with them all his goods, and makes them his family. He sustains his people as the Bread of Life (John 6:32–35, 48–51). He heals them as their physician (Matt. 9:9–13). He guides and protects them as a shepherd and rescues them when they stray (Luke 15:4–7; John 10:11–17; 1 Peter 2:25). He cherishes them as a parent (Mark 10:13–16; Matt. 23:37). His work continues throughout the day-to-day life of believers until he brings them finally to himself in heaven.

As people ask believers who this Jesus is, we first ask them why they want to know. It will do little good to talk at length about him as Savior and Lord to those who need no savior and who love other lords. We must first help them perceive, at least dimly, some need for becoming acquainted with God in human flesh. For those who know their need, we will introduce Jesus in ways that faithfully reproduce the God-man who has introduced himself to us through the pages of Scripture. But we will begin with those characteristics that meet the specific needs of those who are asking. We will help them understand that Jesus Christ is indeed their Savior and Lord, is their God in the situation of their own dilemma and need.

The Author of our Salvation

The writer to the Hebrews called Jesus the one "for whom and through whom everything exists," whose mission was completed through his suffering, the author of the salvation of his people (Heb. 2:10). Salvation, as noted above,[14] encompasses the peace of Eden and the effort that God makes to restore it through his mission of rescue in Christ. The biblical writers described this effort and its results with a number of terms. The most significant, which pierces to the heart of the matter, is *justification,* the subject of the next chapter. The Scriptures use other images and terms to describe God's saving actions, all of which believers should use in their understanding and sharing of his message and gift of salvation.

Rescue

The element of rescue stands foremost in the minds of sinners trapped in evil. God's rescue through his seeking and saving mission (Luke 19:10) assaults his enemies and defeats them (Ps. 44:2–7; 74:12; 80:2; Is. 33:22). This motif of rescue by God's warrior includes a number of results from his victory: he brings joy, removes disaster, deals with the oppressors of his people, saves the lame, gathers the outcasts, changes their shame into praise, and brings them home

(Zeph. 3:17–20). The ultimate rescue of his people, Zechariah confessed, embraced God's rescuing them from the hand of every enemy and above all forgiving them their sins (Luke 1:69, 71, 77).

Redemption

Related to the concept of *rescue* is that of *redeem*. God depicts himself as the one who redeems his people, as one would have bought liberty for a captive in ancient Near Eastern cultures. Behind the English word *redeem* stand several related but distinct concepts in the Old Testament world. In the sphere of private law one person might redeem another from slavery by offering a gift of sufficient value to cover another's debt or obligations; in such a case their ransom might free the other from slavery or from condemnation for a crime, even a capital crime. In this latter case it would buy life itself, not only freedom.

Another kind of redemption in the Old Testament world was that by which a family member reclaimed the freedom, life, or goods of a next of kin, or avenged the murder of a kinsman. God acts in behalf of his imprisoned people; he frees them from their obligations to the condemnation of the law and the claim of Satan. He redeemed his people from their bondage in Egypt, for example (Ex. 6:6; 15:13; Ps. 106:10; Is. 51:10). He promised to redeem them from every kind of evil that would threaten in the present or the future (Is. 35:9–10; 48:20; 52:9; 63:9; Ps. 103:4).

The metaphor of redemption from slavery is problematic if an attempt is made to apply it at every point (generally metaphors dare not be forced to do so, for it is in the very nature of a metaphor that it does not correspond completely to that which it represents). Valid in the metaphor is the result of liberation, of restoration of life. Valid is also the sacrifice of the redeemer to achieve liberation. But both in the Old Testament instance of the Exodus from Egypt and in the supreme instance of human redemption, the sacrifice of Jesus Christ, the metaphor breaks down when it tries to define to whom the price was paid. Egypt, the oppressor of God's people, did not receive payment for their liberation. Its forces were dashed and drowned by the strong arm and mighty hand of the Lord. From his debacle in the midst of the sea Pharaoh did not depart counting the ransom he had gained; the Lord departed, having established his everlasting reign (Ex. 15:1–18). The devil was not heard walking away from Golgotha chuckling at his gain; he had been conquered—not paid off—by the blood of the Lamb (Rev. 12:10–11). The metaphor of redemption expresses the mystery of God's liberation of his people through sacrifice. Explanations pale before the magnificence of the reality of his redemption.[15]

New Birth

Regeneration and re-creation describe what Christ has accomplished for his people with another kind of picture (2 Cor. 5:17). The Holy Spirit's washing of regeneration and renewal take place because he is pouring out the mercy of God through Jesus Christ our Savior, with the result that believers become righteous by his grace and become heirs in the hope of eternal life (Titus 3:4–7).

This new birth places sinners back into God's family, adopted as his children after they had run away from him (Gal. 4:5; Rom. 8:15). This adoption stems from his reconciliation of sinners to himself while they were still God's enemies (Rom. 5:10). God approached those who had fled from him through Christ. Through Christ he did not count their trespasses against them, for he made Christ to be sin (or a sin-offering) even though Christ had no sin of his own. In that process he has justified the existence of sinners, causing them to become righteous before him once again (2 Cor. 5:18–21).

This passage from 2 Corinthians 5 demonstrates how the various perspectives on God's saving act come back to one central focus: Jesus Christ. Here new creation, reconciliation, justification all come together, and they all arise out of what God has done in Jesus Christ. All synonyms of salvation return to the starting point of his crib, cross, and crypt.

How? Atonement Motifs and the Failure of Human Explanation

Christians have often posed the questions, "How does the incarnation work?" "Why did God accomplish the salvation of sinners in the manner in which he did?" "Did some necessity drive him to incarnation, death, and resurrection?"

The church has described just how God came to rescue us from our sinfulness in different ways. These descriptions have been organized into formal "motifs" or "theories" regarding God's saving or atoning action in Christ. Since early in the twentieth century theologians have focused on three "atonement motifs," two of them based on biblical material. These atonement motifs summarize much of the church's attempt to organize answers to such questions.[16] Of course, none of these descriptions can plumb the mind of God and give us an explanation. If we had an explanation, we would have the illusion of control, of knowing as much as God. That is not the case.

Atonement by Christ as Victor

In the early church the emphasis fell on Christ's redemption through his victory over all the powers that opposed and plagued the believer—the devil, hell, and evil people all around. Twentieth-century scholarship designated this atonement motif the "Christus Victor" motif. This victory happened above all in the resurrection of our Lord from the dead. Death is the final enemy, the one that exhibits its power most universally and most dramatically over the life the Creator gave to his human creatures. This victory focused first of all on the threat to our life in God from outside ourselves—although certainly Christ conquered the guilt and shame within us and took them away through his victory over every evil. The second-century theologian Irenaeus, a major expositor of this theme, emphasized Christ's entrance into the darkness in which the human creature was held prisoner. There he destroyed sin as he was tempted and triumphed over Satanic temptation; there he destroyed death as he was buried and triumphed over the liar's death.

Irenaeus taught that Christ "recapitulated" Adam's movement from life into death, so that he might pioneer the way out of death into life for all Adam's descendants. Christ's assumption of humanity because of our falleness provided the setting for his duel with all the forces of sin and death. This engagement became a duel to the death—to Christ's death, but to the ultimate death of Satan's claim on sinners and of death itself. In this triumph Christ won the gift of resurrection for sinners. He shares the life that he won with them. This life is not a new addition to humanity. It is a restoration of

God's original gift of life with him, bestowed first in Eden.[17] Luther loved this picture of God's dueling with Satan to Satan's death.[18]

The "Christus Victor" motif was expressed not only in images from the battlefield. This motif may also employ the psalmists' description of God's victorious intervention in behalf of his people with the picture of his argument against the accuser of sinners in the courtroom. The Jews often thought of God's judgment in terms of a court of justice. The sinner appears in God's court not only as the accused. Sinners also may bring their suits for damages against the enemy before God's court. There Christ argues in their behalf and wins their case against the deities and demons that have claimed God's people as their own. He proves the case that these sinners, forgiven and thus liberated from sin's claim, owe nothing to the false gods and to Satan.[19] Their liberation through Christ's resurrection has won them the victory.

When we think of Christ as victor over every evil and all our sin, we think of him as king. We are focusing upon his exaltation as our risen Lord. We look to our baptisms, in which we were incorporated into his resurrection victory.

As believers use the "Christus Victor" motif, they will remember that the mystery of the atonement is beyond any capturing in human imagery or description. The use of this motif should not so concentrate our attention on external enemies that we forget the enemy within, our own sin and guilt. Christ came not only to conquer enemies outside us. He came also to assume into himself those internal enemies that brought us into the defeat of death.

Atonement by Christ as Vicar and Victim, or the Vicarious Satisfaction

While stressing Christ's resurrection victory over death and all other evils, the believers of the first thousand years of church history did not, of course, ignore his passion and death. However, a new attempt at explaining how God saves us arose in the Middle Ages. It centered on his passion and death. This atonement motif is usually designated the "Vicarious Satisfaction" motif; it speaks of Christ as vicar (that is, a substitute) for sinners and victim in their behalf.

Medieval society was organized in what was called the "feudal" system. The system was based on a series of interlocking oaths between people higher and lower than each other in the society's hierarchy. Peasants swore oaths of loyalty and obligation to nobles, nobles swore them to dukes, dukes to kings and emperors. In turn, the emperor swore to the duke his oath of protection and justice, and the duke swore a similar oath to the noble, as the noble did to the peasant. Saint Anselm, at the end of the eleventh century, viewed all reality from the point of view of the feudal system, as did his European contemporaries. He believed that God and the human creature had had a relationship of a similar sort. When the human creature broke the feudal oath, satisfaction of the obligation was required, even as it would be in a feudal court hearing a dispute between peasant and noble.

The human creature in sin could not render this satisfaction to God's Law, of course, and so sinners could not save themselves. However, satisfaction could justly come only from the human side. Therefore, God had to become human—and a human victim—for only God could perform the satisfaction demanded by the Law, and yet it had to be performed by a human being.

Although Anselm's theory, and similar explanations, do not rely solely on biblical concepts, Anselm proceeded from the biblical writers' clear use of the model of the sacrifice of lambs and goats (e.g., John 1:29; Heb. 9:11–14). Scripture does clearly teach that Christ came to stand in our place under the Law (Gal. 4:4), to suffer the punishment we deserve (Rom. 3:21–26), and to die the death that has fallen upon us (Rom. 5:6–11). Christ came indeed to take our place, to be our "vicar," who stands in for us, to come to terms with guilt and sin and death on our behalf. He is the one who came to give his life as a ransom for many (Mark 10:45), as the Suffering Servant was to do (Is. 53:6, 10, 12).

Thinking of Christ as the sacrificial victim who vicariously took our place helps reassure us that our Lord not only defeated the enemies outside us but that he also has taken away the guilt and shame inside us. He has taken our guilt and shame into himself and buried it in his own tomb, so that we can stand innocent and righteous before his Father on the throne of grace. By taking our place, or by taking our sins into another place, his own body, Jesus has established himself as lord over our sins. He alone has the capacity to eliminate our past faults and flaws. By absorbing them into himself, he consumed them in the fire of his own passion.

We human creatures at least think that we can control our present and our future. But we cannot control our past. It is set; it is done as we have fashioned it. But God can even change our past. He alone is lord of our past. He alone can turn our flaws and faults aside and obliterate them from his own memory, where ultimate reality exists. If our sins are not real to God, then it is blasphemy for us to doubt his Word of forgiveness and to insist that our sins still exist; it is sin to dwell on these sins.

As we talk about Christ's taking our place and satisfying the demand of the Law upon us for our breaking of the Law, we must be careful that we do not make the Law more powerful than God. We dare not take away the important element of God's totally unconditional love by making it seem as though the Law could demand a price for sin from God. The Law's demands fall only on us, God's creatures who were made to live according to his design, as his loving and trusting children. He paid the price of his own Son; his Son paid the price of his own blood and life (1 Peter 1:18–19; 1 Cor. 6:20; Col. 1:20). Yet this price dare never be reduced to a mere commercial calculation. This kind of "price" involves a matter far more profound than mere payment in the usual sense of ransom. God did this not because he had to, but because he loved us, his children. Thus, believers acknowledge that the mystery remains as they praise God for sending his Son to be born under the Law and to make peace through the blood of the cross.

As we focus on what Christ did for us in his passion and death, we remember his role as the priest who is also the sacrificial victim for us. We also recall Christ's humiliation. We focus more on the Lord's Supper, where his body and blood are given for the forgiveness of our sins. We focus more on confession and absolution, where our guilt and shame are placed into Christ's tomb, on his back, and separated further from us than the east is from the west (Ps. 103:12).

"Atonement" by Moral Example

Soon after Anselm's time, another theologian attempted another explanation of how Christ saves. Abelard emphasized Christ's life as a model for good human living. Abelard believed that if sinners would simply follow Christ's example, they would find the good life as God had made it. Abelard did not take sin as seriously as Anselm had. He placed the actual working out of salvation to a large extent in human hands, within our own power.

While the Bible certainly teaches that Christ is our model for the proper performance of the deeds that God designed for his human creatures to do, it does not teach that we are saved by following the model. Abelard confused the two kinds of righteousness and tried to make the righteousness of the horizontal realm operative in the vertical realm. Scripture teaches that we are able to follow Christ's model only because he has saved us through his passion, death, and resurrection. Therefore, although Abelard's theory of atonement by moral example is often discussed alongside the ancient motif of Christ the Victor and the medieval motif of Christ the Vicarious Victim, it does not belong there. Unlike these other two models, it undercuts the grace of God.

Again, it is important to remember that these descriptions of the work of Christ do not explain or define how or why God saved us. They merely point us to his unconditional and immeasurable love.

Atonement by the Joyous Exchange

Martin Luther often employed another image that in some senses combined the two atonement motifs and provided Luther with his own motif (although he never attempted to explain the atonement; he only used the full range of biblical descriptions as he found them appropriate in context[20]). He spoke of the "joyous exchange" of Christ's innocence for the sinner's guilt and sin. With this image he taught that God's Word had effected an exchange of the righteousness and life of Christ for the sin and death of the fallen human creature.

Thus, in his passion and death Christ absorbed into himself all the evil that clings to his people. Substituting himself for sinners, he gathered onto his own back all the sin and guilt that condemn them to death. He took the entire evil of each individual with him into his tomb and deposited it there. This tomb is the only place in God's creation into which the Father does not look. Having assumed our suffering and death upon his own person, Christ trades them for life itself. In his resurrection triumph he won for all sinners the gift of life, as it had been fashioned for God's human creatures in Eden. His Easter victory claimed true human life in God's sight for humanity once again. He restores true life by incorporating sinners into Christ's death and resurrection through Baptism (Rom. 6:3–11; Col. 2:11–15).

In this manner Luther gathered together the fundamental elements of the Christus Victor and Vicarious Satisfaction atonement motifs. He applied them to the daily life of the believer as it is lived out of God's baptismal intervention into the life of the individual believer.

The work of Christ cannot remain merely a historical datum. The one in whom God dwells bodily has made peace by the blood of the cross so that all hostility between God and his human creatures, and among his human creatures, might cease (Eph. 2:11–18; Col. 1:15–22). He had come to rescue them so that they might live out their humanity in the peace for which he designed them in Eden. The "joyous exchange" summarizes this good news not only by bringing together elements of the other atonement motifs but also by expressing them in the baptismal language of justification by God's grace through faith in Jesus Christ.

Notes for Chapter VIII

1. Formula of Concord, Article IX, Christ's Descent into Hell, *The Book of Concord,* trans. and ed. Theodore G. Tappert (Philadelphia: Fortress, 1959), 492, 610.

2. John Calvin, *The Institutes of the Christian Religion,* vol. 1, ed. John T. McNeill, trans. Ford Lewis Battles (Philadelphia: Westminster, 1960), 494–503.

3. Gerhard Friedrich, *"prophētēs," "Jesus," Theological Dictionary of the New Testament,* vol. 6, trans. and ed. Geoffrey W. Bromiley (Grand Rapids: Eerdmans, 1968), 841–48; Oscar Cullmann, *The Christology of the New Testament,* trans. Shirley C. Guthrie and Charles A. M. Hall (Philadelphia: Westminster, 1963), 13–50.

4. Carsten Colpe, *"ho huios tou anthrōpou," Theological Dictionary of the New Testament,* vol. 8, ed. Gerhard Friedrich, trans. and ed. Geoffrey W. Bromiley (Grand Rapids: Eerdmans, 1972), 400–77; Cullmann, 137–92.

5. Werner Foerster and Gottfried Quell, *"kurios," Theological Dictionary of the New Testament,* vol. 3, ed. Gerhard Kittel, trans. and ed. Geoffrey W. Bromiley (Grand Rapids: Eerdmans, 1965), 1039–95; Cullmann, 195–237.

6. Gerhard O. Forde, *Theology Is for Proclamation* (Minneapolis: Fortress, 1990), 107–8.

7. Cullmann, 51–82.

8. Gottlob Schrenk, *"archiereus," Theological Dictionary of the New Testament,* vol. 3, 274–83; Cullmann, 83–107.

9. Wilhelm Dantine, *Justification of the Ungodly,* trans. Eric W. and Ruth C. Gritsch (Saint Louis: Concordia, 1968), 86–88.

10. Martin Luther, *Lectures on Galatians, 1535, Chapters 1–4,* Luther's Works, vol. 26 (Saint Louis: Concordia, 1963), 280.

11. Ibid., 280–81.

12. Walter Grundmann, Franz Hesse, Marinus de Jonge, Adam Simon van der Woude, *"chriō," Theological Dictionary of the New Testament,* vol. 9, ed. Gerhard Friedrich, trans. and ed. Geoffrey W. Bromiley (Grand Rapids: Eerdmans, 1974), 493–580; Cullmann, 111–36.

13. Werner Foerster and Georg Fohrer, *"sōtēr," Theological Dictionary of the New Testament,* vol. 9, ed. Gerhard Friedrich, trans. and ed. Geoffrey W. Bromiley (Grand Rapids: Eerdmans, 1971), 1003–24; Cullmann, 238–45.

14. Ibid.

15. Friedrich Büchsel, *"lutron," Theological Dictionary of the New Testament,* vol. 4, ed. Gerhard Kittel, trans. and ed. Geoffrey W. Bromiley (Grand Rapids: Eerdmans, 1967), 340–49.

16. Gustaf Aulen, *Christus Victor: An Historical Study of the Three Main Types of the Idea of the Atonement,* trans. A. G. Hebert (1931; New York: Macmillan, 1961).

17. See Gustaf Wingren's study of Irenaeus, *Man and the Incarnation: A Study in the Biblical Theology of Irenaeus,* trans. Ross Mackenzie (Philadelphia: Muhlenberg, 1959), 96–98.

18. E.g., Martin Luther, *Lectures on Galatians, 1535, Chapters 1–4,* Luther's Works, vol. 26 (St. Louis: Concordia, 1963), 164; and *Sermons on the Gospel of St. John, Chapters 1–4,* Luther's Works, vol. 22 (St. Louis: Concordia, 1957), 355–56.

19. C. S. Lewis, *Reflections on the Psalms* (New York: Harcourt Brace Jovanovich, 1958), 10; Dantine, 78–79.

20. So argues Ian D. Kingston Siggins, *Martin Luther's Doctrine of Christ* (New Haven: Yale University Press, 1970), 108–13.

Chapter IX

Justification

Paul posed the human dilemma in Rom. 3:10–12: "There is no one righteous, not even one; there is no one who understands, no one who seeks God. All have turned away, they have together become worthless, there is no one who does good, not even one." And no one will become righteous in God's sight by doing the works of the Law (Rom. 3:20).

Human performance does not produce human righteousness; even in Eden, human performance resulted from human righteousness. God's grace fashioned the human creature in the first place. Only God's grace can restore the righteousness of the relationship that he created between himself and humankind at creation. "Since all have sinned and fall short of the glory of God, they are justified by his grace as a gift, through the redemption which is in Christ Jesus, whom God put forward as an expiation by his blood, to be received by faith" (Rom. 3:23–25 RSV).

Justification comes from the Latin word *justitia,* which can be translated both "righteousness" and "justice." The biblical teaching regarding justification defines the right relationship between God and his human creatures. It tells how God restores fallen sinners to that right relationship with himself, rescuing them from sin and death, restoring them to life itself. Human life, in its completeness, embraces at its very core this right relationship with God. Righteousness in his sight is life itself.

Just as God created humankind without compulsion or condition, as a free act of love, so he has re-created humankind without compulsion or condition, as a free act of love. This act of creating anew may be described as salvation or reconciliation or liberation. It is best described as "justification," even though for unbelievers in our culture this term usually means something quite different than the biblical understanding of the word. If I justify myself in modern North American English, I am usually trying to explain why

I had to do something even though it was wrong. When God justifies me, he restores me to my proper place before him. He makes me righteous in his sight.

By Grace Alone

Justification is God's act. He re-creates fallen sinners. He transforms them into his chosen children through his act of bestowing a right relationship with himself. Sinners cannot use God's Law as a guide for restoring their own place before him. Adam and Eve came to the proper place before him through his effort, not their own. Sinners return to that place solely through his effort, not our own. His effort is grace; his effort stems from his grace.

In the Middle Ages the church taught that grace was a gift that God placed within the human creature, a psychological "component part," which added to the sinner what had been lost when another component part, original righteousness, had been lost in the fall.[1] Luther rejected attempts to analyze grace in terms of something added internally to the fallen creature. He defined grace as God's favor, his attitude of mercy, his favorable disposition toward his human creatures. God is gracious in showing his love and in regarding fallen sinners as his own children once again.

God's grace is not compelled; nothing forces God to love his creatures. Nothing created can put its claim upon the Creator. He is indeed sovereign over all that he has made. In relationship to his creatures there can be no "unrighteousness" in God. Paul posed the question: Can there be unrighteousness on God's part? His answer reflects the conviction of all Old Testament people: "Not at all! For he says to Moses, 'I will have mercy on whom I have mercy, and I will have compassion on whom I have compassion' " (Rom. 9:14–15). Nor is God's grace conditional or conditioned by any human action. God's grace and favor are free, freely conceived, freely fashioned, freely given.

Thus, "at just the right time, when we were still powerless, Christ died for the ungodly. Very rarely will anyone die for a righteous man, though for a good man someone might possibly dare to die. But God demonstrates his own love for us in this: While we were still sinners, Christ died for us. Since we have now been justified by his blood, how much more shall we be saved from God's wrath through him! For if, when we were God's enemies, we were reconciled to him through the death of his Son, how much more, having been reconciled, shall we be saved through his life!" (Rom. 5:6–10).

God's grace expresses itself in his setting aside of his wrath. Even God's wrath expresses his love for his human creatures. His anger is directed against them on their behalf. It is anger against their destruction of the heart of their existence, their trust in him. His grace sets aside that anger and restores the righteousness that they lost in their sin.

That righteousness is the righteousness of trust in him. Thus, in humankind, the opposite of God's grace is not God's wrath, but rather the human attempt to reclaim righteousness by human performance. Good works do not save. Human performance can never put a claim on God. God remains Creator and Lord even if the human performance is perfect. The righteousness of human performance matters only in horizontal relationships. It is only the result, not the cause, of our being right with God. In relationship to him we are okay, we are right, only because he has created us as his children. In addition, as we consider our own deeds, we must recognize that the sinner's performance of the works of God's Law is always imperfect. Even our best attempts at righteousness are still like a filthy rag (Is. 64:6), permeated as is every attempt at righteousness with a lack of perfect trust in Yahweh.

Thus, the whole Christian life rests on God's gracious disposition, the attitude and expression of his favor, toward us. His grace is sufficient for us. His power is made perfect in our weaknesses, and in our weaknesses his power and the favor of his love are revealed (2 Cor. 12:9). God's grace causes Christian behavior (2 Cor. 1:12). All believers confess with Saint Paul, "By the grace of God I am what I am, and his grace to me was not without effect. No, I worked harder than all of them—yet not I, but the grace of God that was with me" (1 Cor. 15:10).

This grace means that we do nothing. That "we do nothing" means death for the person who presumes that doing something saves, or secures God's grace.[2] God is Creator, and for us to be in relationship with him presumes that he remains the one who gives and sustains life without condition. Without any merit or worthiness in us we receive his grace.

Justified by His Gracious Word

God created the worlds by his Word. He spoke, and all that exists came into being (Genesis 1). Likewise, God speaks fallen sinners righteous. He re-creates through his Word.

The term "to justify" had at least two different shades of meaning, both in the Greek of the New Testament and in the German of Luther's day.[3] Usually, Lutherans have understood clearly its meaning, "to pronounce righteous." God acts as gracious judge in pronouncing the fallen sinner innocent. The word of a courtroom judge determines reality for the defendant. The person guilty of serial murder may for all practical purposes roam the streets of the city freely once the judge has pronounced him or her innocent. The person who has committed no crime experiences the reality of guilt—prison, fines, probation—if the judge has pronounced him or her guilty.

God's Word determines reality also. When God pronounces the sinner innocent, the sinner does not remain a sinner. The sinner becomes righteous. God's regarding us as his children means that we are his children. He has said so. That is good enough for him. It must be good enough for us also.

"To justify" means not only "to pronounce righteous, in the manner of a courtroom judge," however. It also means "to do justice to." When God justifies the sinner, the sinner receives justice. Most believers would protest: no, sinners receive mercy and forgiveness. We do not get what is coming to us when God justifies us. However, Paul describes justification in precisely such terms. He climaxes his description of justification in Romans 3–8 with his affirmation that as God justifies the sinner, in Baptism, the sinner is baptized into Christ's death (6:4). We have been united with him in a death like his (6:5). "Our old self was crucified with him so that the sinful body might be destroyed, and we might no longer be enslaved to sin. For he who has died is freed from sin" (6:6–7 RSV).

In the process of burying us—who were dead in trespasses and the uncircumcision of our flesh—with Christ in Baptism, God has also made us alive together with him. In dying and rising with Christ in Baptism, believers have been given the cancellation of the bill of indictment that stood against them with the demands of the Law. It has been nailed to Christ's cross. There Christ disarmed the enemies of the believers, making a public example of them, triumphing over them (Col. 2:11–15).

Sinners must die; it is what they have earned from their sin (Rom. 6:23). Sinners do die. God does justice to them in justification. He buries them. He buries them with Christ. Christ has taken the sins of the world and hidden them in his tomb, the only place in his universe where the Father's glance never falls. Sinners do not exist before him any longer, for Christ has let his grace overflow into the lives of sinners, as he shows them mercy (1 Tim. 1:15). Those who were sinners before his justifying Word did justice to them are now his saintly children. Christ's blood shed for his people has blotted out their sins, forgiving them in the riches of his mercy and grace (Rom. 3:25; 1 John 2:2; Eph. 1:7; Col. 1:14, 20).

Lutherans sometimes debate whether it is proper to translate *justify* as "make righteous"—as well as "pronounce righteous." The concept of "making righteous" has often been used to designate the righteousness that "actually" is present in the righteous deeds of the horizontal relationship. For this reason Lutherans have often emphasized that the better translation is "to pronounce righteous." However, the Word of the Lord *is* acting in justification. It creates as it speaks; it does what it says. It makes sinners righteous as it pronounces them righteous. We truly are what God declares us to be; we are truly refashioned as children of God when his Word creates the new reality of the forgiveness of our sins and the gift of life in Christ for us.

This message of forgiveness of sins stood at the heart of the message that the first believers brought to the sinners around them, a message of liberation from guilt and from sin's reward, death (Luke 24:47; Acts 5:31; 13:38–39; 26:16–18). God had raised them from the dead with Christ to newness of life, for he rose—having obliterated their trespasses by absorbing them into his death—so that they might become righteous once again (Rom. 4:25). Believers consider themselves dead to sin and alive to God in Christ Jesus because they know that in his death and resurrection they have the assurance that they shall not die again (Rom. 6:8–11).

Thus, the fundamental reality of the life of believers lies in God's gift of death as a sinner and resurrection as God's child and heir (Rom. 8:17). God's Word, which kills and resurrects, stands at the center of both the understanding of justification as God's pronouncement and the understanding of justification as God's re-creating through his Word. God's Word effects the verdict of innocent. God's Word effects death and life.

Thus, justification in the biblical sense is labeled "forensic justification." *Forensic* means "belonging to courts of judicature or to public discussion and debate." It refers to activities of public speaking, and specifically to judgments rendered in court. Thus, God's Word, which bestows righteousness as a pronouncement of innocence and as a re-creative act, can be called "forensic."

Some Lutherans have understood Luther's teaching regarding the pronouncement of righteousness upon the sinner in an unclear manner. They have thought that Luther was suggesting that "God says I am righteous, and we will let him believe that. But that is not really the case. The fact of the matter is, I am a sinner. But I will be glad to let God think otherwise even if his view of me is not the real me." This "unreal" understanding of God's justifying Word tends to place the center of human reality in human consciousness, in human activity. Luther did not believe that was the case.

Luther placed the highest level of reality in God's Word and in his gracious disposition toward his children. When God says that we are righteous, that we are his children, nothing can be more real. All reality came into being through God's Word. We still experience how sin permeates all our thoughts, words, and deeds, weakening the best of our own righteousness (Is. 64:6). But that experience does not determine the ultimate reality of our life, even here and now. God's Word, which has re-created us through its pronouncement of our innocence and righteousness, is the ultimate reality of our lives.

By Faith Alone

That word of righteousness, bestowed upon us, promises us life. Promises elicit trust. Through faith or trust we receive the gift of justification by God's grace through the redemption God put forward in Christ Jesus as an expiation by his blood (Rom. 3:25). It is the nature of a promise that it cannot be proven. Control over the promise rests not in our proving it but in the reliability and faithfulness of the one who promises. The original relationship of Adam and Eve with God in Eden rested upon the free exchange between him who loved them and them who trusted him. Christ has come to restore that relationship of trust. Righteous children of God trust him. Their faith is the core and engine of their entire existence. They live by faith; trust constitutes and sustains their entire life.

Human faith, as noted above, stands at the very core of human existence.[4] Faith cannot be compelled. It can only be drawn forth by a reliable object. Faith is—at one level—a psychological phenomenon. It combines a knowledge of its object, a knowledge that can grow and develop, with an emotional commitment to that object. Faith in a person always involves a relationship. Faith is a relationship. Yet the Christian faith is different from other faiths. It has a different object, a different content—Jesus of Nazareth, and the God who he is and reveals. It originates not merely in the knowledge and emotion of the human creature; it arises out of the Holy Spirit's working upon the individual's knowledge and emotion. Its very nature is receptive. It receives the gift of life in Jesus Christ.

Faith in Jesus Christ is elicited by him, by his promise, because he is reliable. The Holy Spirit creates our trust in him and his reliability. God graciously grants us the ability to believe in Christ, just as he grants us the ability to suffer for his sake on the basis of that faith (Phil. 1:29). Only through the Holy Spirit's power can sinners come to recognize in faith that Jesus Christ is their Lord (1 Cor. 12:3).

The Holy Spirit re-creates the relationship between God and the fallen sinner by putting his claim upon the sinner through his Word, as he does in Baptism. But that relationship grows on its human side as people hear God's Word of forgiveness and life, and as they gain information about him through that Word. They cannot believe in him of whom they have not heard. Faith grows out of hearing, and hearing springs from the sharing of God's Word (Rom. 10:14). Faith may not fully comprehend the mystery of God's speaking to us. Faith cannot always explain everything about God's attitude and action in our behalf. For faith is the assurance of things for which we hope; it is the conviction of that which we do not see (Heb. 11:1). Fundamentally, faith is the relationship with the God who cannot be fully comprehended by his creatures, particularly when their minds are still suffering the damage of the fall into sin.

Because God is the object of our faith, we can be utterly sure in trusting him and his promises. There is no uncertainty here, no "maybe yes, maybe no." "For no matter how many promises God has made, they are 'Yes' in Christ. And so through him the 'Amen' is spoken by us to the glory of God" (2 Cor. 1:20). The Hebrew word *amen* confesses "that's the way it is." It expresses the confidence believers have in their utterly faithful God.

This trust in God is, of course, more than "mere knowledge" or "mere faith." "Mere knowledge" is possible in regard to things that make little difference to us. We can have "mere faith" or a purely intellectual recognition of the fact that Augustus Caesar ruled the Roman Empire some two millennia ago. It is impossible, however, to have "mere faith" in a person. The emotional aspects of the personal relationship demand more than purely intellectual knowledge of another person. Above all, when the one who claims to be Creator of all life says, "I love you," the reaction of "mere faith" is not possible. God's approach to us in the death and resurrection of Christ may cause sinners to laugh or to flee from such an absurd claim. It may cause sinners to quake in fear before a God who found it necessary to die for us. But "mere knowledge" or "mere faith" in reaction to God's message will turn quickly to an emotional reaction of one kind or another. God turns it to loving trust.

Thus, simply at the word of Jesus the official from Capernaum "believed the word that Jesus spoke to him," confident that Jesus' promise of healing for his son was reliable (John 4:46–54 RSV). The centurion at Capernaum was not used to relying on other people; he was used to being in charge. But he had confidence that Jesus' word would be reliable. He said to Jesus, "Say the word." That was sufficient for him (Luke 7:1–10). The Canaanite woman was not even put off by Jesus' silence or the disciples' nastiness. She trusted that Jesus would want to throw her at least a crumb. Jesus did, with admiration for her faith (Matt. 15:21–28). All who trust in him join these believers and Paul in confessing, even when suffering tests faith, "I know whom I have believed, and I am sure that he is able to guard until that Day what has been entrusted to me" (2 Tim. 1:12 RSV).

God's Law, which is open to human testing on the basis of experience, is not a matter of faith. Paul stated, "The law does not rest on faith" (Gal. 3:12 RSV). Faith rests upon the person of our God, through his revelation of himself as Jesus of Nazareth. Faith rests upon the good news, which he is and brings.

From God's perspective this relationship of faith is of one piece. It exists, or it does not exist. It is not a matter of degree. The relationship with God stands on the basis of his promise, and the psychological characteristics of that faith do not alter the nature or strength of the relationship. God is faithful even when we are not, "for he cannot disown himself" (2 Tim. 2:13). He is faithful and will sanctify us wholly (1 Thess. 5:23–24). When we are failing, he is faithful and strengthens us and guards us from evil (2 Thess. 3:3).

However, from the human perspective we feel the knowledge of God and his Gospel message for us grow—or escape our memories. We feel the emotional commitment to him wax and wane. The father of the boy with seizures cried out, "I do believe; help me overcome unbelief!" (Mark 9:24). Christ observed Peter's "failing" faith (Matt. 14:31), and he commented on the Canaanite woman's "strong" expression of trust in him (Matt. 15:28). Such fluctuations in an individual's psychological experience of the relationship with God do not indicate that the relationship is stronger or weaker. The variations in the internal and external expressions of faith among individuals do not indicate that one believer actually is closer to or further from God than another. God stands by all his people, whatever the psychological cast of their created being, whatever "shape" that cast gives the psychological side of the relationship with God. For, as important and vital as faith is to our life as God's children, it is the God of peace, not we, who equips us so that we may do his will. He is the one who works in us what is pleasing in his sight through Jesus Christ (Heb. 13:20–21).

Righteous and Sinful at the Same Time

Faith is the assurance of things not experienced. Sinful believers often experience their own sin and the power of evil in their lives. The fullness of the trust Adam and Eve experienced in Eden escapes us. Because sin continues to bite at our heels, we do not yet enjoy life fully even though, from Baptism on, we have eternal life. Nonetheless, we are not always quite so sure. We focus on our own daily failures and wonder if God's Word is really working. That phenomenon of faith led Luther to teach that we are fully righteous and fully sinful at the same time (Latin: *simul justus et peccator*). With that phrase he meant that in God's sight we have become perfectly righteous, without any fault or flaw, because our sins have been taken away from us by Christ and deposited in his tomb. At the same time, we honestly recognize that even the best of our human works still suffers from the imperfections wrought by our sin (Is. 64:6; Rom. 7:15–20). Nothing we do is as pure in motivation or in execution as we wish it were. Nonetheless, we can be confident that the Lord's Word about us—that we are righteous—will prevail.

Thus, we commit blasphemy when we wallow in our guilt or let it immobilize us into wondering whether we will make the right decision about one thing or another. Instead, we will rejoice in God's liberation from our sin. He has freed us from every evil, including the evil that paralyzes us by making us doubt that we are free to praise God by loving our neighbor.

Luther's double perspective on the Christian life helps believers in two ways. We can be brutally honest about our own sinfulness. We can confront it and confess it without fear. Acknowledging its existence does not separate us from God. It is the first step in daily dying and rising as his children. It forms only the backdrop to acknowledge at the same time that God regards us as his righteous and innocent children.

The acknowledgment of our sinfulness is made always with the consciousness that this is only half the story, and the smaller half at that. Better, the acknowledgement of sin is the foreword to the Word of God, which re-creates us fully in the image of his Son, dead and risen to new life. Thus, even when we are experiencing our own imperfection and worthlessness, we know that we simply press on toward our own resurrection, in which we shall obtain the fullness of God's grace and our own perfection—because Christ Jesus has made us his own people (Phil. 3:8–12).

God Assures Us that We Are Righteous

God continues to bombard us with his message of grace through faith in Christ at every point at which we encounter the Gospel. He has designed three ways of reassuring us that nothing can separate us from his love in Christ Jesus (Rom. 8:38–39), that he who began his good work in us will complete us on the day on which our Lord comes to end this sphere of our existence (Phil. 1:6).

He gives us that assurance, first of all, as the Holy Spirit brings us to faith and keeps us in faith. The Spirit accomplishes his life-restoring work through the tools of his re-creating trade, the means of grace. We know that God loves us as individuals because we have been baptized. All of us who have been baptized into Christ Jesus have been baptized into his death (Rom. 6:3). For "all of you who were baptized into Christ have clothed yourselves with Christ" (Gal. 3:27). We know that God loves us as individuals because we hear his forgiveness through the absolution our pastor pronounces and that his people share with us. We hear God's love as it is proclaimed in his congregation. We know that God loves us because we individually receive Christ's body and blood for the forgiveness of our sins. Through the means of grace the Holy Spirit assures us that we are righteous before God.

We also know that God loves us because he has invested himself in our humanity. The incarnation of the second person of the Trinity is the second source of assurance for us as individuals. We are confident that God has not become incarnate in vain. We are certain that Christ's death and resurrection have swooped us up individually into the company of God's family. We are confident that Christ Jesus died for each one of us, for God wanted every human creature to be saved and to come to a knowledge of the truth, that Jesus Christ has given himself as a ransom for all (1 Tim. 2:4–6). For, as John wrote, Christ died not only for "our sins" but also for the sins of the whole world (1 John 2:2). In deepest despair the struggling faith can look to this assurance: the circle cannot be drawn in such a way to exclude me from those for whom Christ died.

Third, God assures us that we are righteous in his sight by assuring us that nothing we can do determines whether we are his righteous children or not. He has chosen us before the foundation of the world, in the mystery of his love in Christ Jesus. No further reason is needed or given. God's election of his own family remains a mystery. The fact remains: God foreordained us to be his children, and nothing can separate us from his love in Christ Jesus (Rom. 8:29–39).

The Proper Distinction of Law and Gospel

The extravagant riches of God's good news seem to set him up for abuse. The unconditional Gospel of Jesus Christ seems almost to invite sinners to say, "Let us sin the more, so that grace may increase." Paul tells us that such an attitude is impossible because we are baptized (Rom. 6:1–3). Nonetheless, it happens that sinners turn the Gospel into a license to sin. The solution comes not in altering the conditionlessness of the Gospel. It comes in distinguishing this Gospel from Law, and in distinguishing arrogant or secure sinners who would abuse this Gospel from the broken sinners who can hear it and receive life through it. The secure sinners cannot understand the Gospel any more than the typical North American can understand the Swahili language. In vain will we try to communicate effectively with secure sinners through the Gospel. Secure sinners understand only the crushing language of the Law. It alone confronts or undermines their sinful security in language that can crack and destroy the sin.

Broken, despairing sinners, on the other hand, understand the Law's language altogether too well. They have heard it. It has made its point. But it has opened them to the possibility of hearing what God has to say to them in Jesus Christ. That unconditional word of grace transforms them. It swoops them into Christ's death, and it gives them new life with him in his resurrection. In the vertical relationship the re-creating word of justification obliterates their sinful records before God the Father. It sets them completely righteous and innocent before him, their names recorded in indelible ink in the book of life (Phil. 4:3). In the horizontal relationship that Word of re-creation begins to put to death the habits of hell, and it begins to cultivate the habits of heaven.[5]

Because the struggle goes on between sin and faith within the Christian (Romans 7), the continuing dialogue between Law and Gospel dare not cease in this life. Daily, believers need to be reminded of their need to die to sin and their need to be raised again to newness of life. The Law must continue to condemn desires in us that oppose God. The Gospel must continue to restore our flagging and failing consciousness of God's presence in our lives and his love for us.

Believers talk with one another and with those outside the faith on the basis of their estimate of whether their hearer needs to hear some form of God's Law or some form of his Gospel. They establish why their hearers are asking the questions or posing the problems that set the agenda for their conversation. Only then can they discuss either Law or Gospel aptly and appropriately.

Christ Alone

This Gospel, and all that "justification" means, is comprehended in the person of Jesus of Nazareth, the second person of the holy Trinity. When you have said Jesus, you have said it all, Paul was convinced. "I resolved to know nothing while I was with you except Jesus Christ and him crucified" (1 Cor. 2:2). In Christ alone Paul found all there is in life that gives us ultimate identity, security, and meaning: "May I never boast except in the cross of our Lord Jesus Christ, through which the world has been crucified to me, and I to the world" (Gal. 6:14). Death and life are all comprehended in Jesus alone.

Children of God are those who simply trust in Jesus the Messiah (1 John 5:1). They are those who have died and have their lives hidden with him (Col. 3:3). God chose us to be his children through Jesus Christ. In Christ we have redemption through his blood, the forgiveness of our trespasses, according to the riches of his grace, which he lavished upon us. God set forth his purpose for us in Christ and unites us to himself in Christ (Eph. 1:3–14). For we have life in the name of Jesus the Messiah (John 20:31).

Living the Justified Life

Since we are justified through faith, we have peace with God through our Lord Jesus Christ. Through him we have obtained access to life in God's favor. This brings us joy as we live in the certain confidence and hope that we shall share in the glory of God. That joy is present even when we are caught in the midst of the sufferings of daily life because God's love has been poured into our hearts through the Holy Spirit (Rom. 5:1–5). Christ bestows peace upon us by putting us to death as sinners and raising us up to newness of life. That peace recognizes that God is relaxed with us, his children. If he is relaxed with us, we need no longer be uptight about ourselves. We can relax in his presence, and we can turn our focus to the lives of our neighbors, where he wants us to focus, so that we can carry his love and care to them. Thus, our trust in his love inevitably produces deeds of love for others.

We are righteous in God's sight because of his grace and favor. That was true in Eden. Adam and Eve were righteous in God's sight not because of what they were performing but because God loved them as his children. Redeemed children of God are righteous in God's sight because Christ has given them his own righteousness and innocence. What makes us right in the vertical relationship of our lives is always God's favor. It is always the righteousness of another, of God in Jesus Christ. Therefore, this righteousness is called "alien righteousness" or the righteousness of someone else (*alienus* is the Latin word for "another"). What makes us right in our horizontal relationships is the righteousness of our own performance. This righteousness, since it takes form in our own actions, is called "proper" righteousness (*proprius* is the Latin word for "one's own").

The confusion of these two kinds of righteousness can have disastrous results for our understanding of salvation. Too often Christians have understood righteousness one-dimensionally and thus presumed that proper righteousness is necessary to make sinners acceptable in God's sight. They have thus invented ways of defining grace as that which makes our deeds righteous enough to please God. God is pleased only with those whom he makes his children, apart from any performance of their own. Alien and proper righteousness are not separable in the life of the believer. The former is always producing the latter, imperfect though the latter may be. But the two must be kept distinct in our understanding if we are to preserve a proper understanding of God's grace and his justification of sinners through the death and resurrection of Christ.

Christ Died for All

Christ's death and resurrection have objectively covered the sins of all people. He is the expiation for our sins, and not for ours only but also for the sins of the whole world (1 John 2:2). God reconciled the whole world to himself in Christ (2 Cor. 5:19). God sent Jesus Christ because he loved the whole world (John 3:16). Just as Adam's trespass led to condemnation for all people, so Christ's act of righteousness leads to acquittal and life for all (Rom. 5:18). Objectively, Christ has won righteousness for all.

Subjectively, he comes through the one whom he sends, the Holy Spirit. He teaches us all things (John 14:17, 26). He bears witness to Christ (John 15:26) even as he convicts the world and guides God's people into all truth (John 16:7–15). The Holy Spirit re-creates and renews them by pouring out God's mercy in the washing of regeneration, which conveys the benefits of Christ's death and resurrection to the baptized, justifying them and making them heirs in the hope of eternal life (Titus 3:4–7).

God's Election of His Own

God wants all to be saved and to come to know the truth (1 Tim. 2:4). Not all do. Why are some saved and not others? That question has plagued believers at least as long as the church has tried to make the Gospel intelligible in the world of Greek thought.

Chosen by God

Jews had less problems with God's sovereign choice of his own people; in this regard Paul echoed the whole Old Testament when he affirmed that God has the right to have mercy upon those upon whom he wants to have mercy (Rom. 9:6–33). The question "why are some saved and not others?" is only a special form of the entire question of theodicy. The mystery of the workings of a good and almighty God in an evil world will not be pierced at any point. Thus, this question is called "the cross of theologians." It crucifies all pretensions of those who want to be able to supply all the answers about God to those who ask. It reminds theologians that their powers have limits, and their pride dies right at this most critical question.

But God has affirmed as part of the good news for his chosen people that they are secure as his children because he has chosen them to be his own. Christians sometimes seek assurance that they are truly God's own people in a variety of false ways. Some look to their own good works; they believe that if they are doing God's will, they can be assured that they are God's children. That assurance vanishes with the failure of our works or even with the failure of our confidence that our works are good enough. Tender consciences develop such scruples with ease.

Some trust their own feelings about God for their assurance that they will remain his children. Feelings are fickle. Such trust can be blown off course by contradictory feelings and shipwreck our faith. Others try to count external blessings as God's assurance that they are truly saved. God gives assurance under the cross; if we could count on anything external, we might more likely count lack of external blessings as assurance of God's presence in our lives. But neither earthly fortune nor earthly misfortune can assure us of his love. Not even our own faith can give us that assurance, for the psychological strength of faith waxes and wanes. Only the Word of the Lord can assure us that we are his children. His Word, as it comes to us in the various forms of the Gospel, the means of grace, tells us that we, as individuals, belong to God. It explains that we are his children because he chose us to be his children.

Before the foundation of the world he chose us to be holy and blameless before him. Because he loved us, he predestined us to be adopted as his children through Jesus Christ, simply on the basis of the good pleasure of his will—because he wanted to have us as his children. Through Christ he freely bestowed on us his glorious grace. In Christ we have redemption through his blood, the forgiveness of our trespasses, according to the riches of his grace which he lavished upon us. In preaching the Gospel to his people he makes known the mystery of his will; in the means of grace he presents his purposes, which he executed in Christ. Christ is his plan for the fullness of time as he unites all things in him. Thus, in Christ, according to God's purposes, as he carries out his own will, we recognize that our hope in Christ springs from God's plan for predestining and appointing us to live to praise his glory. To carry out this purpose the Holy Spirit brought the word of truth, the Gospel of our salvation, to us, and he brought us to trust in Christ (Eph. 1:3–14). Paul could not separate his discussion of God's gracious choosing of those whom he wanted to adopt from the name of Christ and from the Holy Spirit's action in the means of grace.

Paul discussed God's election of his chosen people in Rom. 8:28–39. There he noted that God works for the good of those who love him in everything that happens in their lives. Those who love him, by Paul's definition, are those whom he has called according to his plan or purpose. Those whom he has called are those whom he has predestined to be conformed to the image of his Son, those whom he intended from before the foundation of the world to incorporate into Christ's death and resurrection. The predestined are those whom God foreknew.

God's foreknowledge differs from the kind of foreknowledge human creatures might have. You, as you read this book, might look ahead to page 257 to read about the doctrine of the church. You could "peek ahead" to know what is coming. My student could come into my office and find an examination I had written and "peek ahead" to see what questions he would have to know. God did not "peek ahead" into human history to check on who might believe or who might do good works. As author of this book, I know that I intend to be writing about the doctrine of the church when I get to page 257. I have the book outlined, and my intentions are set before I ever execute them with the actual words of chapter XVI. Before the exam is put on paper, I know which questions will be on it. When I foreknow that students should study a certain topic for the test, that foreknowledge creates what will exist on the question sheet. When the students "peek ahead," their foreknowledge comes from a glance at what I have already designed and executed. God is the author of the new life of his people. His foreknowledge of his elect designs their salvation and executes his decision to choose this individual and that one for his church, to be his own child. God's foreknowledge is not the kind of foreknowledge that depends on its object. It creates its object.

Paul traced the process in Romans 8. In the mystery of his loving purpose and plan for us he foreknew us. By his foreknowledge he planned to make us his own, without any reference to our faith or our performance. He referred only to Christ as he designed our re-creation. Out of that creative foreknowledge came his predestination of those who would be his children.

Human parents conceive but cannot specify and design their children. God our Father not only conceived of us but specified and designed the shape of our lives. He is the Creator. Those whom he predestined, he calls through the Gospel, and those whom he calls, he justifies. This is the way his plan unfolds. Those who have received this gift of righteousness anew through Christ will be glorified. Thus, no charges can be brought against those whom God has chosen in Christ. God justifies those whom he foreknew and predestined through Christ's death and resurrection. Christ now intercedes for us at the Father's right hand. Therefore, nothing shall separate us from God's love in Christ Jesus our Lord. We are more than conquerors through him who loved us (Rom. 8:28–39).

Paul was convinced that God's power resided in the Gospel of the God who saved us and called us. Its power rests not on the basis of what we do, but on the basis of his own plan and the grace he bestowed upon us before time began. This grace he made known with the appearance of our Savior Christ Jesus (2 Tim. 1:8–10). Paul accumulated Old Testament witnesses to that understanding of how God has acted in behalf of his people in Romans 9. From Mal. 1:2–3 he cited God's sovereign choice of Jacob and not Esau to fulfill his purposes. For, as Paul observed, Rebecca's two children had not even been born: they had done nothing either good or bad to put a claim on God's choice of one or the other, when he chose. Paul recognized that this was so "in order that God's purpose in election might stand: not by works but by him who calls" (Rom. 9:6–13). He cited Ex. 33:19 to reinforce his claim that God will have mercy on those whom he chooses for mercy; "it does not, therefore, depend on man's desire or effort, but on God's mercy" (Rom. 9:14–16). For, Paul knew from Is. 29:16 and 45:9, God regards himself as a potter who molds one vessel for beauty and another for menial use (Rom. 9:19–24). God has created his beloved people out of those who were not his people, according to Hosea (2:23, 1:10). According to Is. 1:9, he distinguished Israel from Sodom and Gomorrah only on the basis of his free choice (see also Rom. 9:25–29). God has chosen his own. Thus, Luke could recognize that when the Gospel was proclaimed in Antioch of Pisidia "all who were appointed for eternal life believed" (Acts 13:48).

The doctrine of election too often confuses and discourages people, particularly in Western culture, where human creatures are supposed to function responsibly and control their own destiny. But God has given us the gift of being his children—just as human parents bestow the gift of being a child—without any contribution from us children. God intends this teaching regarding his choosing us to comfort us, to assure us, to carry us beyond any doubt that something can separate us from his love in Christ Jesus. We properly use this teaching only when it bestows this comfort and assurance.

It is designed to give God glory for his love and care for his children. It should direct us only to Christ and to the means of grace. There God "does his choosing" in effecting his eternal plan for us by calling us and giving us Christ's righteousness as our very own. Any other use of this teaching leads us astray.

Thus, the doctrine of election dare never become an invitation to speculate about whether we or others are truly elect children of God. The means of grace answer that question for us without recourse to such speculation. To use the doctrine of election as an entryway into that kind of speculation is to substitute poison for potatoes. It can only harm faith. God chose us so that he might build faith.

Nor can believers use the doctrine of election as a false kind of assurance that permits them to "go on sinning so that grace may increase." The doctrine of election dare not be discussed with someone who is claiming that the grace it offers permits the elect to sin. What Paul said regarding Baptism in Rom. 6:1–3 pertains to the doctrine of election. When someone tries to use the excuse that they can sin without worry because they are elect, we must explain that they will not sin precisely because they are elect. Only in such an instance does the doctrine of election permit itself to be dragged into use as a law that condemns.

When someone asks, "Am I among the elect?" Christians respond, "why do you want to know?" Those who wish to use the doctrine of election as an excuse or license for sin will not understand what it means to be God's chosen child. Such people need to hear God's Law as it crushes their sinful pretension. Those who fear they have so offended God that they can never be or become his children are crying out for God's assurance that he has chosen them to be his own.

The doctrine of election is good news. It announces God's unconditioned love. It contradicts every despairing attempt to abandon hope in Jesus Christ on the basis of deductions about past performance or future failures and potential apostasy. The biblical teaching on God's unconditioned choice of us to be his own assures us that he who has begun his good work of re-creating us as his own in us will bring it to completion at the day of Jesus Christ (Phil. 1:6). For nothing can separate us from God's love in Christ Jesus (Rom. 8:39).

The Conundrum of Election

Martin Luther understood God's unconditioned choice of his people as a word of Gospel. It was good news that our being God's children stands completely apart from anything in us. In us uncertainty reigns. Only God gives assurance that we are safe in God's hands and shall remain so. At the same time Luther steadfastly resisted the temptation to pierce the mystery of election and answer the question why some are saved and not others. Instead, he focused on the specific and immediate need of the sinner. To the secure sinner the Law—not the doctrine of election—must be presented. Secure sinners need to hear God's word of Law, which holds them responsible for their own misdeeds and their own denial of God. Only to the broken and despairing sinner can the words of comfort come, which the doctrine of election is designed to bring, according to Luther.[6]

Double Predestination. John Calvin, who tried to follow Luther's teaching, missed the context of his understanding of God's choice of believers to be his own: Calvin separated the doctrine of election from the proper distinction of Law and Gospel. Thus, he taught a doctrine of double predestination. He believed that God has fashioned some human vessels to receive mercy as his children and other human vessels to be destroyed in hell.[7] Without a strong doctrine of the means of grace, this approach fails to give some the assurance that they were among the elect.

God wants all to be saved and to come to a knowledge of the truth (1 Tim. 2:4). He gave Christ to be the expiation for the sins of the whole world (1 John 2:2). A doctrine of double predestination adjusts the logic of the matter, but it fails to deal with the tension involved in the mystery of evil in the presence of a gracious, omnipotent God. It makes it difficult to deal sensitively and properly with the difference between secure and broken sinners. Thus, it not only leaves itself open to offer security to arrogant sinners who count on election to cover their willful sins (as does every proclamation of grace). It leaves itself open to crush despairing sinners who cannot determine whether they are chosen or damned by God's "horrible decree"—and such sinners generally tend to use the doctrine only to deepen their own despair.

Synergism. Another logical solution to the question, "why are some saved and not others?" is expressed in the view called "synergism" ("cooperationism"). Synergists insist that God saves by his grace, but that the human creature ultimately either accepts or rejects that grace. God's choice of his children cannot become effective without human acceptance, according to this cooperationist view.

Some Lutherans among Luther's students and much of later Protestantism, particularly in the Anglo-American religious ghetto, accepted this explanation. It places the burden of the Law squarely on the back of the believer. The eternal destiny of believers rests upon their own decision. This recipe for uncertainty only superficially solves the problem, for it places a condition on God's grace at the key point at which it begins to be operative in the human creature's life. The ability of God's grace to draw the believer to God depends on whether the human creature permits it to work or not. Such a view contradicts the Lord's explanation that new birth, not human decision, brings God's children into his family (John 3:1–12). Such a limited grace fails to deliver the comfort despairing sinners need.

Universalism. Others have solved the problem of why some are saved and not others by denying its premise: that some are not saved. In several eras of church history "universalists" have taught that God will save all. In contemporary Christianity there are those who argue that "anonymous Christians" have been saved by Christ even though they have not believed in him. The apostles taught that only through the *name* of Jesus Christ can sinners be saved (Acts 4:12). Only one access leads into the presence of the Father: Jesus alone is the way, the truth, and the life (John 14:6). God's earthly punishment of the wicked only foreshadows a fate like that of the fallen angels, who were cast into pits of nether gloom (2 Peter 2:1–10). Christ will separate those who have lived for him from those who have not. The latter will depart from him into eternal punishment (Matt. 25:46). There they shall experience weeping and wailing and gnashing of their teeth (Matt. 8:12; 22:13; 24:51; 25:30).

Such reminders of God's judgment warn us of the seriousness of his wrath against all that disrupts the life of the human creatures whom he made to be his own. God has arranged to restore them to righteousness. He has done so according to his plan, which he set down before the foundation of the world. That plan brings death to sinners and restores life to them through the life, death, and resurrection of Jesus Christ. Through us, his people, he calls others to be joined to the chosen family of his elect people. As the instruments of the Holy Spirit, we bring God's saving, re-creating, justifying Word to those around us.

Notes for Chapter IX

1. *Canons and Decrees of the Council of Trent,* trans. H. J. Schroeder (Saint Louis: Herder, 1941), 29–46.
2. Gerhard O. Forde, *Theology Is for Proclamation* (Minneapolis: Fortress, 1990), 136.
3. Gottlob Schrenk, *"dikaioō," Theological Dictionary of the New Testament,* vol. 2, ed. Gerhard Kittel, trans. and ed. Geoffrey W. Bromiley (Grand Rapids: Eerdmans, 1964), 211–19; Wilhelm Dantine, *Justification of the Ungodly,* trans. Eric W. and Ruth C. Gritsch (Saint Louis: Concordia, 1968), 21–36, 55–123; Werner Elert, *The Structure of Lutheranism,* vol. 1, trans. Walter A. Hanson (Saint Louis: Concordia, 1962), 73–90.
4. See ch. I, p. 7–8.
5. C. F. W. Walther, *Law and Gospel,* trans. Herbert J. A. Bouman (Saint Louis: Concordia, 1981); Bo Giertz, *The Hammer of God,* trans. Clifford Ansgar Nelson (Minneapolis: Augsburg, 1973).
6. Martin Luther, *Lectures on Genesis Chapters 26–30,* Luther's Works, vol. 5 (Saint Louis: Concordia, 1968), 42–50.
7. John Calvin, *The Institutes of the Christian Religion,* vol. 2, ed. John T. McNeill, trans. Ford Lewis Battles (Philadelphia: Westminster, 1960), 920–64.

Chapter X

The Holy Spirit and the Conversion of the Sinner

In order that we may obtain the faith through which we are righteous in God's sight God instituted the ministry of teaching the Gospel and administering the sacraments. For through the Word and sacraments, as through instruments, the Holy Spirit is given, and the Holy Spirit produces faith, where and when it pleases God, in those who hear the Gospel.[1]

With those words the Augsburg Confession continued its discussion of justification—and its presentation of the work of the Holy Spirit—in its fifth article. Sometimes Lutherans are charged with not paying much attention to the Holy Spirit. As a matter of fact, the Augsburg Confession itself, the basic definition of what it means to be Lutheran, says quite a bit about the work of the Holy Spirit even though it is as modest as the Spirit himself is about himself. The Holy Spirit inspired the Scriptures, but in its pages he focuses on Jesus Christ rather than on himself.

The third article of the Augsburg Confession, later entitled "the Son of God," makes clear that Jesus Christ works through the Holy Spirit. He had promised to do so when he told his disciples that he would the send "the Counselor" or "the Comforter" (John 14:16–18; 16:7–14). Through the Holy Spirit, the Confession states, Christ sanctifies, purifies, strengthens, and comforts all believers. In its fifth article Lutherans confess that the Holy Spirit works faith in believers through their receiving the Gospel in Word and sacrament. The Augsburg Confession goes on to treat the life of faith that the Holy Spirit works in believers in articles six and twenty, and in articles seven and eight it treats the church, the family into which the Holy Spirit incorporates believers through Word and sacrament.

The Lord and Giver of Life

The Holy Spirit is indeed true God, a distinct person of the Holy Trinity. The Spirit does God's work in re-creating us through the washing of regeneration and renewal of our Baptism (Titus 3:5). Against the Holy Spirit people can commit blasphemy, the sin of insulting or defaming God (Matt. 12:31). Christ (Matt. 28:19) and Paul (2 Cor. 13:14) placed the Holy Spirit on the same level with the Father and the Son. The early church confirmed that the Holy Spirit is true God, the distinct but inseparable third person of the Holy Trinity, as it condemned the contrary belief of Macedonius at the Council of Constantinople in 381.[2]

The Holy Spirit comes to restore fallen human creatures to their original relationship with God, so that they might live again in righteousness as heirs of eternal life (Titus 3:3–7). He accomplishes this re-creation through Baptism (Titus 3:5) and through the hearing of the Gospel (Gal. 3:2, 5). God's instrument of his creation at the beginning of the world was his Word. His instrument of re-creation at the beginning of the renewed relationship with individual believers is again his Word. This Word takes various forms as the "means of grace." Through the means of grace the Holy Spirit delivers the grace to acknowledge Jesus Christ as Lord, as the primary source of identity, security, and meaning (1 Cor. 12:3).

Trusting in Jesus Christ as Lord enables believers to live the kind of life God designed for them in the first place. The Holy Spirit comes to dwell in God's chosen people and make them his temples. Their lives serve and praise God (Rom. 8:9–11; 1 Cor. 3:16; 6:19; 2 Tim. 1:14). Believers do not find the Spirit. They do not take possession of him and hold him as their own. He comes to us, to take possession of us, to take up residence in us. He comes to us as a gift (Acts 10:45; 11:17). He is present in our lives as the first installment, or guarantee, of God's pledge that we belong to him (2 Cor. 1:22; 5:5; Eph. 1:14).

Righteous in the vertical relationship through this faith, believers then practice the fruit of the Holy Spirit's presence in a life of love, joy, peace, patience, kindness, goodness, faithfulness, gentleness, and self-control (Gal. 5:22–25). He functions as our Counselor, the one who stands by us and who brings us the truth (John 15:26). The second person of the Trinity became God's Word in human form and flesh. The third person of the Trinity bears the forgiving and re-creating Word of God, but he has no human form and flesh of his own. He must borrow our lips and hands, our voices and loving touch, if he is to accomplish his work. Believers become the tools of his work in this world.

When we describe the work of the Holy Spirit, we often label it with the term *sanctification.* Most often North American Christians today use this term, which means "making holy," for the human response to God's Word. In his Small Catechism Luther, on the other hand, did not define sanctification as the result of the Spirit's work in us. He defined sanctification as the process of the Spirit's work in believers. The Holy Spirit calls, gathers, enlightens, and sanctifies us within God's family, his church. He does so through the Gospel. He sanctifies us as he forgives us all our sins, and he will complete this task as he raises us from the dead and grants us who believe in Christ eternal life.[3]

The term *sanctification* may be used in either sense, with the believer or with the Holy Spirit as its subject. Each respective emphasis focuses on the same fact of daily life. The Spirit takes those who have been bought with a price and re-creates their entire lives as temples in which the praise and honor of God is conducted (1 Cor. 6:19–20). The Holy Spirit always points our lives to Christ and centers them in him. Thus, Paul can also say that our lives are lived with Christ dwelling in us; it is he who lives in me, and not I myself, who lives out the life of faith (Gal. 2:19–21).

The Holy Spirit Works
through the Means of Grace

The Holy Spirit re-creates, as God created in the first place, through his Word. The Word comes in several forms, collectively called "the means of grace." Some Christians put less stock in the instruments of the Word than do Lutherans. Lutherans believe that the Word of the Gospel of Jesus Christ does not merely share information or point toward a heavenly reality. Lutherans believe that the Gospel we convey with our words, in various forms, actually convey God's power for saving his people (Rom. 1:16).

God Works through Selected Elements of the Created Order

Some Christians have followed ancient Platonic philosophy in regarding anything material, or created, as merely a shadow of a heavenly reality. For them, the best that human language or sacramental elements can do is direct our spiritual gaze toward the reality of God's love in heaven. Lutherans teach that God uses the material creation, the created order, to express his will and power. He has selected certain elements of his created order to be the instruments of his power. He is truly present among his people in Word and sacrament. His power and presence do not rest in the strong wind, which tore up the mountains in Elijah's sight as God led him to a cave (1 Kings 19:9–18). God's power is not to be experienced in earthquake or fire. It rests in the still small voice that brings the presence of God into the middle of our lives. God's voice comes from God, not from within our own murky emotions. It comes from outside us. It speaks to us from God's mouth; it is not the voice of our own imaginations. As God's Word, it comes with power (Rom. 1:16). It shall not return to him empty; he does not speak in vain. His Word accomplishes his purposes, and it prospers in the matter for which he sends it (Is. 55:11).

Some people have sneered at those who believe that God has revealed himself in the human language of the Scriptures. They say that those who trust God's Word in the Scripture put God in a box. The Bible, of course, is not a box. Its natural position is open, so that the Word can flow out of it with its power. God has placed his power for new life in the Scriptures. It takes other forms as well, in certain created elements that he has chosen as his instruments for making us truly alive again. He began that process by choosing to come in human flesh. The fully human Jesus of Nazareth is the second person of the Trinity. In him God's presence and power is enfleshed in human form and personhood. As one who is fully human, like us in every respect but our sinfulness, he reveals God's Word. He shows us who God is and what plans of love and mercy he has for us.

He chose human language as his tool for coming to be present among us, as the speaking God, God in communication with us, God calling and gathering us through his Word as his family.

God also chose certain elements to link with his Word to convey his power to save us in more extravagant fashion. He loves to bombard us with his love from all sorts of directions, through more than simply our sense of sight or hearing. He comes to touch us with water, to feed us with the bread that bears Christ's body and the wine that bears his blood. In these forms he re-creates and restores and empowers his children through the Word, which accompanies the water and the bread-body and wine-blood. Through them he renews believers in his own image as forgiven children of God.

Finally, he has also chosen human creatures to bear the Word and share it with one another. In the office of the public ministry of the Word he has selected some to be special bearers of his Word. He has called every reborn member of his family, the church, to witness to the wonders of his love. As we bear the Word to others, we are agents of the power of God, who works saving faith through that Word.

The Word in All Its Forms

Often the means of grace are summarized with two words: *Word* (usually thought of as the Scriptures) and *sacrament* (Baptism and the Lord's Supper). In the Smalcald Articles (article four of section three) Luther listed five ways in which God offers his power or resources and help against sin in the richness of his grace: First, through the spoken word [the sermon], by which the forgiveness of sin (the peculiar function of the Gospel) is preached to the whole world; second, through Baptism; third, through the holy Sacrament of the Altar; fourth, through the power of keys; and finally, through the mutual conversation and consolation of Christians with one another.[4] First, we note that Luther did not mention the Bible itself. There are three possible reasons that might explain why Luther left the Scriptures off his list. Above all, the Bible is present in all five of these means by which God conveys the power of his forgiveness. There is nothing to proclaim or to use in consoling one another if we are not delivering the Word that God gives us in the Bible. Second, many people in Luther's day were still illiterate and had to depend not on their own reading of the Scriptures but on hearing it. Third, Luther was deeply convinced that believers need to be applying God's Word to the lives of other human creatures directly, with all the sensitivity they can bring to the task.

There is no magical power that arises simply from the words on the Bible's printed page. The content of the Gospel contains and delivers God's power for salvation as it creates faith and speaks to it. Just as we have great difficulty in removing the speck from the eye of another, yet do not even notice the log that is stuck in our own eye, so we often need a fellow believer to apply the good news of Christ's death and resurrection to our hurts and aches. Flipping through the pages of the Bible and chancing upon one verse or another may deliver the wrong message. If we would just hand the Bible to someone depressed under the assaults of God's Law and one or another form of evil, he might open by chance to a passage like Eccl. 4:1–3 and concur altogether too quickly with its judgment that "the dead, who had already died, are happier than the living, who are still alive."

The Living Voice of the Gospel

Luther called this personal delivery of God's Word "the living voice of the Gospel." It involves the lovingly fashioned response of that part of God's Word that applies to our hearers. That Word may often need to be the Law. It will finally be the Gospel. That Word of God must in any case be individually fitted and fashioned to be most effective and appropriate.

Therefore, Luther steered his readers toward the oral expressions of God's Word of love when he wrote the Smalcald Articles. That does not mean that the text of Scripture itself or other written forms of conveying its message cannot deliver the power of God's re-creating Word. The inspired Scriptures and the published works of other Christians who guide our encounters with God's Word deliver its forgiveness and power effectively. Nonetheless, Christians must be aware that God has called them to be conversing with others and consoling them with God's good news in Christ. They must be aware that God lavishes his love upon us in the several forms in which he has placed his Word.

Those forms can be classified in several ways. The means of grace can be summarized in one word: the Word. They can be listed as the five Luther mentioned in the Smalcald Articles—the sermon, Baptism, the Lord's Supper, absolution, Christian conversation—and written forms of the Word, both the inspired Scriptures and other Christian writings derived from them. And now, within the last few decades, electronic media have joined these other channels of conveying the biblical message. However we classify the means of grace, we recognize the three basic forms in which God's Word is conveyed out of the Scriptures to us: written, oral, and sacramental. God bombards us with his love, as it comes to us in his Word. He wants us to be using this Word in all its forms as much and as best we can.

The Sacramental Forms of the Word

The sacramental forms of his Word, Baptism and the Lord's Supper, are not grouped together in the New Testament. The church has fashioned the category and chosen the term for these two forms of the Word on the basis of biblical teaching about them. The Latin word *sacramentum* referred originally to the oath that Roman soldiers took, pledging their faithfulness to the state. The Christians used the term to translate the Greek word for "mystery." In Baptism and the Lord's Supper, mysterious expressions of God's love and forms of his verbal power that we cannot completely understand, God takes his oath and pledges his faithfulness to his chosen children.

Protestants have followed Augustine's understanding of the word *sacrament* as meaning "gift."[5] God gives his forgiveness to his people in the sacraments. He does so under external forms or means through his Word. The sacraments are practiced because Christ has given them to us and commanded us to use them. These three elements, forgiveness, external means, and Christ's command, constitute the Lutheran definition of the term *sacrament*.

Sacraments convey God's Word of power, the Gospel of the forgiveness of sins. They do so regardless of the personal character of the person who administers them. In the early church some Christians challenged the validity of the sacraments if they were performed by people who did not fit a certain mold, a certain definition of what a good priest should be. The church rejected this view, that of the Novatians and the Donatists, because God's power lies in his sacramental word whether the person who administers the sacrament fits the definition of a desirable dispenser of the Word or not.[6] The pastor does not determine the presence of the power of God; the Word does.

Indeed, if those who receive the sacraments reject that power of God to forgive, or dismiss it in unbelief, then they do not receive its benefits. Like the hearing and reading of the Word, receiving it sacramentally works faith and works through faith. Without faith the benefits do not penetrate our lives. Thus, we must distinguish the benefits of the sacraments—and other forms of the promise of forgiveness—from their nature and their validity. God's Word remains his reliable promise whether faith receives it or not. But it does not work magically (in the Latin phrase of the medieval church *ex opere operato*, simply by virtue of performing the sacramental act). God's Word both creates and sustains faith.

Christians have disagreed on the number of acts that should be designated with the term "sacrament" because they have not always shared a common definition of the term or a common understanding of certain sacred acts. From the time of Peter Lombard (ca. 1100–1160) many Western Christians defined seven such sacred acts as sacraments: Baptism, confirmation, the Lord's Supper, penance, extreme unction, ordination to the priesthood, and marriage. In the Reformation era Protestants rejected all but two or three of these as sacraments. All Protestants retained Baptism and the Lord's Supper, although some Protestants redefined them as symbolic rites rather than sacraments that convey forgiveness of sins. Luther taught that confession and absolution is also a sacrament but then changed his mind and called confession and absolution a continuation of Baptism rather than a separate sacrament.[7] Since his time Lutherans have differed on whether confession and absolution should be considered a third sacrament or the continuation of God's baptismal action of killing and making alive.

The sacraments remind us most clearly that God does use selected elements of his created order to save us. Their very material character helps remind us that our salvation is anchored outside ourselves, that God comes to us from outside ourselves, that his still, small voice is his voice and not merely a feeling welling up within us. "The self is a bottomless pit, a black hole, endlessly sucking everything within and crushing it. The internal self constantly defeats and swallows"[8] what we might call the "mere words" of preaching and Christian conversation. The sacraments keep the Word from being swept into this "black hole" of the self, of our own internality. They refuse permission for letting the Word dissolve into our own good (or lack of good) feelings. The promise of God in Baptism remains, no matter how the bedraggled spirit of the Christian feels about it. The sustenance of the Lord's Supper wakes the Christian from the coma of doubt and despair as the sacramental elements cross the lips. They help open the ears to the promise of the Words of Institution "given for you," "shed for you." "It is the very concrete externality of the Word and the sacrament embedded in it that calls for and supports faith. Faith is not centered on itself. . . . Faith is precisely a faith in the God who comes in the Sacrament. Faith depends on, clings to, stands on, just this externality." If it does not, it turns inward to cling to itself, to feed on itself—and it may suffocate or starve itself. God must come externally. Nowhere is that clearer than in the sacraments and in their external elements on which the Word rides.[9]

Setting our minds on his Word means setting our minds and our lives on him, on that which is above, on God and his gracious will for *us*. There can be no separation of the way in which we think of God's coming to us in Word and sacrament from the way in which we live out our Christian lives.

The Means of Grace Call Believers into New Life

No one can confess faith in Jesus Christ as Lord apart from the Holy Spirit's power (1 Cor. 12:3). The Holy Spirit regenerates and renews believers through the washing of Baptism (Titus 3:5) and other forms of the Word. Sinners enter the Kingdom of God as little children (Matt. 18:3); they must be born again (John 3:3–8). God changes or converts sinners into his newborn chosen children. God takes the dust of those who are dead in trespasses in sins, those who have turned their backs on the Author of Life, and he breathes into them the forgiveness of sins through his re-creative Word (John 20:22–23).

Not by our Own Reason or Strength

Sinners cannot by their own reason and strength believe in Jesus Christ or come to him on their own. In sin—apart from the Holy

Spirit—people do not receive the gifts of God's Spirit. God's way of thinking, and our thinking about God as he truly is, seem folly to them. Only through the Spirit can God's truth be discerned (1 Cor. 2:14). Those who live apart from the Spirit set their minds on their own agenda; only those who have received life from the Spirit set their minds on his agenda (Rom. 8:5).

The thrust of much of Western thought has opposed a biblical understanding of how God brings people out of living apart from him to himself. The "Greek tradition" lacks a strong sense of a Creator God—and thus lacks a strong sense of human sinfulness and responsibility for what goes wrong in life. Because of this, people in our culture often insist that the individual stands on his or her own two feet and takes of his or her own needs. There is simply no "god" there to do it for us in the underlying presuppositions of our culture. Because of this even Christians have fallen into the trap that emphasizes that we can pretty much take care of ourselves. God's total responsibility for our lives contradicts total human responsibility, it seems. Therefore, this dual message from the Scriptures is simplified, and only the human side of our responsibility is treated in the popular thought of our culture.

Thus, the understanding of God's grace, which is found in the Scriptures, is sacrificed—to a greater or lesser extent—to the cultural understanding of human responsibility. Outside the church that means that voluntarists insist that for better or for worse human creatures have the whole world in their hands. Determinists believe that human creatures eke out an existence at the mercy of their genes or their environment.[10]

Pelagianism. Inside the church this means that some believe that human contributions add to God's grace or are strengthened by God's grace in order to achieve a measure of righteousness. Such a view is named for the fourth-century monk Pelagius. Against Augustine he advanced the view that believers take the initial and fundamental steps toward their own salvation by their own efforts. Once they have begun the process, God adds his grace to bring these efforts to perfection. Pelagianism emphasizes human works at the expense of God's grace.[11]

Semi-pelagianism. Semi-pelagianism tries more to balance God's grace and human effort. It teaches that grace is always necessary to complete, if not to initiate, the process of becoming righteous. It mixes grace and works in various measures, trying to preserve some role for grace and some role for human effort. Both pelagianism and semi-pelagianism limit human righteousness to the righteousness of adult performance. They both ignore the distinction between the two kinds of righteousness.

Synergism. Synergism is a view that confesses that sinners are saved by grace alone. But this view operates with a model for the interaction between God and the sinner that presumes that the transaction that delivers God's gift of grace takes place according to the pattern by which adults receive gifts. They must reach out their hands to receive a gift. They must stop by the post office to pick up what God sends—even though he sends it without cost to the receiver. This view sets aside Christ's description of our entering God's kingdom as "new birth" (John 3:3–8). This view sets aside the judgment that sinners are much more than sick or in a state of disrepair when we live apart from God. We are dead in trespasses and sin (Eph. 2:1).

In contrast, conversion as Christ describes it is a matter of new birth, not of concluding an agreement or reaching out a hand, however weakened by sin it might be, to receive the gift. Such descriptions were certainly available to Jesus and Paul. They chose instead to assert our need to die and be reborn (Rom. 6:3–11; Col. 2:11–15); they chose to describe our coming into the Kingdom of God as new birth (John 3:5). The Holy Spirit re-creates—regenerates and renews—the human creature who has been dead in sin when he gives the gift of faith, the relationship of the child with the heavenly Father (Titus 3:5–8).

Conversion: God's New Creation

The mechanics of how sinners return to fearing, loving, and trusting God above all things once again must remain a mysterious event in the final analysis. Nonetheless, the parallels between God's creation of Adam and Eve and his re-creation of those who do not exist in his sight as righteous creatures help explain the conversion of these sinners. God took the dust and breathed into it the breath of life, and Adam became a human creature. God is the sole subject of the action. No pile of dust volunteered to become the human creature. God did not seek out one pile of dust that would make a decision to accept God's offer and commit itself to the task of receiving God's breath. God created—by his own power, without any help from the dust. Similarly, using Christ's description of "new birth," no sinners contribute to the decision of their own salvation any more than they have contributed to the decision to conceive and give them birth physically. Our parents do not invite us to join them in conversations about our own conceptions. They do not ask us whether we want to be born. They give us the gift of life without our asking.

To return to the analogy between creation and re-creation, God's sovereign action transformed the dust into humanity through his breath. The difference between dust and a human creature is quite obvious. Nonetheless, the elements of both are the same physical elements. The dust was transformed, but its chemical makeup remained in the newly fashioned human creature. When adult human creatures are re-created, God fashions his own children from those who were dead in trespasses and sins. Nonetheless, the psychological elements of his human creatures do not disappear after the fall into sin. They remain a part of the person who is converted.

For this reason the preachers of God's word proclaim, invite, and command repentance. They know that this re-creative Word works through the minds and wills of those who are dead in trespasses and sin. Just as Christ commanded the dead Lazarus to come forth from his tomb (John 11:43–44), so the language of command can be used as God converts or re-creates sinners. He does not void or ignore our humanity. He works with us as the psychological beings he created. Just as metal has the characteristics that allow it to be melted and refashioned but does not have the ability to melt and refashion itself, so the sinners have the characteristics—in their rationality and wills—to be reborn as God's children, but they do not have the ability to give themselves new birth.

God is in control of conversion. He re-creates by his sovereign act as he shapes our minds and wills to receive the gift of his favor and love. God claimed to have formed Israel as his own people. He affirmed that he had redeemed Israel, and the re-creative breath of his mouth, his Spirit, had "swept away your offenses like a cloud, and your sins like the morning mist" (Is. 44:21–22). The Holy Spirit re-creates minds and hearts that were set on things he had made instead of on him (Rom. 8:5–11). The Holy Spirit leads sinners out of lives focused on immorality into true life, which produces the fruits of the Holy Spirit. That path leads through death to the old way of thinking and living, through crucifixion of the passions and desires that rule human flesh in the death of sinfulness (Gal. 5:16–24; cf. Eph. 2:1–10).

The old way of thinking and willing is set aside as the Holy Spirit moves our psyches—as he re-creates them once again in Christ's image. Jeremiah knew that the return of God's rebellious people depended on his bringing them back that they might be restored (Jer. 31:18). No one experiences this change, this conversion, unless Christ draws the person out of unfaith into faith (John 6:44). Only by God's power do those who have fled from his presence become his children once again (John 1:12–13). He raises those dead in trespasses and sins to new life (Eph. 2:1, 5–6; Col. 2:12). In desperation over his own weakness Paul could cry out, "What a wretched man I am! Who will rescue me from this body of death?" His answer: "Thanks be to God—through Jesus Christ our Lord!" (Rom. 7:24–25).

Nonetheless, the psychological being does experience mental and emotional change as the Holy Spirit re-creates this person by moving mind and emotions. Thus, sinners experience "accepting" Jesus Christ as their Lord and Savior. They "commit" their lives to him with heart and mind. Two things must be remembered in this connection. First, far more important is God's acceptance of us as his children and his commitment to be our God and Father. Second, the Holy Spirit enables and empowers our minds and hearts to accept and commit. It is he who remakes us and not we ourselves.

From Death to Life in Christ

The Holy Spirit raises the dead to life through his re-creative Word, as it comes in all the forms of the means of grace. In adults God first works a sense of death. Sinners perceive the seriousness of their situation before their wills are moved by the Holy Spirit to want to do anything about it. God's plan for human life, his Law, reveals in all sorts of ways that life on our own apart from God has failed (Rom. 3:20; 1 Cor. 15:56). The Law breaks the spirit of self-sufficiency and rebellion without directly accusing and condemning many unbelievers. A slowly growing sense of inadequacy can bring people to sense their desperate need for change, for conversion, just as effectively as a sudden crisis, in which old ways of life fall apart. Both may be more effective than the direct accusation voiced by Christians.

That direct confrontation is sometimes necessary, but it can also make sinners act even more perversely. "Some, who hate the law because it forbids what they desire to do and commands what they are unwilling to do, are made worse thereby. Accordingly, in so far as they are not restrained by punishment, they act against the law even more than before."[12] But in whatever form the Law puts the squeeze on life lived in reliance on false gods, it attacks the sinner's falsely placed sense of identity, security, and meaning. It calls into question a way of life based on false gods and false goals. It ultimately challenges the idolatry that pretends we can secure life on the basis of someone or something God has made, not on God himself.

Paul noted that this confrontation with the law "grieves" sinners. He rejoiced in that, not because the Corinthians grieved but because they "were grieved into repenting . . . For godly grief produces a repentance that leads to salvation and brings no regret" (2 Cor. 7:9–10 RSV). In this passage Paul spoke of the repentance that believers experience, but the "grief" of sinners who repent for the first time is similar. The Holy Spirit himself uses the Law, in its various forms, to convict sinners of their false belief and of their false conduct (John 16:8–11).

People may be tempted to ask—in one last attempt to contribute something to the process of their own rebirth—what they have to do to be worthy of God's grace. The biblical answer is "nothing," both in the realm of the Law's doing the sinner to death and in the Gospel's bringing the person dead in trespasses to life again. Some Christians believe that they must at least push themselves into the vicinity of God's grace by mustering a sufficiently sincere and genuine sorrow to make themselves look pitiful enough to attract God's mercy. Contrition—sorrow over sin—is necessary in the life of the new child of God. But grasping for the Gospel comes psychologically not out of some desire to please God but simply out of the fear that our existence is threatened, that life is going or gone. The destruction of our old mindset, our old idolatries, requires nothing but that fear the law induces. It may induce it through threats of many kinds. A certain psychological level of terror is no prerequisite;

neither is a certain quantity of grief and sorrow. "Contrition is not even a good work. The contrition which precedes faith is only something suffered by man. It is anxiety, pain, torment, a being crushed that is produced by God through the hammer of his law."[13] Sinners do not generate this fear in themselves. Life as God has created it hems and squeezes and finally crushes those who try to break out of its form. That hemming, squeezing, and crushing brings sinners into the consciousness of their own death. That suffices to open them for the Holy Spirit's bringing of the Gospel.

The Holy Spirit can use the wide variety of human experience with flaws and failures to convict unbelievers of the inadequacy of their old ways of life and their old gods. He comes with the Gospel revealed in Jesus Christ and conveyed through the Scriptures to raise those dead in trespasses to new life in Christ, lived out in trust in him (John 15:26; 16:14–15). God has made the dead come to life by exchanging their death and his, by substituting his reclaimed, resurrected life for theirs (Eph. 2:1–10). He has taken those who were "no people," and through the blood of Christ has brought the alienated and strangers, the dead, into his own living family (1 Peter 2:10). There they find peace as the Holy Spirit makes them his dwelling place (Eph. 2:11–22). This he does by speaking a word, which makes them righteous once again. He re-creates as he created, through the power of his Word, which proclaims new life in Christ (Rom. 10:17; 1 Peter 1:23). "For God, who said, 'Let light shine out of darkness,' made his light shine in our hearts to give us the light of the knowledge of the glory of God in the face of Christ" (2 Cor. 4:6). Thus, he opens hearts through preaching (Acts 16:14). When it seems that we are working out our own salvation through the acts of our minds and hearts, it is God who is at work in us (Phil. 2:13).

The Lifelong Rhythm of Law and Gospel

The Word comes through the proclamation or sharing by other human creatures. Believers must hear both the Law and the Gospel in connection with their calling to witness to God's saving power in Jesus Christ. The Law reminds believers that they must prepare themselves for effective witness. That places two burdens upon them. They must study the Scriptures diligently so that they know

God's message well. They must be sensitive to the precise needs of those to whom they are bringing God's Word of Law or Gospel. The Gospel for believers who are witnessing reminds them that the Holy Spirit is in charge of the entire witnessing process. He guides and gives to both the one who is witnessing and the one who is receiving the witness. He works sometimes in spite of us, his people, more than through us. Believers must avoid not only a synergism of the one whom the Spirit is converting. Believers must also acknowledge the total sovereignty of the Holy Spirit over the one who is witnessing as well. We are indeed the Spirit's tools and even co-workers (1 Thess. 3:2), but we contribute nothing to the conversion of the other person. God is working in, with, and under us as we speak his Word.

The process of re-creation is instantaneous and at the same time lasts throughout human life. God establishes his relationship with us through his promise. His promise stands sure. Yet the psychological weaning from false gods and the dawning of knowledge and the emotional commitment that builds on the knowledge of Jesus Christ continue throughout life on earth. "When our Lord and Master Jesus Christ said, 'Repent,' he willed the entire life of believers to be one of repentance."[14] When he calls us, he calls us to follow him into death.[15] Some have received the promise who are still struggling with doubts and thus believe that they do not believe. Others lose some of their confidence or some of their knowledge in Christ and question whether they are still in a faithful relationship with their Lord.

Our responses to those caught in such quandaries must be exercised within the distinction of Law and Gospel. We will respond to their questions only when we know why they want to know. For those who are resisting faith, the Law must be used to remind them that there is no God but Yahweh, revealed in Jesus Christ, and that our whole lives must rest in him. For those who are broken in their confidence and seeking a new source of ultimate identity, security, and meaning, the Gospel must bring reassurance of God's love and favor. Only in and through this Word can faith be created.

This word springs from the Word of the Lord as it comes in Baptism and absolution, in preaching and Christian conversation, in the Lord's Supper and in tracts and books and media of other kinds. These channels convey what God has revealed in Jesus Christ, as we learn from the Scriptures.

Notes for Chapter X

1. Augsburg Confession V, 1–2, *The Book of Concord,* trans. and ed. Theodore G. Tappert (Philadelphia: Fortress, 1959), 31.
2. J. N. D. Kelly, *Early Christian Doctrines,* (New York: Harper & Row, 1960), 258–63; Jaroslav Pelikan, *The Christian Tradition: A History of the Development of Doctrine, 1: The Emergence of the Catholic Tradition (100–600)* (Chicago: The University of Chicago Press, 1971), 211–20.
3. Small Catechism, Creed, 6, *The Book of Concord,* 345.
4. Smalcald Articles III:IV, *The Book of Concord,* 310.
5. As Luther understood Augustine's broad definition of this term; cf. Ian D. Kingston Siggins, *Martin Luther's Doctrine of Christ* (New Haven: Yale University Press, 1970), 156–64, on Luther's use of Augustine's pairing of "sacrament" and "example" for Christ.
6. Kelly, 409–17; Pelikan, 308–13.
7. Martin Luther, "The Babylonian Captivity of the Church, 1520," *Word and Sacrament: II,* Luther's Works, vol. 36 (Philadelphia: Fortress, 1959), 81–91, 124.
8. Gerhard O. Forde, *Theology Is for Proclamation* (Minneapolis: Fortress, 1990), 159.
9. Ibid., 159–62.
10. See ch. III, p. 48–49.
11. Kelly, 357–72; Pelikan, 307–18.
12. Smalcald Articles III:II, 2, *The Book of Concord,* 303.
13. C. F. W. Walther, *Law and Gospel,* trans. Herbert J. A. Bouman (Saint Louis: Concordia, 1981), 126.
14. Martin Luther, "Ninety-Five Theses or Disputation on the Power and Efficacy of Indulgences, 1517," *Career of the Reformer: I,* Luther's Works, vol. 31 (Philadelphia: Fortress, 1957), 25.
15. Dietrich Bonhoeffer, *The Cost of Discipleship,* trans. R. H. Fuller (1937; New York: Macmillan, 1959), 99.

Chapter XI

Holy Scripture

"Men moved by the Holy Spirit spoke from God" (2 Peter 1:21 RSV). God's Word took shape first in oral form. He talked with his people through his prophets (e.g., 2 Sam. 23:2; Is. 6:8–10; Jer. 1:7–8). How the Word of the Lord came to the prophets is not explained. False prophets also spoke, but in some way the Holy Spirit guided the people of God to recognize true prophets even while many followed the false prophets (Jer. 23:9–40). Then, God turned the prophetic Word to written form. He commanded Jeremiah to record all the words that he had spoken to the prophet, for he wanted his Word, delivered to Jeremiah, to be at the disposal of his people when he later restored their fortunes in their land (Jer. 30:1–3). The apostles' message was also recognized as God's Word (1 Thess. 2:13), not only in its oral but also in its written form (Eph. 3:2–6; 1 Cor. 14:37). In this authoritative, utterly reliable form God delivers his Word to the church today.

The Nature of Holy Scripture

The Scripture is quite modest about itself. It mentions itself seldom, and it never explains the mechanics of its origin. Its occasional references to its origin and nature assure us, however, that its writings, like Jesus Christ, are fully divine and fully human, completely God's Word and completely human language.

The Inspiration of Scripture

"All Scripture is God-breathed" or inspired (*theopneustos*) (2 Tim. 3:16). The nature or process of verbal inspiration is not described. It is simply presumed. The Jews knew that God's Word spoke to them from pages of the Scriptures in the days after authoritative oral prophecy ceased and that Scripture is therefore the

Word of God, as he delivered it to his people. Some Christians have posited theories of how inspiration might have worked. These theories can direct attention and trust to the process rather than to the Lord who speaks the words of Scripture. Such speculation about God's means and methods is unnecessary. Human speculation will not secure God's Word. God himself has made his prophetic word more sure through his revelation of himself in Jesus Christ (2 Peter 1:19).

Believers simply trust God as he speaks through every word of the Bible. They remember that the Bible, because it is God's Word, is not their own playground, and they dare never turn his Word into a wax sculpture, which they shape according to their own inclinations. For "no prophecy of Scripture is a matter of one's own interpretation" (2 Peter 1:20 RSV). The Holy Spirit moved those whose prophecies are conveyed to us in Scripture's pages; human activity—human thinking and then human speaking and then human writing—was involved. But the impulse from which those words came lay with the Holy Spirit (2 Peter 1:21).

Some Christians are uncertain that God has really selected certain elements of his created order to convey his re-creative power and to serve as his instruments. They believe that the Word of the Lord may be sought in the Scriptures but that the entire Scripture is not God's inspired Word. They believe that God would have no interest in telling us, for instance, that Nimrod was a mighty hunter (Gen. 10:9). The exact significance of this information at this point in the text is not clear to me. Whatever it may have been, it need not serve some greater purpose in the vertical realm to be the Word of the Lord. God the Creator takes an interest in all of his creation.

God is present in the pages of Scripture. God is not imprisoned or boxed up in these pages, but God is there, waiting for readers who encounter his power in words of both Law and Gospel. He condemns sin and expresses his wrath from its pages although fallen human creatures encounter the crushing or irritating power of his Law throughout life. He bestows his promises, and through them life, in its pages as well, as the Scriptures testify of Jesus Christ (John 5:39). God bursts forth from the pages of Scripture to do his work. God's presence not only stands behind the words of the Bible by virtue of the Holy Spirit's inspiration. God's presence remains in the Scripture as he works through it to deliver the power of salvation in the Gospel to all who use it in their own lives and in the lives of others.

The Human Nature of Scripture

The verbally inspired Scriptures are at the same time cast in human language, composed under the Spirit's inspiration by human beings who were writing these documents as other documents were written at their time. God acts in history. He revealed himself by sending "a strong east wind" to divide waters and thereby save his chosen people (Ex. 14:21–29). He directed his people's exile and their return from exile (Neh. 1:8–9). He was born as a fully human creature, a Jew, at a specific time in human history to be "crucified under Pontius Pilate," as believers confess and thereby anchor God's primary revelation firmly in human history. So also God reveals himself in Scripture's pages in a totally human way. He has taken human language written in normal human fashion, set in specific contexts in human history, as the means by which he conveys his saving truth and power to us.

Thus, the writers of the Scriptures give us glimpses of the human side of the process by which they wrote. John was writing to his fellow believers on the basis of what he had heard, seen, and touched (1 John 1:1), and he was writing because it gave him pleasure to share the Word of life with others (1 John 1:4). The process of writing the gospel of John included selection of certain materials from a vast array of incidents to report (John 21:24–25). Luke had turned eyewitness accounts into an orderly narrative on the basis of his research (Luke 1:1–4). The biblical writers used good Hebrew, Aramaic, and Greek grammar and syntax. They used specific literary genres from their time periods, well aware of how their message could be framed for their hearers and readers and how their ideas could be effectively conveyed. They wrote aware of their historical situations and bound by them, even as the Holy Spirit gave them words they could not have found on their own because those words conveyed the mysteries of God.

In its original expression in Hebrew, Aramaic, and Greek, and in any good translation, what God has written is apprehensible to any reader. God's writers did not use any mysterious code. There is no secret in the Scriptures that cannot be recognized by the average reader. God's language is plain, straightforward human language.

God's revelation of the mystery of his love is not so readily comprehensible, however. The human mind can relatively easily understand that the author—John in the prologue to his gospel, for instance—was claiming that God has come in human flesh. But the human mind cannot grasp or comprehend that this can be true, apart from the Holy Spirit's aid (1 Cor. 12:3).

Nonetheless, God's use of human language is not magical even if it conveys mystery. It is not some special "gnostic" revelation that lies outside human apprehension. The Holy Spirit inspired the authors of the books of the Bible to write within their times, with the knowledge available to them, in forms that were used in their cultures to convey information. It is wrong to dismiss the Scriptures as merely human words. It is just as misleading to assert their divine nature but to trap the inspired texts in some literalistic theory of language that reduces their words to symbols for any stray thought a believer may have. Fundamentalistic interpreters of the Scriptures do make them into a wax nose when they ignore the historical circumstances in which the biblical writers were inspired. Such interpreters reduce the Bible's words to their own playthings when they impose meanings upon the biblical language that it did not have in the author's use of the language of his time.

Thus, believers strive to know as much about the world in which the biblical authors wrote as possible. Archeological and linguistic studies improve our ability to hear the Holy Spirit's voice as it comes through the message of the writers whom he inspired.

The Purpose of Scripture

In the message of the inspired writers comes the re-creative Word of the Lord. John admitted that he could have written more about Jesus' life. What he did write was enough, however. It was written so that its readers "may believe that Jesus is the Christ, the Son of God, and that by believing you may have life in his name" (John 20:31). Similarly, John wrote his first epistle so that his readers "may know that you have eternal life" (1 John 5:13). "You have known the holy Scriptures, which are able to make you wise for salvation through faith in Christ Jesus" (2 Tim. 3:15). The purpose of the Scriptures is to bring fallen sinners to salvation. They do so by acquainting them with Christ Jesus and cultivating in them God's gift of faith. They convey the Gospel of Jesus Christ. In so doing they function as God's power in the lives of believers (Rom. 1:16).

Alongside this central purpose of making believers "wise for salvation," the inspired Scriptures also are useful "for teaching, rebuking, correcting and training in righteousness" (2 Tim. 3:16). Believers use them to learn more of God's gracious will and wondrous ways. They use them to rebuke and correct false ideas, which inevitably interfere with a proper understanding of God's Word. They use them to grow in the practice of the godly life. The goal of the church's use of the Scriptures is that believers may enjoy the fullest renewal of their humanity possible—that they may become complete or mature—and thus be equipped for every good work (2 Tim. 3:17).

As the biblical message comes to believers through apostles, prophets, evangelists, pastors, and teachers, the saints are equipped for the work of ministry. They are edified so that they might become one in their faith, in their knowledge of God's Son, and thus that they might be mature by the measure of Christ. This means that the Scriptures will prevent them from being tossed to and fro with every wind of cunning, crafty, deceitful views of life. Instead, they will be growing up in Christ, and they will speak God's truth to one another in love, joined together as they are in Christ's body, which he supplies with the power of his Word in order to make sure that his body continues to grow (Eph. 4:11–16).

This maturity, which the use of the Scriptures cultivates, is grounded in trust in Jesus Christ and the sure hope in his continuing presence in our lives. "For everything that was written in the past days was written to teach us, so that through endurance and the encouragement of the Scriptures we might have hope" (Rom. 15:4).

The Word of the Lord, as conveyed by apostles and prophets, forms the foundation of the whole church and of its individual members' lives. Thus, this Word from God binds believers together in God's temple (Eph. 2:19–22). The "apostles and prophets" mentioned here may be the apostles of the New Testament and the prophets of the Old Testament. Or the passage may refer to two New Testament offices that were bringing the Word of the Lord to Paul's contemporaries. In either case, the message of those apostles and prophets is delivered to Christians at the turn of the twenty-first century only through the Scriptures. The apostles continue to exercise their office as ambassadors of the Lord through their writings.[1]

Interpreting the Scriptures

Believers proceed from certain fundamental principles to interpret the biblical message. Out of the Lutheran Reformation and Luther's practice of the task of biblical interpretation arose an approach to reading the Scriptures embraced in four principles.

The Clarity of Scripture

First, the Scriptures are clear. This principle of the clarity, or, as it is called, the perspicuity of the biblical text, is not always clear to those who read it. The principle intends first to posit that the Scriptures contain no mysterious language, as noted above. Its words are apprehensible to the average reader, even when its message can be accepted only as a gift through the Holy Spirit. God's wisdom is foolishness to those who operate apart from faith, with a rationalistic or empirical epistemology (1 Cor. 1:21–25). Paul acknowledged the necessity of destroying arguments and obstacles to the knowledge of God in order that the thoughts of believers might heed Christ (2 Cor. 10:5). Nonetheless, what the biblical writers convey is available to the apprehension of the average reader.

That does not mean that every believer will understand and master every passage of Scripture. The wisdom of God is deep and unsearchable and even inscrutable at points, also for believers (Rom. 11:33). Peter found some of what Paul had written difficult to understand (2 Peter 3:16). Believers do not trust in their own mastery of Scripture for their ultimate sense of identity, security, and meaning. They trust in the Lord who is present in his Word as it is found in the pages of Scripture. They place their lives in the hand of the Lord who is speaking in his Word even when they cannot explain to their own satisfaction every phrase he has caused to be uttered.

Nonetheless, Scripture is clear in its statement of the message that lies at the heart of God's concern for us. It is able to make us wise to salvation through faith in Christ Jesus.

The Sufficiency of Scripture

And, in this regard—and there can be no other concern for the believer who approaches the Word of the Lord—it is sufficient. Jesus observed, as he put words in Abraham's mouth in telling the story of Lazarus and the rich man, that "they have Moses and the Prophets; let them listen to them" (Luke 16:29). God has given his human creatures dominion in his creation to learn how much of life works in the horizontal realm apart from his specific revelation of himself. He comes to us in his special revelation, with the specific knowledge we need to be restored to our vertical relationship with him. For this, the core of human life, the Bible contains all we need to know, even if it does not contain all we always want to know.

The Power of Scripture

Third, the Scripture is powerful, for it instructs us in salvation through faith in Jesus Christ. The word of the prophets could be compared to fire and to a hammer that breaks a rock in pieces (Jer. 23:29). The words of Scripture rise from the page to pierce hearts (Heb. 4:12). John's words about the Word made Flesh were written to bring life to those who read them (1 John 5:13; John 20:30–31). They continue the creative speaking of God as they bring sinners to new life in Christ.

Scripture Interprets Scripture

Finally, Scripture interprets Scripture. The Word of the Lord alone can govern how his Word is to be understood. The one who listens to God is "trapped" within what some call a "hermeneutical circle." There is no way for the hearer of God's Word to grasp it at either "end" and twist it to his or her own liking. It remains an authoritative voice from outside our control. Therefore, the words of Scripture must be read as human words, but at the same time their content and significance cannot be judged merely by human criteria. They must be understood within the context of God's revelation of himself within the biblical text.

All sorts of historical and literary research enrich our understanding and apprehension of the text. If the texts of the Bible are not viewed in their historical context, they will be misunderstood. A wooden, overly-literalistic use of biblical language does not listen to God but twists the words of the biblical page around the preconceptions of the culture that informs the mind of the reader.

Nonetheless, the reader always stands under the biblical text, not over it. Human judgment cannot be exercised against the meaning and message of the text; human judgment can be exercised only in its service. That, of course, is a difficult line to draw, even among believers who in good faith wish to place themselves under the text. Cultural presuppositions ambush even the most faithful of believing interpreters and divert them from what the author wrote. Therefore, the whole life of the interpreter of the Scriptures must be a life of repentance.

Contemporary Methods of Interpretation

In these latter days much discussion of biblical authority has centered on the use of particular methods, particularly those labeled "historical critical methods." Believers must remember that every method is devised, and arises, from certain ideological presuppositions. That does not mean that a method may not be used by people with other presuppositions than those of the method's inventors. It does mean that methods must be examined on the basis of their presuppositions as well as their operational guidelines and practice.

Believers must also recognize that the Gospel of Jesus Christ has shone through good methods of biblical interpretation and bad, and that good methods and bad have been used to obscure that Gospel. A good tool guided by false presuppositions will not produce the correct results. Using a faulty method, the allegorical method of medieval Christianity, some teachers of the faith proclaimed God's grace in Jesus Christ, and some did not. Using the same methods of interpretation, reformers of different confessions in the sixteenth century came to different conclusions on important teachings, for instance, on the sacraments. The dogmatic presuppositions that interpreters bring to the text, as well as the conceptual frameworks within which they work, determine to a large extent what they find, whatever method they may use.

Often "method" can be a vehicle of dogma as well as "mere" method. Much of what has been practiced under the label "historical criticism" has arisen from one kind of biblical study at the end of the eighteenth and beginning of the nineteenth centuries. Such study was conducted by people who came to the text with the dogmatic presuppositions of the Enlightenment. This view presumed that the biblical text was not God's Word. It presupposed that human reason as defined by "enlightened" European minds at the time was superior to every other cultural system of thought—to say nothing of words that claimed to be the revelation of God himself. It dismissed the possibility of the miraculous and thus refused to consider the resurrection of the dead (and anything else that diverged from the scientific knowledge of the time) to be true—or even possible. It presumed that human reason "is the measure of all things."

Such presuppositions combined with antisemitism in the thought of an early "historical critic" like Hermann Samuel Reimarus (1694–1768) to produce a fierce attack on the authority and credibility of the "Hebrew" Bible. Much of nineteenth- and twentieth-century biblical study was not able to free itself from the direction and framework set in place by Reimarus and his contemporaries. Their stance of placing the reader above the text, however, must be distinguished from the legitimate methods used to ascertain the meaning the author—and thus, the Holy Spirit—set down. Proper historical and literary examination are necessary for hearing the text itself. Such methods, sometimes relabeled under the term "historical grammatical method," are indispensable in listening to the voice of God in the pages of Scripture.

All methods of biblical study may be abused if presuppositions falsely direct their application. The study of literary form, for example, is indeed helpful in understanding what the authors of the Bible intended to say through their use of specific words, phrases, and forms. For instance, scholars have noted that the gospel writers use a literary form to tell about Christ's performance of miracles that parallels the form used by pagan authors to describe the miracles of pagan miracle workers. "Form criticism" as practiced by some would suggest that this has to mean that the evangelists invented such stories in order to convey their opinion of Christ's greatness. Believers can just as easily recognize in the use of such forms the evangelists' desire to communicate what Christ actually did in performing miracles in a familiar form, so that their readers would clearly understand what had actually happened as he touched the sick and made them well. Believers should not flee from the use of such methods just because they have been used for false purposes.

The Historical Grammatical Method. Believers must recognize, however, the necessity of placing the text in its historical context. A literalistic interpretation of words on the page, ignoring historical context and literary form, leads the hearer and reader far from the text. Such an approach puts the text as much at the mercy of the interpreter as do those presuppositions that deny God's presence in the words. Apart from that context, its meaning will be obscured if not obliterated. God inspired writers in the Hebrew culture of the centuries before Christ in their language. He inspired writers in the Jewish and Hellenistic culture of Christ's and Paul's time in the Greek language. He is a God who has anchored himself in the history of his human creatures. He will be misunderstood if readers carelessly transpose the words of his inspired authors into a contemporary cultural situation.

Likewise, his words will be misunderstood if they are simply and literally limited to the forms in which he spoke them. He charges the church with the lively and living translation of his Word into the cultures in which he has placed his people. For example, believers in most of Christian history have believed that they could love their neighbors only if they abstained from any form of charging interest, in correspondence with the law as laid down in Lev. 25:36–37. For centuries Christians did not include this command as part of that law of God for Old Testament believers that Paul set aside and abolished for the church (Col. 2:16–17). In the past century most believers have come to recognize that in a capitalist system interest can be paid and charged without necessarily breaking the underlying concern that led to that command from God for his Old Testament people. Believers recognize that the command that women cover their heads in church or that men not wear their hair long (1 Cor. 11:2–15) conveyed a principle in forms not necessary for every cultural situation in which the church has found itself.

Challenges in interpretation such as these should not obscure the fundamental truth regarding the Scriptures. They record the Word of God, as it has come to human authors, for the salvation of his people.

Notes for Chapter XI

1. Oscar Cullmann, *Peter: Disciple, Apostle, Martyr,* trans. Floyd V. Filson (Cleveland: World, 1953), 215–23.

Chapter XII

The Living Voice of God's Word

"How can they believe in the one of whom they have not heard? And how can they hear without someone preaching to them? ... Consequently, faith comes from hearing the message, and the message is heard through the word of Christ" (Rom. 10:14, 17). God has called his people to take the words of Scripture, which convey his message for humankind, and to pass their content on to one another and to those outside the faith. Through those who speak his Word he gives faith, and thus life.

The Proclamation of the Word

Believers serve as agents of his re-creative word as they share this Word of life. They serve as the priests who build bridges of life from God's Word, with its message of new birth in Christ, to the specific kinds of dying that plague those whom they encounter. They speak God's Law, and they give living voice to his Gospel, as they take his universal message and focus it on individuals. For congregations this takes place in the sermon. For individual acquaintances it occurs in the conversation and consolation that believers share with one another and with unbelievers in the situations of daily life. Believers listen first, so they can understand those to whom they want to speak. Then their words let loose the power of God, to kill and to make alive, in the lives of those around them.

The Sermon

This word is spoken and shared privately and publicly. The public sermon stands at the heart of the congregation's common experience each week. Other public teaching of the Word brings God's people together in one body to share together insights into his message for them. Some biblical scholars have emphasized the distinction between proclamation and teaching.[1] The borderline between these forms of public exposition of the Word seems hard to draw. Some sermons are largely didactic; some teachers often proclaim as they teach. The difference between the two lies in the form of address, the way in which the connection between God in his Word and the hearer is made. The proclamation of Law or Gospel does address the sinner directly. It is primary discourse; it involves first- and second-person conversation. "I am the Lord your God"—his people cite him as they speak to one another and to those still outside the faith. "In the stead and by the command of my Lord Jesus Christ I forgive you all your sins." Direct discourse between God and his human creatures: that is what is happening when proclamation takes place. It puts a claim upon the sinner, the claim of death or the claim of life.

Teaching about Law or Gospel provides information and insight. It takes place in secondary discourse, in third-person descriptions of what God has done and what he expects from his human creatures. Through such teaching God does let loose his power in his people's lives. But his intention toward us expresses itself more clearly and directly in proclamation. Its direct address sharpens the condemnation of the Law and deepens the comfort of the Gospel. Teaching in this culture may be expressed in an authoritative manner, but it presumes the freedom of the hearer to accept or reject. Proclamation is sacramental; it is pure gift. It announces God's disposition and effects God's action toward his children.[2]

Proclamation is a verbal noun, as is *teaching*. Paul linked the delivery of the message with its content as he spoke of his proclamation in 1 Cor. 2:4–5: "My message and my preaching were not with wise and persuasive words, but with a demonstration of the Spirit's power, so that your faith might not rest on men's wisdom, but on God's power." The folly of Paul's proclamation serves as God's instrument of saving his people (1 Cor. 1:21), the instrument of building their faith and knowledge of the truth (Titus 1:2–3). In other passages Paul defined his proclamation by its content: Jesus Christ (Rom. 16:25) or the resurrection of Christ (1 Cor. 15:14).

The sermon formally conveys God's power to save (Rom. 1:16) to the assembled body of believers. They are commissioned as priests to carry that message to others informally as is appropriate in all situations of life. The several Great Commission passages (Matt. 28:18–20; Luke 24:46–49; John 20:19–23; Acts 1:8) give the charge to share the Word of repentance and the forgiveness of sins to the whole church. Called pastors exercise that charge publicly; all believers are also called by God to share his Word as appropriate, wherever appropriate.

Proclaiming Law and Gospel

The appropriate sharing or application of God's Word to the lives of hearers rests upon the proper distinction of Law and Gospel. Sinners come in two varieties, spread out along a gradual spectrum between absolute security with false gods and self-destructive despair when the old gods have failed. Those who live in relative security with a false system of identity, security, and meaning remain deaf to an offer of a different gospel. They must have their security broken by the Law. The Law need not always be voiced by the Christian. The Law impinges upon human life at every turn. Some sinners manage to make truces with the Law and not feel its crushing power. Many, however, are preoccupied with dodging and ducking—or perhaps denying—that power day in and day out.

Such people experience the Law's power because they have been abused and battered by others, by the "system," by the forces of nature. They are experiencing alienation and loneliness. They are finding no meaning in life. They are struggling with shame and guilt. They are trembling under the terrors of death. Believers who encounter such people have no obligation to say some specific words or to make certain that the accusing force of the Law has imposed guilt upon our hearers. Believers only have to gauge whether the sinner is broken enough to begin to feel a need for the Gospel of Jesus Christ.

The Law operates as the description of what human creatures perform. The Law is functioning when human creatures are the subject of the sentence and human actions are the subject of its content. Therefore, it always places the burden upon the human creature. The Gospel describes what God does for his human creatures. The Gospel is functioning when God is the subject of the sentence and his gracious actions in behalf of his fallen creatures are the subject of its content. The Law imposes conditions upon the human creature, and therefore the grammatical mood of the Law is often the imperative ["Do this . . . "] or the conditional ["If you do this . . . "]. However, any description of human action places the crushing burden of the Law on us. It makes little difference whether we say, "we should," "we ought to," "we must," or even "we shall" do this or that particular good work. In all these cases, the burden falls on us. Only the Gospel of Jesus Christ shifts the focus from our performance to our identity, from our works to God's work in establishing and re-establishing our identity as his children.

In Christian preaching and conversation the proper distinction of Law and Gospel must always be functioning. Believers must ask, "Why do you want to know?" in order to identify who is asking—secure sinner or despairing sinner—and in order to know what the agenda of the conversation partner really is. Only when secure sinners hear the Law, and despairing sinners hear the Gospel, will the Word of God pierce hearts appropriately. Believers must remember that they are called to do their best in sensitively applying the Word. They dare never forget that the Holy Spirit controls the witnessing process and works through us when he can and in spite of us when he must.

Confession and Absolution

God has called his church to serve as his hit men, to deliver the death-dealing Law to secure sinners. God has called his church to serve as his midwives, to deliver life to despairing sinners through the Gospel. God has called his people to retain and remit the sins of others (John 20:23). Christ has commanded this process of dealing death and dispensing life. Its power lies in the Holy Spirit's use of believers to retain and remit sins. He has selected believers as specific elements of his created order to carry out these tasks that bring sinners back into the family of God. Christ commissioned believers to bind sins and to loose them (Matt. 18:18), to open or shut heaven for others through the use of the Word (Matt. 16:19). This exercise of the keys of the Kingdom of God is entrusted in the formal, public life of the church to pastors. All believers are called to be calling fellow believers and unbelievers to repentance and to be announcing the forgiveness of sins and God's love in Christ Jesus to the repentant. The Office of the Keys is exercised in the various forms of confession and absolution.

Confession of sins is a dirge of death. Confession of sins admits the justice of God's condemnation, or the correctness of the observation that we are dead without the Author of Life. Confession of sins repeats the burial with Christ in our Baptisms.

Absolution looses or frees us from the condemnation and the death. Absolution brings us to life in Christ. Absolution washes us by dissolving all that threatens us—sin, guilt, shame, alienation, the Law's verdict, death itself. It restores sinners to being children of God caught up on the Father's lap, there secure from all evil.

The church practices the confession of sins in a variety of ways. Most often Christians practice the secret confession of the heart, laying their sins before God and thus placing their lives at his mercy. The problem with such secret confession is that it may be difficult to identify the log or speck in our own eye, and it may be difficult to hear comfort from our own absolution. Christians ideally use a confessor—formally the task of the pastor, informally the calling of all believing friends—who in private confession aids the believer in identifying the sins that beset us. Confession of sins may take place in small groups of believers who come together for Bible study and prayer. The practice of confession and absolution in such groups may bring the power of the Gospel to his people in a special way. Finally, Christians confess their sins in public. On rare occasions a matter of offense may be confessed by an individual before the congregation. When such an offense has taken place, caution must be used that the public confession be an experience that edifies the sinner and others, not a spectacle the sinner can use for self-justification or the congregation for self-congratulation. Much more common is the common confession of the public worship service, in which believers confess their sins together and receive absolution together.

The advantages of the common confession in public worship and of secret confession center around their accessibility. They are necessary because they provide confession and absolution at a minimal expense of time and travel. But ideally every believer should confess sins to another believer individually and receive from that individual the forgiveness of sins and the assurance of God's love in other ways as it comes to us individually through Jesus Christ.

211

The Lutherans of the sixteenth century boasted that they practiced individual private confession and absolution.[3]

Absolution tailors the Gospel to the individual. In private confession of sins the one who hears our confession comes to understand our personal battles against temptation and can apply the Law and the Gospel to those struggles with an insight and an objectivity that we often lack ourselves. When we know that a believing friend also knows about the sin to which we are often tempted, we confront that sin no more alone, but with the knowledge that our confessor's prayer and God's Word of strength stand alongside us in the battle against this evil. That fellow believer can also give voice to the Word of God's forgiveness and support that we, in our discouragement or despair, may not be able to sound for ourselves. Thus, the comfort of the Gospel is immensely strengthened by the practice of private confession and absolution.

Mutual Conversation and Consolation

In the Smalcald Articles Luther included the "mutual conversation and consolation" of Christians with one another as one of those means by which God "offers counsel and help against sin." He expected that normal Christian contact in the home, in the workplace and school, in the neighborhood and social group, in the congregation, would include conversation that conveyed God's Good News in Jesus Christ.[4] Luther presumed that believers would be consoling one another with the announcement of the forgiveness of sins in Jesus Christ as they went about their daily lives.

This conversation and consolation can be structured within a congregation as it organizes small groups for Bible study, prayer, and the sharing of the forgiveness of sins. It takes place more often as believers live out their callings in daily life. Such conversation demands the preparation of the believer's normal engagement with Scripture. It requires prayer for those whom we encounter as they face the needs they share with us. But it requires no highly sophisticated knowledge or sensitivity. It simply expresses the faith in the normal and everyday contacts of the believer's life.

Through such conversation and consolation God brings the presence of his love to his people. He repeats his baptismal claim upon his people as they speak the Gospel to each other. He rein-

forces all that he accomplishes through public preaching and absolution and through the Lord's Supper as he lets his Word loose
in lives through such conversations.

Witness to the Gospel for Those outside the Faith

In the course of normal conversations believers also witness to
their faith in the presence of unbelievers. Christians are called to
build the bridges that convey the Gospel into the lives of those
around them. Such witness can take place in formal evangelism
programs in the congregation. They always are taking place as believers live out lives in situations that bring them into contact with
unbelievers.

Believers do not choose whether to witness to unbelievers with
whom they have contact. To unbelievers who know that we are
believers, we are always making some statement about our faith in
Christ. We may often be witnessing to his lack of importance for
us, to our indifference to him for daily life. But we are stating something with our words and deeds about our faith, even if we are
making it look small and unimportant for us. Those who get to know
us but who do not know we are Christians also receive a witness
regarding our faith from us. They soon form an estimate of what is
holding our lives together, what is most important for us. They sense
quite quickly what provides us with an ultimate sense of identity,
security, and meaning. Therefore, believers do not choose to witness
or not to witness. They choose either to sharpen their witness or
to let it convey a misimpression of our Lord.

Christian witness can happen in any situation. The Holy Spirit
can use a hit-and-run speaking of his Word to good effect. But
normally the Gospel is most easily heard, humanly speaking, when
believers have created a climate of trust in a relationship with the
unbeliever. Although they will not (as the song states) "know we
are Christians by our love"—for unbelievers often love very effectively—our love builds a foundation on which speaking the Gospel
can be built.

Believers must listen carefully to ascertain whether those with
whom they are speaking need to hear Law or Gospel. They need
to listen sensitively to determine how to formulate the Law or the
Gospel most effectively, in a form the unbeliever can hear and

understand most easily. Believers must show tremendous patience as they convey the Word of the Lord. They must be willing to speak and then wait in silence, repeatedly, as it dawns on the sinner that reliance on other sources of identity, security, and meaning spells death. Then, as our hearers test the Gospel—and test us and our patience at the same time—we repeat the good news in Christ as the Holy Spirit creates new life—though often too slowly for the impatient schedules of our love.

To these tasks of being God's hit men and midwives, we are called. We give his Word its living voice. The Holy Spirit gives believers the blessing of serving as his instruments in bringing sinners into death and the children of God to life once again.

Notes for Chapter XII

1. E.g., C. H. Dodd, *The Apostolic Preaching and Its Development* (London: Nisbet, 1936).
2. Gerhard O. Forde, *Theology Is for Proclamation* (Minneapolis: Fortress, 1990), 1–9, 147–58.
3. Apology of the Augsburg Confession, XI, *The Book of Concord*, trans. and ed. Theodore G. Tappert (Philadelphia: Fortress, 1959), 180–82.
4. Smalcald Articles III:IV, ibid., 310.

Chapter XIII

Baptism

"Baptism ... now saves you also" (1 Peter 3:21). Peter was quite direct. Baptism saves. Scholars believe that the apostle may well have written his first epistle on the basis of a sermon delivered in connection with the Baptism of new Christians, adults and infants, at Easter time. Whether that is the case or not, Peter leaves no doubt about what he regards Baptism to be—the instrument of God's salvation. Peter explains how Baptism saves. He has mentioned God's delivery of Noah and his family through water and finds some correspondence with Baptism in that act of God. God acts through Baptism and thereby creates a clear conscience, which can stand before God with its appeal. That conscience is cleared through the resurrection of Christ. Baptism connects the baptized with Christ's rising from the dead.

There can be no doubt about the importance of Baptism for the life of the early church, on the basis of the glimpses Luke gives us. Repeatedly, in his account of the early history of the church, he mentioned the central role Baptism played in Christian preaching and living (Acts 2:38, 41; 8:12–13, 36–38; 9:17–18 [cf. 22:16]; 10:47–48; 16:15, 33; 18:8).[1]

God Kills and Creates New Life in Baptism

The concept that Peter here takes for granted is expressed more fully by Paul, in two passages in which he links Baptism with Christ's resurrection—as well as his death. Paul builds upon the proclamation of God's grace, which he set before his readers in chapters 3–5, as he moves to the subject of Baptism in Rom. 6:3–11. In Baptism God's grace actualizes itself in the lives of believers, and Paul continues to discuss how he had experienced that grace that Baptism brings, in chapters 7 and 8.

Dying and Rising in Baptism: Romans 6 and Colossians 2

God brings sinners into death, Paul reported, by joining them in Baptism to Christ's death. He buries sinners in Christ's tomb, the only place in his universe where he no longer looks. Then he raises up these sinners to new life as his children. The old self is crucified in Baptism by God's Word, and in this death that Christ shares with us, we die to sin and are thus liberated from it. Through this baptismal death and the resurrection, we have new life. The "with him" of the believer's dying to sin and rising to new life in Romans 6 begins a theme that Paul used to conclude this section on the Christian life in Rom. 8:17. There he returned to that theme of being "with Christ" as he spelled out what baptismal incorporation into Christ would mean for the Christian: becoming an heir with Christ, suffering with Christ, being glorified with Christ.

Paul explained the Christian life in these terms to the Colossians as well. In this epistle, too, Baptism occupies the key position between God's action in Christ (1:11–20; 2:9–10) and the life Christians lead, raised to new life in Christ (2:16–4:6). In Col. 2:11–15 he wrote of the new circumcision, which incorporated God's elect into his family. The old circumcision brought Israelites into God's people (Gen. 17:9–14; Lev. 12:3). The new circumcision, Baptism, has taken place with the death and burial of the "body of flesh" (Col. 2:11 RSV), the sinful person, as God canceled the bill of indictment by nailing it to Christ's cross. New life comes to those whom Christ freed from death as he rose from death to disarm principalities and powers, making public sport of them as he led them in a triumphal victory procession. Thus raised with Christ, through God's baptismal action that placed us in death and then hid our true life in Christ (3:1–3), believers live in the shadow of their baptismal death and resurrection, experiencing death to immorality and the assumption of a godly life (3:5–11, 12–17).

New Birth in Baptism: John 3 and Titus 3

Baptism is a matter of death and life, according to Paul. God acts in Baptism. God accepts sinners as his own through this Word of life that he joins with water. God commits himself to those whom he has chosen to make his own through this gift of new life. Baptism is a preenactment of Judgment Day, where God puts sinners to death. Baptism is a reenactment of Creation Day, where God brings us to life through Christ's resurrection. In Baptism he delivers to us the goodness and lovingkindness that he revealed in sending Jesus to save *us*. For his restoration of life is not based upon our doing the right thing, but on the basis of his doing the right thing.

He has acted on the basis of his mercy alone. That mercy has come into our lives through the "washing of rebirth and renewal"— of re-creation—through the Holy Spirit, as it is called in Titus 3:5, a phrase early Christians could only have understood as a reference to Baptism. That washing of re-creation is poured out upon us through Jesus Christ, our Savior, the one into whose death and resurrection we are incorporated through this washing. We were dead in the foolishness and disobedience of sin, led astray into passions, pleasures, malice, envy, and hatred. The washing, God's Word and the water together, have given us new life. It justifies us— it makes us righteous—in God's sight and therefore makes us heirs in the sure hope of eternal life (Titus 3:4–7).

That life begins with the action of God in water and the Holy Spirit, as Jesus told Nicodemus (John 3:1–15). Whether John 3:3 is translated "unless one is born again" or "born from above" makes little difference. It is clear that Jesus was insisting on a new birth for those who are dead in trespasses and sin, and that new birth comes from above, from God. Jesus emphasized the mystery of how the Holy Spirit works to bring new life: as difficult as it is to chart the wind or master it, he said, so impossible is it to harness the Spirit's power. But the Spirit comes through the Word. God uses the Word as his instrument for creating all things. He uses the Word to re-create those who have lost true human life by turning their backs on the Author of Life. He combines that Word with water, and Baptism becomes the watersack from which new life emerges, as those who were dead in sin are born anew, as God gives new life from above. Only in this way can one enter God's kingdom; only in this way can God's children become members of his family (John 3:5).

By calling this return to his realm "new birth," Christ emphasized that new life is God's gift; it is not earned or won by the child of God. Neither our consent nor our contribution was necessary—

or possible—for our physical birth from our mother's womb. Likewise, our consent or contribution is neither necessary nor possible for our being turned from sin to new life in Christ. Birth, or life, is pure gift. Salvation in Christ is pure gift.

No precise equivalent of Baptism is found in the Old Testament, although circumcision and ceremonial washings foreshadow it in part and in different ways. Paul compared Baptism to circumcision (Col. 2:11), the rite by which God incorporated infant boys into his people. But circumcision did not employ water. Ceremonial washings had become a part of Jewish ritual, but these "baptisms" required repetition and carried no promise from God with them. The baptism of John the Baptist stems from this Jewish custom. The Scriptures do not clearly spell out the relationship between John's baptism and that Baptism Jesus inaugurated through his disciples (John 3:22; 4:2), nor do they define the precise nature of John's baptism. It was a baptism "of repentance for the forgiveness of sins" (Mark 1:4; Luke 3:3). John's baptism served to point the way to Jesus, and it, like him, moved offstage when Jesus arrived (John 1:29–34).

The Baptism Jesus gave to his disciples saves because it is an instrument of God's saving power, his tool, which re-creates. God has chosen human language and water, combined in this sacrament, to be the means by which he crucifies sinners and raises them up to new life. The richness of his grace has provided this form of the Word along with others to provide life.

Cleansing in Baptism

The church has often emphasized the cleansing nature of this washing of regeneration. Fouled with sins of all kinds, the Corinthian Christians were then "washed . . . sanctified . . . justified in the name of the Lord Jesus Christ and by the Spirit of our God" (1 Cor. 6:11). Christ demonstrated his love for his church by cleansing her "by the washing with water through the Word" (Eph. 5:26).

But more significantly the New Testament focuses on water's deadly destructive power visited upon the sinner and its nutritive, life-giving power, which raises up the children of God to new life (Rom. 6:3–11; Col. 2:11–15; John 3:3–6; Titus 3:3–6). Neither water nor the Word can stand alone here. God has joined them together. The Enlightenment recaptured some of the spiritualism of ancient

Platonism, and some of its adherents practiced a "baptism" of rose petals; that was no Baptism. Some Christians use "holy water" as a religious symbol apart from God's Word; that is not Baptism, either. You cannot have one without the other and have the sacrament of Baptism.

Making Disciples through Baptism: Matthew 28

According to Christ's command in Matt. 28:18–20, the church baptizes in the name of the holy Trinity, Father, Son, and Holy Spirit. Baptisms have taken place in the name of Christ, but there is no reason to depart from the words of Christ in his commissioning of the church to make disciples through Baptism. For we receive our names, and our new identities as God's children, from him whose name is God: Father, Son, and Holy Spirit. We are incorporated into Christ's death and resurrection, and thereby into the Father's family, as the Holy Spirit effects his regenerating and renewing work in Baptism. We confess the entire work of God when we baptize in the name of Father, Son, and Holy Spirit.

Water and Word do not work together in some magical process, however. God works with us as the creatures whom he has made. God's Word—whether it comes initially in baptismal form, or in written form, or in oral form—re-reates us as the human creatures we are. It transforms us from deadly sinful beings into living trusting creatures. It transforms us as the people God made, with all the psychological characteristics at work in us as God effects this transformation. We do not know what that means for the psychological processes of the infant, to whom God gives the gift of life as he establishes the baptismal relationship. We do know that as the Word embraces the adult, it bestows the gift of faith as the Holy Spirit moves mind and heart to respond to God's accepting us as his own and committing himself to us. Thus, for adults, the biblical writers connect Baptism with the psychological experience of being turned away from sin and being turned toward God, that is, with repentance (Acts 2:38).

Faith stands at the heart of human existence, as we have shown above. Thus, Baptism's re-creation of the sinner into a child of God can never be separated from faith. But the psychological aspects of faith do not exhaust what it means for us to be in relationship with

God. When we sleep or are in a coma, when our mental capacities are undeveloped—as in infants—or wear out—as in the senile—God still maintains the relationship he has established through his baptismal Word, whether we can respond or not. He has turned us toward himself and will never let us go. His Word is certain, for it establishes reality.

Baptized into Christ's Body, the Church

God turns us toward himself in Baptism. He brings us into his family. His baptismal action establishes the basis of our relationship with all the other people in the body of Christ, the church. God calls his followers through other followers, whom he commands to be on their way to "make disciples" (Matt. 28:18–20).

As he discussed how Christians live together, Paul reminded the Corinthians that they function together with each other, since they are like members of the same body because they belong to Christ. "For we were all baptized by one Spirit into one body—whether Jews or Greeks, slave or free—and we were all given the one Spirit to drink [through Baptism]" (1 Cor. 12:13). Believers live united by the Holy Spirit in the bond of peace, for the Holy Spirit has created this one body, calling believers to a common hope under a common Lord, in a common faith, on the basis of a common Baptism, the gift of the common God and Father of us all (Eph. 4:4–6). Because of Baptism believers are family, the family of God.

Putting on Christ

Like any good parent, God is concerned about clothing his children. The children of God, baptized into Christ, have been "dressed" in him. That makes them equal in God's sight. He no longer takes our sin into consideration as he looks at us, nor does he take our earthly characteristics into account. Among his people it does not count in his reckoning whether we are Jew or Greek, slave or free, male or female. We who have been baptized into him are one in Christ Jesus (Gal. 3:26–29).

God sees us through Christ-colored glasses. In the vertical relationship his Word has killed us as sinners—stripped us of our torn and tattered garments of sin—and buried us in Christ's tomb.

His Word of resurrection in Christ has brought us into a new existence before him in the new clothes of Jesus' innocence and righteousness. We are as holy and as innocent as Christ in the Father's presence. We are his perfect children, because he has said so. His pledge to us in our Baptisms clears our conscience completely. At the same time we still experience the ravages of sinfulness in our daily lives. In our horizontal relationships we still encounter temptation, and we still succumb. Baptism initiates a lifelong process of dying to the habits of hell and rising to the habits of heaven in the daily struggle against the sin that destroys our humanity.

Recalling God's baptismal promise to be our God and to hold us as his children strengthens us for that process, that struggle. Paul described the process in Colossians. Having been buried and raised with Christ (2:12), believers seek the things that are above and therefore put to death immorality, impurity, passion, evil desire, and covetousness, which is idolatry (3:1–5). Dressed up in a new nature, having shed the old through this baptismal death and resurrection, believers experience God's renewal of their lives according to the image of the Creator (3:9–10). We are therefore clothed in godly characteristics, compassion, kindness, humility, meekness, patience, and all the other attitudes and actions that Christ has bestowed upon those whom he has raised up with himself (3:12–17). For he has raised us up to newness of life (Rom. 6:4). "These two parts [of Baptism], being dipped under the water and emerging from it, indicate the power and effect of Baptism, which is simply the slaying of the old Adam and the resurrection of the new man, both of which actions must continue in us our whole life long."[2]

The Abuse of God's Baptismal Grace

Those who cannot grasp the biblical teaching on Baptism will sometimes ask, "What about the abuse of Baptism by those who claim that they can do whatever they please because they have God's promise in Baptism?" The question is much larger: What about the abuse of God's grace by those who claim that they can "sin all the more" because God's grace covers their sin? Paul had an answer. He had discussed God's free gift of life and salvation in the 3d, 4th, and 5th chapters of Romans. The extravagant goodness of God is not depicted more clearly anywhere in Scripture. Inevitably, Paul knew, someone would raise the question, "Why then shouldn't I go on sinning so that grace may grow even larger?" His answer to that question is "Baptism!" It does not make sense—it is not possible!—Paul told the Romans, to go on sinning because Baptism has rendered God's verdict on our sin and has transformed our identity from sinner to child of God (Rom. 6:1–3).

It could be said that the Gospel of God's grace—expressed, among other ways, in Baptism—is defenseless against the sinner. But, of course, this defenseless Gospel is the very power of God for salvation. When others ask about the significance of their Baptism for their daily life, believers ask why they want to know. To those who say, "My Baptism permits me to sin without fear," the proper division of Law and Gospel leads us to reply, "Your Baptism leads to death as a sinner. You are rejecting God's Word for you in your Baptism when you sin." God's promise in Baptism to be our God and to have us as his children is, of course, ever valid because it is God's re-creative Word. His commitment to us remains firm. But it is a word of Gospel, and thus it cannot be understood by those who want to live by their own devices, that is, in the realm of Law. Paul answers our dilemma of the abuse of Baptism by returning us to what God says about his powerful Word at work in Baptism.

Frustrating as it may sometimes be, we can do no better than to rely on the crushing power of the Law, also in Baptism, to meet the desire of the sinner who wants a license to sin instead of wanting the joy of being God's child. For when God came to bury us as sinners and to raise us up new in his own sight, he came with the power the Holy Spirit employs day by day to bury us as sinners in the sight of those around us and to present us to our acquaintances as newborn loving children of God.

Therefore, as they experience the action of Law and Gospel in their lives, believers are brought back to their Baptisms. They die again, and they rise again as they confess their sins and receive absolution, as they acknowledge their sinfulness and trust in God's forgiveness day after day. The entire life of the Christian is a life of repentance, of the Spirit's repetition of his baptismal action.

The Mode of Baptism

Christians have sometimes disagreed among themselves about the manner in which Baptism is to be performed. Some have insisted that the Greek word for baptizing meant "to dip," and that the baptized should therefore be "immersed" in the water of Baptism. It is true that the original meaning of the Greek verb *baptizo* involved "dipping" or "immersing." But by the time of Christ the word was used much more generally for any application of water. For instance, tables were "baptized" when they were wiped off with a wet cloth. The kind of washing that the Pharisees expected Christ would do before dinner did not involve immersion of his entire body (Luke 11:38), but there the word *baptize* is used for the usual "washing your hands" of Jewish daily life.[3]

The mode of the application of the water is not the important thing. God's Word with the water is. Immersion reminds us more powerfully of our burial with Christ. Pouring water over the forehead suffices, however. Water and the Word together save.

Infant Baptism

Because some Christians do not view Baptism as God's action, an event in which he is working, but rather see it as a human response to God, they do not believe that infants should be baptized. However, the overwhelming majority of believers throughout church history have baptized infants, for good, biblical reasons.

In Baptism God Accepts His Children and Commits Himself to Them

First of all, Baptism is not merely a human rite, a human commitment to God, a human response to his Word in other forms. Baptism brings the re-creating Word of God and all the power of his Gospel to the sinner who is being baptized. God has selected elements of his created order to use as instruments in his saving action in behalf of fallen sinners. He chose human flesh when he became Jesus of Nazareth, and through his incarnation he has saved us. He chose human language as the means by which to pronounce the good news of salvation upon us. He has chosen us to use that human language of the Gospel to bring one another into faith and the family of God. He has placed that human language together with bread, which carries his body, and wine, which carries his blood, for the forgiveness of our sins. He combines that Gospel with water in re-creating us through his baptismal action. Therefore, there is no reason not to interpret literally what we read in 1 Peter 3:21, or Rom. 6:3–11. Baptism actually saves. God actually buries us as sinners in Baptism, and from his perspective—the perspective from which reality is determined—he raises us to a new life, a new existence in Christ through Baptism.

Infants Need the Gift of Life

Second, children need to be brought into God's family. They are infected with sin from conception (Ps. 51:5), and their mortality proves that they receive the wages of sin (Rom. 6:23). Although passages such as Matt. 18:3 or Luke 18:15–17 do not speak directly of Baptism, the words of Jesus that we must become like little children to enter the kingdom of God do state his expectations clearly. Not adult achievement or commitment but the passive reception of newborn infants marks our passage into God's kingdom. Its doors open for those who enter through the baptismal womb (John 3:3–5). In Baptism God establishes a relationship with children that saves (1 Peter 3:21) without requiring the psychological activity—even though psychological activity is part and parcel of adult response to God's action. He buries and resurrects those whom he has chosen to bring into his family through Baptism because he loves them, not because they are able to perform acts of acceptance or commitment. Important as such human responses are for the adult faith, his acceptance of us and his commitment to us dwarf their importance—at the same time they make these human responses possible.

Evidence for Infant Baptism
in Scripture and the Early Church

Most Christians have believed that infants are naturally included in the "all nations" of Matt. 28:19 or the "family" of the jailer of Philippi, in which most certainly infants were present (Acts 16:33). Those whose presuppositions separate them from this biblical way of thinking will reinterpret these passages to exclude infants. Argument over the interpretation of these passages will avail little so long as one presumes that Baptism is fundamentally a human action and that infants do not need to have a relationship with God established through Baptism.

Likewise, the evidence from the practice of the early church is open to some variation in interpretation.[4] The charge against the early Christians that they practiced infanticide strongly suggests that pagan neighbors heard them talking about the deaths of their infants in Baptism. Paul's comparison of Baptism with circumcision, the rite exercised upon infant males to bring them into the people of Israel, suggests strongly that the church was practicing Baptism at the same time as the Jews practiced circumcision (Col. 2:11).

Infant Faith

Indeed, infants do not express a "faith" in the same way in which adults do. We know relatively little about their cognitive capacity, a bit more about their strength of will. Recent studies seem to indicate that there is more memory and understanding present in infants than earlier investigators had recognized. But the "problem" of infant faith cannot be solved by trying to claim that the relationship of the infant with God is psychologically identifiable with that of the adult. For that focuses on the less important side of the relationship. God has commanded Baptism. God acts in Baptism. God kills and makes alive in Baptism. He does that to infants and adults alike. For he is Lord of death and life.

The Church's Use of Baptism

God exercises his lordship through his people. His people designate leaders, pastors, who normally carry out their functions on their behalf. So it is with Baptism. Pastors baptize, and normally and ideally they baptize within a worship service. For the child is being joined not only to the body of Christ's death and resurrection but also to the body of his church. The act takes place most suitably in the midst of the congregation of that body. There is nothing invalid about Baptisms that take place outside worship services. But the people of God like to be there when a newborn enters the family. Because of the critical nature of Baptism for the conveying of God's grace, lay people may baptize in emergencies. For the validity of

Baptism hinges on the Word of God, not on the person who speaks it.

Since the early church, Christians have chosen sponsors for those who are baptized. Sponsors aid baptized believers in the Christian life that lies before them. Adult converts who are baptized need sponsors as badly as do infants, perhaps more so, in our society. Sponsors serve as more than witnesses to the Baptism. They pledge themselves to pray for the baptized and to work for the baptized's growth in faith in Christ and in godly living. If families cannot find those who can honestly pledge themselves to work for the edification of the baptized, they should not call them baptismal sponsors but only witnesses. Sponsors share the confession of faith into which the child is being baptized.

Baptisms must involve the combination of water applied to the body of the baptized along with the Word, summarized in the words, "I baptize you in the name of the Father and of the Son and of the Holy Spirit." Other customs that enhance the conveying of the Gospel to the assembled congregation and to the baptized and their families rightly adorn the baptismal service. Particular note should be made of the "rebirthday" within the calendar of the church year. You might, for instance, select the third Sunday of Easter (rather than, say, April 27) to celebrate Baptism. Tying Baptism to the specific date within the church year on which the individual was baptized is a useful device in remembering both the Baptism and the church's own perception of time.

Baptism is worth remembering. There God takes the dust of a person born in sin and breathes new life into this child of his through water and the Word. Those who are born dead in trespasses and sin come to life as the children of God, members of his baptized family.

Notes for Chapter XIII

1. Albrecht Oepke, "baptō, baptizō," Theological Dictionary of the New Testament, vol. 1, ed. Gerhard Kittel, trans. and ed. Geoffrey W. Bromiley (Grand Rapids: Eerdmans, 1964), 529–46. See also Edmund Schlink, The Doctrine of Baptism, trans. Herbert J. A. Bouman (Saint Louis: Concordia, 1972).
2. Large Catechism, Baptism, 65, The Book of Concord, trans. and ed. Theodore G. Tappert (Philadelphia: Fortress, 1959), 444–45.

3. Oepke, 530.
4. Two views of the evidence are presented in Joachim Jeremias, *Infant Baptism in the First Four Centuries,* trans. David Cairns (Philadelphia: Westminster, 1962); and Kurt Aland, *Did the Early Church Baptize Infants?* (Philadelphia: Westminster, 1963); with Jeremias' reply to Aland in *The Origins of Infant Baptism,* trans. Dorothea M. Barton (Naperville: Allenson, 1963).

Chapter XIV

The Lord's Supper

People need to eat. People love to eat. Meals do much more than sustain life. They do that, to be sure, but they also provide the occasion for families to feel at home with one another. They serve as expressions of thankfulness and celebration. God loves us, his children, so much that he has provided us with his life-giving Word in the setting of a meal. God not only comes to give us new birth through the most common element of life in his creation, water, joined to his Word. He also feeds us, the most common event in human life, by joining his Word to bread, which carries the human body of Christ, and to wine, which carries his blood. His love embraces us as his Word reaches into our lives in all its various forms.

The Names of the Supper

Like the meals of daily life, the Lord's meal has occupied a central place in the lives of his people throughout most of Christian history. The meal is called by several names. It is his meal, and so believers have called it "the Lord's Supper." There he is both chef and entree. He prepares the supper, and he is the supper. Because the church celebrates this meal at the altar, it is also called the "Sacrament of the Altar." It is often called "Holy Communion," for there are three kinds of "unity" or "union" that take place in this feast. There is the union of bread with body and of wine with blood, as Saint Paul mentioned in 1 Cor. 10:16. There is the union of Christ with his people as he gives them his body and blood (Matt. 26:26–28). This meal also unites Christ's people with one another, one body in one loaf (1 Cor. 10:17).

Christ called his meal a new *diathēkē*.[1] This Greek word can mean "covenant," or "last will and testament." If the word is understood as covenant, it must be understood as the kind of covenant that is given by the king to his vassals. The king offers; the king imposes. The covenant is his gift to vassals who have no claim on his protection and rule. Christ's Supper is likewise pure gift. We do not bring the groceries for him to prepare. He and he alone gives. He gives the relationship that arises from his death and resurrection, as it is applied to our lives. In that sense there is the coming together of two people here. But one of them gives and the other receives. Thus, it is better to think of the Lord's Supper as a last will and testament. Here Jesus bestows all his blessings, the blessing of forgiveness and new life, the blessing of his presence, upon his people.

The term *Eucharist* is also used in connection with the Lord's Supper. The term comes from the Greek word for "thanksgiving." Because the Lord acts in the Lord's Supper, giving us the meal, and with it forgiveness and life, the Supper itself cannot be called the Eucharist. Only the response of God's people in the liturgy, which surrounds the Supper, is thanksgiving. God's gift is sacrament.

The church has linked Baptism and the Lord's Supper in the category of "sacrament." They bear many similarities, beyond the basic definition of a means that Christ has commanded to convey forgiveness and life through the joining of Word and physical element. They both bring God's children into death as sinners and into new life through Christ's resurrection. They both join us to the other members of Christ's body, the church. They both bring God's Judgment Day into the midst of this realm of existence, and they both repeat his "let there be life" from Creation as they create life for us in the midst of the deadly sinfulness that besets us.

But the category of sacrament does not impose upon these two sacraments complete uniformity. New birth is not repeated; the meal is. Gustaf Wingren suggested an explanation for this on the basis of parallels from the Old Testament and from daily life. The children of Israel crossed through the waters of the sea but once; they repeated the Passover meal again and again. We experience physical birth but once; we eat each day.[2]

The Elements of the Supper

The meal consists of bread and wine. Christ used unleavened bread as he instituted the Supper because he did so during the Passover celebration, "the day of Unleavened Bread" (Luke 22:7). After that festival season had passed, the disciples continued to use bread, even when it was not unleavened. Christ used the "fruit of the vine" (Matt. 26:29), a term used, in a culture without refrigeration and preservatives, for grape juice in the only possible form in which it could be found within minutes of picking the grapes—wine.[3]

Christians must anchor their use of the Supper in the historical revelation of our God. He came as a Jew some two thousand years ago, in a historical situation that led him to be crucified under Pontius Pilate's administration. He used bread, and he used the fruit of the vine. Substitutes generalize and abstract Christ's specific historic action, and thus they pull the fact of God's intervention into history out of history. Cookies and soda pop do not make a sacrament. The attempt to be relevant with such substitutes usually narrows the frame of reference for God's historic action in behalf of his people. On the other hand, specific forms of bread and the fruit of the vine should not become legalistic criteria for a valid sacrament. Only the Word of the Lord makes the Supper God's instrument of forgiveness and new life.

The Real Presence of the Body and Blood of Christ in the Supper

In his Supper Jesus gives us his body and his blood.[4] For most of the history of the church, in most parts of the world, Christians have simply believed the words of the Lord when he said, "This is my body," and "This is my blood." But not all Christians agree how his body and blood are present in the bread and wine of the meal. Indeed, not all Christians agree *that* his body and blood are present in that bread and wine.

Presuppositions for the Real Presence

Lutherans define the presence of Christ's body and blood in the Lord's Supper on the basis of four presuppositions.

The Literal Interpretation of the Words of Institution. First, we believe that the Words of Institution, "This is my body," and "This is my blood," should be interpreted literally. We do not believe that all passages in Scripture should be interpreted literally. God uses a variety of genres and figures of speech in conveying his Word to us. But like most human language the language of the biblical writers should be understood literally unless there are compelling reasons for interpreting them otherwise. It is true: we do not have other instances in which bread and human flesh come together; human blood does not normally come in the form of wine. It is also true: scientifically, with a chemical analysis in the laboratory, we cannot establish the presence of human cells in the bread or the wine. Christ's words here cannot be proven empirically, nor do they make sense on the basis of our experience or logic. Nonetheless, there is no compelling reason to submit the gift of the Lord to these criteria. He who combined his Godness with his humanness is certainly able to combine his body with bread and his blood with wine. There is no compelling reason not to take him at his word in the Words of Institution. Although we cannot understand how Christ's human body can be conveyed by the bread of the Supper, we believe that God can do this. Here human reason fails us, and faith clings to the mystery of God's love and presence in the bread and wine.

God Works through Selected Elements of His Created Order. Second, we presume that God does convey his saving power through selected elements of the created order. We presume that he has chosen bread and wine and body and blood to be linked with his forgiving, re-creating Word in the Sacrament of the Altar. Some Christians have traded a biblical point of view for a spiritualistic presupposition from ancient Greek thought. This spiritualistic point of view insists that the finite—the earthly and material creation of God—is not capable of bearing the infinite power and presence of God. The biblical writers believed that God had selected certain elements of the created order to convey his power. They believed that the infinite God could bear the earthly and material in his hand as instruments through which he delivers his power to forgive and restore life. He chose human flesh in his incarnation to effect salvation. He chose human language as the medium of his good news of deliverance from sin. In similar fashion he chose bread-body and wine-blood as elements that could be combined with his Word to deliver forgiveness and life to his people.

The Communication of Christ's Attributes. Third, Lutherans presuppose that the characteristics of Christ's human nature are shared with the characteristics of his divine nature in the person of the God-man. Therefore, we presume that this communication

231

of attributes between the two natures makes it possible for the human nature's body and blood to be present wherever and in whatever form God wills.[5] Christ's human nature and his divine nature continue to exist, but they do not exist apart from each other. Therefore, as they function together in the mystery of the personal union that makes him the person he is, they share attributes. As God he is able to be present in specific ways wherever he wishes to be present. Christ's body and blood are not present in all bread and wine, even though he is present as provider whenever people consume bread and wine and all food and drink. But in a special mysterious way he places his bodily presence in the blood and wine of the Sacrament of the Altar, as it is joined by the Word.

The Mystery of the Real Presence. Fourth, Lutherans presume that God's action through his Word in the Sacrament is a mystery. Neither human reason nor scientific investigation will ever penetrate this mystery of his love.

The Definition of the Real Presence

Sacramental Presence. Therefore, on the basis of these presuppositions, Lutherans define the real presence of Christ's body and blood in the bread and wine of the Lord's Supper by calling it a sacramental presence. The word *sacrament* in Latin is used to refer to a mystery. The sacramental presence of our Lord's body and blood is, therefore, something that cannot be explained in terms of human physics or chemistry or even metaphysics. Human reason cannot get its grasp around the mystery. "Sacramental presence" means, "His body and blood are here in the elements of bread and wine. We take him at his word even though we cannot explain the presence."

Some Lutherans have used the phrase "in, with, and under" to define the relationship of body to bread, blood to wine. Luther said it most simply and straightforwardly in the Smalcald Articles when he wrote, "The bread and wine in the Supper are the true body and blood of Christ."[6] This sacramental presence indicates that God is at work in the Supper. He has instituted it for his saving purposes. "The body and blood of Christ are present for us in the supper because his incarnation, death, and resurrection have made permanent alteration in the structure of reality."[7] He has altered our existence as sinners decisively; as he does so, he is able and has chosen to be present with us in his human body in the bread and in his human blood in the wine.

Oral Partaking. The second phrase Lutherans use to define the real presence of Christ's body and blood in the Lord's Supper is "oral partaking." We receive Christ's body and blood through the mouth, not in some transaction between God and the soul. His body and blood move across our tongues as we ingest the body in the bread and the blood in the wine of the Supper.

Partaking by the Ungodly or the Unworthy. Third, we define the real presence by confessing that his presence depends on the Word of the Lord, not on the faith of the person who receives the Supper. Even unbelievers receive Christ's body and blood when they partake of the Supper even though they do not receive its benefits apart from faith. We call that reception by the ungodly or unworthy. The presence of Christ's body and blood does not depend on us. It depends on God's Word.

Paul wrote in 1 Cor. 10:16 that the cup of blessing in the Sacrament—and this means the wine, which the cup holds—participates, or has communion with, the blood of Christ. The bread of the Sacrament participates, or has communion with, the body of Christ. In bread and wine Christ comes to us with his body and blood, as his Word works its forgiving and re-creating power upon us.

Alternate Views of the Real Presence

There are other views of the Real Presence within Christendom. Luther accepted the medieval catholic affirmation of the Real Presence, but he objected to its attempt to explain how the Real Presence is possible. Medieval teaching affirmed the doctrine of the Real Presence but tried to explain it in terms of the physics of Aristotle, the physics taught in the schools of Luther's time. Aristotle had taught that everything in this world had an inner substance, which determined its basic nature, and also had accidents, which give the specific individual item its own characteristics. According to this system of thought, all chairs are chairs because they have the inner substance of "chairness." Each individual chair has the accidents of wood or plastic or metal, of specific colors and shapes, etc. Medieval theologians wanted to explain the mystery of Christ's presence. They said that the substance of the sacramental bread and wine are replaced by the substances of Christ's body and blood even though the outward accidents of bread and wine remain. They called this process "transubstantiation." Luther believed that the presence of Christ is a mystery, which ought not be explained. He believed that trying to explain it exalts the human mind above the word of the Lord. He wished to accept the mystery of the presence of Christ's body and blood in faith.

Consubstantiation. Therefore, it is wrong to suggest that Luther taught "consubstantiation," a view held by a few medieval theologians. That view states that the substances of both Christ's body and the bread, of both Christ's blood and the wine, are present in the Supper by virtue of the power of God's Word. That view still uses Aristotelian physics to try to explain the presence, and Luther insisted it remain a mystery, outside the mastery of human reason.

Symbolic Understanding. Some Christians reject the possibility of Christ's actual body and blood being present in the bread and wine. In the Reformation era the Swiss reformer Ulrich Zwingli represented this view. Although he moved toward a concept of the "spiritual presence" of Christ toward the end of his life, for much of the preceding decade he had argued with Luther over the Real Presence. He had received an education that framed his thought with Platonic conceptions of reality. Therefore, he believed that earthly elements could only point to—symbolize—the heavenly reality. He thus taught that the bread and the wine only symbolize what Christ had done in the past. He separated God's action on the cross from his delivery of the benefits of Christ's death and resurrection through his Word. Therefore, at most the Supper recalls the sacrifice on the cross.

Spiritual Presence. Another sixteenth-century Swiss reformer, John Calvin, taught that Christ is spiritually present in the Sacrament. According to Calvin, Christian souls partake of Christ as their bodies receive the bread and wine. Here, too, the influence of the spiritualizing presuppositions of Platonic philosophy reveal themselves. The soul operates at a heavenly level while the body consumes the merely earthly elements. Although closer in some respects to Luther's view than was Zwingli's symbolic definition of the Supper, Calvin's view nonetheless was determined by his Platonic presupposition that God's power for salvation cannot come through the earthly, material elements.

It is important to note that speaking of the "presence of Christ" is insufficient to convey the entire biblical concept of what God is doing for his people in the Lord's Supper. It is necessary to speak of the "presence of Christ's body and blood" to convey fully what the Lord has told us of his approach to us in his meal.

Receptionism or Consecrationism

Some North American Lutherans have recently focused on whether the bread and the wine become the body and blood of the Lord when the Words of Institution are spoken to consecrate the elements or when the elements are received by the communicant. The Scriptures do not define the process of God's work in this regard, and the church does well not to press the issue.

Behind each position lie certain valid concerns. In the sixteenth century Lutherans reacted against medieval scholastic arguments over the properties of the leftover elements of the sacrament. Thus, many favored the "receptionist" view. Others were concerned to preserve the focus on the power of God's Word and favored the "consecrationist" view. Still others wisely thought such questions were best left unspecified since the Scriptures do not speak directly to them. Indeed, some find that the implications of what the Scriptures do say lead them to one conclusion or the other. They should maintain their defense of biblical teaching without false reproach to those who agree with them on biblical teaching but differ from them in drawing or not drawing specific implications from it.

Broken and Shed for You

For the Forgiveness of Sin

In his Supper Christ serves his people his own body and blood. In so doing he joins them to himself, to his own death and to his own resurrection. He gives us there the body that he gave into death for us on the cross. He gives us there the blood that was poured out for the forgiveness of sins (Matt. 26:28). God views us as his innocent

235

and beloved children as we receive his Son's body and blood. God sees us pass out of existence as sinners once again when we receive this body. In receiving the blood that was poured out on Calvary in our behalf, we sinners are received into the tomb into which his lifeless body was placed. Into that tomb God will not look. But this body and blood belong to the one who has risen from the dead. So, as we receive his body and blood in his Supper, we also receive the gift of life. He takes away our sins and hides them in his tomb, so that we can join in the celebration at his Father's table. We join in his meal as children of God, raised to newness of life through the power of his Word. That Word comes here with bread-body and wine-blood to transform us from sinners into children of God.

Luther sharply rejected the popular medieval conception that Christ's sacrifice was somehow repeated in the Supper. Connected with that view was the popular belief that somehow human merit became involved as God's priest—if not his people—performed this repetition of the sacrifice. Luther insisted that the Supper is pure gift—no human contribution to its giving of death and new life at all. Indeed, the Lord's Supper, as every other form of God's re-creating Word, does bridge the gap between the historical sacrifice of Christ on the cross and his resurrection from the crypt. That sacrifice and resurrection was "not just a once-upon-a-time but a once-for-all event," and it therefore "must bring with it some fundamental and permanent alterations."[8]

Many contemporary Roman Catholic teachers have shifted from viewing the Mass as a repetition to viewing it as a re-presentation of Christ's sacrifice. Nevertheless, if they focus on human roles in the celebration of the Sacrament, they miss the point Luther made. Luther objected to any view of what happens in the celebration of the Sacrament as a human opportunity for contribution. The Lord's Supper effects the death of every human pretension and claim of activity in rebirth. It effects life without any contribution coming from the baby. It feeds the newborn children of God without sending them first into the field to do some harvesting.[9]

The Supper feeds believers; it feeds their faith. Luther also rejected the popular misrepresentation of the medieval theological maxim that the sacraments work *ex opere operato*. That phrase was designed to teach that the sacraments work on the basis of the Word, not on the basis of some other factor in the humans who are performing the sacramental action or receiving its benefit. By Luther's time, many Christians believed that it meant that faith played no necessary role in the beneficial reception of the sacrament. God's Word, Luther insisted, works on its own power, without depending on human contribution or participation. But it works faith. God speaks for no other purpose than to bring fallen sinners into a relationship of trust and love with him once again.

He hosts the Supper only so that he might draw back into his own family those who have become disoriented by trusting in false gods. Family means faith. The Supper cultivates trust in God. The Word of the Lord, with the bread-body and the wine-blood, does not work "magically" to place some charm or amulet upon the recipient. It engages us in conversation. It pronounces us dead as sinners and alive in Christ. It maintains and sustains the relationship a loving Father wants to have with his children. No magic: just the good relationship of parent and child together enjoying the meal the parent has paid for and prepared.

Faith does not make Christ's body and blood present in the Sacrament, any more than the infant's appetite makes the oatmeal present in the dish. God does create faith so that we may receive the benefits of the meal, however, just as the parent's love must move the child to open wide and receive—rather than spit out—the breakfast. In the Supper God calls on us to trust him. We trust him there for the forgiveness of our sins and the gift of new life. We trust the way he has chosen to act. Even if it seems out of the ordinary, this is one way that he has chosen to convey the promise of life to us. So unpretentiously he approaches us with the assurance of forgiveness and life.

Thus, faith leaps to his table. Faith knows that receiving Christ's body and blood sustains and uplifts and strengthens. Faith cannot walk away from this table without recognizing how good God is. He has not only given himself into death that we might have life. He has shared that death and life with us. He has done so in several ways, also by coming to feed us with life itself. Believers cannot help but take deep delight in the love of such a Father.

Remembering Christ's Death and Resurrection Together

Approaching the Father's table with and in front of other Christians adds to that delight. In coming to Christ's Supper believers confess their faith and share their confidence in his forgiveness with others. "Whenever you eat this bread and drink this cup, you proclaim the Lord's death until he comes" (1 Cor. 11:26). Just because some Christians see only a memorial meal in the Lord's Supper does not mean that we should ignore this important aspect of the Supper. Together we remember what Jesus has done for us, even as he conveys the benefits of his death and resurrection to us in his meal.

United with Other Believers in One Loaf

Furthermore, we enjoy being linked with one another through this meal. He has made us here to be one loaf (1 Cor. 10:17). Perhaps, quite honestly, we do not always enjoy being linked with those with whom God joins us at his altar. The Supper does make us family not only with the Father but also with his other children. It establishes and reminds us of the unbreakable association God has forged between us and them. Sometimes God brings us to the same table with people we do not like. We learn there to love them because he loves them, even when we do not always like what they are doing. Since he has reconciled us to himself, we know that he has reconciled us to them and them to us as well. Thus, the Supper serves as God's instrument for reconciliation among his people.

Fellowship at Christ's Altar

Because the Supper both symbolizes and effects unity among Christ's people, the church has normally been quite strict about who communes together. From the earliest period of its history the church has used the Lord's Supper as a means of discipline as well as a means of grace.[10] It has refused to let those who are deceiving themselves about the nature of God's Word or of the Christian life believe that there is unity of faith or life where that unity is broken, or even cracked. Therefore, the church "excommunicates" and the church practices the fellowship or communion that draws lines of exclusion as well as inclusion.[11]

Throughout most of its history the church has normally practiced "close" communion, that is, gathering the family of the congregation and those who share its confession of the faith into the Supper's circle and asking those who are not part of the family not to partake. The practice of "open" communion—in which all are freely admitted to the Supper—arose relatively late in Christian history and in those areas in which the doctrine of the real presence of Christ's body and blood, and the significance of the Sacrament in general, were not highly prized. In the early church those who had not yet been baptized were asked to leave the assembly after the sermon, before the reception of the Lord's Supper. This practice of the church reinforces the significance of what God does in the sacraments for his people.

Dress Rehearsal for the Eschatological Banquet

Finally, believers delight in the Supper of the Lord because they recognize it as a dress rehearsal for the eschatological banquet, which will last forever at his heavenly throne (Matt. 8:11). Dressed in Christ through Baptism (Gal. 3:27), we come to celebrate the future as well as the present blessing of his promise. Christ promised that he would drink together with his disciples on "that day when I drink it anew with you in my Father's kingdom" (Matt. 26:29). God's rule, of course, already is breaking in upon us as his death sentence is executed upon us in Baptism and in receiving the body and blood of Calvary's sacrificial victim. God's rule has established itself in his children as he shares with them the body and blood that came back from death to give them life. But the Supper focuses our attention on the completion of God's killing and resurrecting work in our lives. Jesus' picture of heavenly life with God as a banquet (Matt. 8:11) is repeated in the Lord's Supper. We look forward to banqueting as members of his family when dying to sin will no longer be necessary, when life will be confirmed for us forever.

Celebrating Together

Because the Lord's Supper occupies so important a spot in the weekly rhythm of the life of God's people, it is necessary to look at some of the practical aspects of our assembling at God's table.

The Whole Congregation Receives Together

The Lord's Supper gathers God's people together. Therefore, they eat together as a congregation. Although the church has always taken the Supper to those who were ill and infirm and thus unable to join the congregation, it has not deemed the Supper appropriate for private use or for use by small groups within the congregation. The Supper unites the whole congregation and should not be used to "do something special" for a group within it. The church has justly tried to avoid such groupings, which consider their own way of doing things superior to the common, ordinary life of the majority within the congregation. To use the Lord's Supper to reinforce such a party spirit abuses the Lord's invitation.

Thus, the pastor of the congregation is the one who consecrates the elements and leads the Supper of the Lord. In the person of the pastor the unity of the congregation is expressed and observed. Lay assistance in distribution does not violate this principle. Scripture contains no rules or procedures for distribution, and lay people may distribute Christ's blood without offending God's plan for his Supper. The pastor must consecrate and, as the congregation's representative, should admit the communicants to Christ's Table. That ordinarily means that the pastor should distribute Christ's body.

The Consecration of the Elements

Proper consecration requires the proclamation of the Words of Institution. The church has always set them within a liturgy. That liturgy may have a variety of forms. None of these forms is necessary for the proper observation of the Supper.

The elements should be received and disposed of reverently, whether one holds a receptionist or a consecrationist view of the presence of Christ's body and blood in them. In either case, they are vehicles that God uses in a special way. We cheapen the Lord's approach to us through these elements if we treat them casually. Reverent treatment of the elements may vary from congregation to congregation, depending on local perceptions.

Frequency of Communing
and "Worthiness" for Reception

Children like to eat at their parents' table. Not only do they enjoy the food; they enjoy the company. Believers like to come to the Father's table to feast upon the body and blood of their Lord. There they receive sustenance for daily life, and there they enjoy the company of their God and their fellow believers. Much of Christendom throughout history has celebrated the Lord's Supper weekly. Luther believed that people could not be considered Christian if they did not receive the Sacrament at least three times a year,[12] but his church celebrated the Lord's Supper weekly. Many Wittenbergers received the Lord's body and blood each week.

Some Christians fail to do so because the Supper is so strange; it does not fit into their conception of reality. Others feel relatively little need because their sensitivity to their own sinfulness has become dulled. Some do not understand what the Sacrament accomplishes in their lives—that it bestows forgiveness and life, first and foremost, but that it also links us with God and fellow believers in the family circle, and that it builds anticipation and hope as we await the promise of the perfect celebration at God's heavenly table. Some Christians avoid the Lord's Supper because they fear receiving it unworthily.

Worthiness for receiving the Sacrament consists of our recognition that we are unworthy, that we need God's love and forgiveness. Luther suggested that if the devil, the world, and the flesh still threaten to tarnish or take away the joy of our faith, we need the Sacrament. Christ offers it to the hungry, not to the satisfied. It is Christ whose worth is at issue in the Lord's Supper. The meal is planned for those whose worth has disappeared, who need the gift of worth.

Paul insisted that believers examine themselves (1 Cor. 11:28) as they come to the Supper. That examination, Paul continues, includes the recognition of what God is giving in the Sacrament. Those who do not discern the Lord's body receive judgment (1 Cor. 11:29). Although some have suggested that this body is the body of Christ, the church, the context, particularly verse 27, prevents that interpretation. This judgment that we can receive in connection with an unfaithful use of the Lord's Supper is no different than the judgment that falls upon those who hear his Word in a frivolous or apathetic manner.

Because of Paul's command to examine ourselves, the Western church has offered the Lord's Supper only to those who are able to do so. The Eastern church has communed infants as soon as they are baptized. There is no biblical warrant for this practice. Baptism and the Lord's Supper are not to be equated even though the church has placed them both in the category of "sacrament." There has been no general agreement on the proper age for admission to the Lord's Supper. In Luther's own time children began to commune at an earlier age than they normally do today.

"Examination" in preparation for the Lord's Supper recognizes no more and no less than who God is as he comes to us in the Supper and who we are as we receive it. We recognize with joy and thanksgiving that God gives in the Sacrament and that we receive. We recognize that we need the blessings God gives in this meal of life. We recognize that our own unworthiness draws us to the Lord's life-giving body and blood. Believers approach the Lord's Supper craving not only the forgiveness of sins but also the power to live out God's callings in daily life. The spirit of repentance guides us to come to receive death and to be raised to genuine human life once again. At his Supper our God feeds us for living.

Notes for Chapter XIV

1. See, e.g., Luther's interpretation in "A Treatise on the New Testament, That Is, the Holy Mass," *Word and Sacrament: I,* Luther's Works, vol. 35 (Philadelphia: Fortress, 1960), 79–111.

2. Gustaf Wingren, *The Living Word: A Theological Study of Preaching and the Church,* trans. Victor C. Pogue (Philadelphia: Muhlenberg, 1960), 160.

3. No absolute necessity of the interpretation of this phrase as wine is found in Friedrich Büschsel, *"genema," Theological Dictionary of the New Testament,* vol. 1, ed. Gerhard Kittel, trans. and ed. Geoffrey W. Bromiley (Grand Rapids: Eerdmans, 1964), 685.

4. Luther's teaching of the Lord's Supper is presented in Hermann Sasse, *This Is My Body: Luther's Contention for the Real Presence in the Sacrament of the Altar* (Minneapolis: Augsburg, 1959).

5. See ch. VII, pp. 127–134.

6. Smalcald Articles, III:VI, 1, *The Book of Concord,* trans. and ed. Theodore G. Tappert (Philadelphia: Fortress, 1959), 311.

7. Gerhard O. Forde, *Theology Is for Proclamation* (Minneapolis: Fortress, 1990), 176.

8. Ibid.

9. Ibid. 172–73.

10. Werner Elert, *Eucharist and Church Fellowship in the First Four Centuries,* trans. Norman E. Nagel (Saint Louis: Concordia, 1966).

11. See ch. XVI, pp. 265–266.

12. Small Catechism, Preface, 22, *The Book of Concord,* 341.

Chapter XV

The Sanctified Life, or New Obedience

God's Word re-creates sinners into people who live out a new life in Christ. The Holy Spirit moves into believer's lives to make them temples of God, where worship goes on (Rom. 8:9; 1 Cor 3:16; 6:19; 2 Tim. 1:14). Paul can also say that it is Christ who lives in us. Through him our desires to live life apart from God are put to death, and he bestows the power to live free, as God made us to live in Eden (Gal. 2:20). The Holy Spirit empowers Christian living on the basis of the hope we have in Christ (Rom. 15:13; cf. Acts 1:8). This revival of true human living, often called sanctification,[1] takes place through faith. Faith in Jesus Christ grasps a whole new perception of human life and of its Creator.

As we think about the sanctified life, we think about attitudes and actions, about motivation and structure.

Sanctified by Faith

The Holy Spirit brings a new attitude to the believer's mind once he has made Christ its focus. Believers reap and produce the fruit of the Holy Spirit's presence as their minds are turned to the attitudes of love, joy, peace, patience, kindness, goodness, faithfulness, gentleness, and self-control. These attitudes flow in when self-centered passions and desires have been crucified in Christ (Gal. 5:22–24). These products of the Spirit's presence give believers the mind of Christ (Phil. 2:5). This mind produces the fruits of faith, or new obedience, or good works. These are the result of the saving message of salvation in Jesus Christ and the faith it produces (2 Tim. 3:15–17; cf. Eph. 2:10).

This life lived in faith in Christ is often called a life of new obedience. It is new because the old way of life, which turned us inward on ourselves, is put away. We are liberated by Christ's word of forgiveness to "live a new life" (Rom. 6:4). It is a life of obedience because faith now turns its ear to listen to God's Word. Life comes as we are brought out of our deafness to his word of love. We are no longer deaf to his call to live in peace, with him and with fellow human creatures. The Hebrew word *shama'* means "to hear," but it was also used as an expression of the concept of obedience. To hear God is to obey him. Faith, listening once again to the Lord, cannot help but respond with praise in thought, word, and deed.

In the Apology of the Augsburg Confession Philip Melanchthon twice set forth brief explanations of how faith produces works.[2] Too often Lutherans have taken the link between faith and works for granted. Particularly in our age, as conscious of motivation as our society is, we ought to remember that faith does motivate new obedience to God's design for human life in ways that can be analyzed psychologically. To be aware of this can only help our practice of the Christian life. We live out our new life as the psychological and physical beings God created us to be.

Therefore, we understand that trusting in Jesus Christ does change our attitudes in fundamental ways that enable free human action, action determined by selfless love. The fruit of the Spirit is at work in believers, moving them and training them in the practice of horizontal righteousness.

First, faith recognizes God's unfathomable goodness and gives thanks. Thanks takes many forms. It begins with verbal praise and gratitude, in the congregation of God's people and in personal prayer. Thanks then flows over into words of love and deeds of kindness to those around us.

Second, the faith of God's children cannot keep secrets; it is a contradiction in terms to tell a child a secret. As God's children glow in their appreciation of his love, they cannot contain it within themselves. They reflect that love. The secret of God's love bubbles out from within them, not only in words but also in deeds. They share the secret with those around them by touching others' lives with God's kind of care and kindness.

Third, faith has confidence in Christ's providing and protecting presence. Therefore, believers dare to risk what God has given them to serve others. They no longer believe that they have to hang onto material possessions or time or anything else God has given in order to secure their own lives. Faith gives them confidence that God will supply their needs and support them as they carry his love and concern into other people's lives.

Fourth, faith recognizes that God's plan for human life differs significantly from the plans we had made for ourselves when we still had to search for the ultimate source of our identity, security, and meaning on our own. Faith perceives that God has "succeeded" by submitting himself to the evil that afflicts his people and by surrendering and sacrificing himself. God has fleshed out the perfect human life in service and suffering. So faith takes its cue for good living from its Savior and God. Faith submits to the call to service and suffering in self-surrender and self-sacrifice. Therein we find the joy of being God's people.

Motivated in such fashion by faith, believers can live out the Christian life in the midst of the struggle against the call of sin to draw us back into ourselves. Believers struggle to live the cruciform life, arms reached out to others, because they are freed by Christ to live in faith and to live out their faith in him.

That life is permeated by conversation with God. God's children do not speak with him regularly because they believe that their prayer has the power to dictate to him what he must do. They do not pray because they regard prayer as a magic formula to get what they want. Nor do believers dismiss prayer as empty words since God already has made his unchangeable decisions regarding the course of human life. Believers do recognize that their prayer cannot add to God's knowledge since he is omniscient. But they do want to talk with their heavenly Father, and they know he wants to hear from them. So they pray, early and often. Their prayers respond to God's goodness and to human need as his Word engages them and as those around them cry out for help.

The Structure of the Life of New Obedience

As noted above,[3] God has designed human life quite carefully. He has created his human creatures to live in two kinds of relationships (or communities), with himself and with other parts of his creation, above all other human creatures. He created human creatures to exercise the dominion of service under other parts of his creation and to praise and serve him through their care of others.

Called to Serve in Home, Occupation, Society, and Congregation

In the horizontal relationships, with the rest of creation, he has structured four situations for human service. These are the situations of home, occupation, society, and congregation. In each of these situations God has fashioned responsibilities for his human creatures: "response-abilities," which enable his creation to function through human activities. They respond to needs within the communities God has designed for their daily life (Gen. 2:18).

These responsibilities extend God's care and concern and direction into daily life. These responsibilities include our roles, as spouse or parent or child or member of an extended family in family life; as homemaker or worker or foreman or CEO on the job; as neighbor and friend, as voter and taxpayer and member of a political organization in society; as worshiper and witness, and Sunday school teacher or pastor or committee chair or altar guild member in the congregation of God's people. In each of these roles human responsibility takes shape in specific functions, from changing diapers and washing dishes in the home, to distributing campaign brochures or writing legislation in the political part of society.

All human creatures find that life fits into these situations—although some societies combine two situations into one institutional form. But Christians recognize in their responsibilities the calling of God. Therefore, believers regard their responsibilities as "vocations," not just in the occupational realm but in all four situations of human life. God calls his people, as he assigns all human creatures, to be doing his work in loving and caring for the rest of his creation. That is how he works. Luther called us "masks of God," for he stands behind us to take care of the world he has made.

Recognizing this structure does not determine which actions believers will perform in any given instance. The structure reminds us of the general shape of God's plan for human life, and it reminds us that He is Creator and Provider. But within this structure human creatures—and even believers—may disagree among themselves on just how God's love, care, and concern should rightly be demonstrated in a given instance. Believers often disagree on whether one course of action corresponds to God's plan for fruitful life together in the family or whether it contradicts that plan. Different cultures have developed different forms for successful governance of life in the family or in society, and in each society the institutions and customs that shape daily life within each of these situations are often in a state of development and flux. Therefore, believers need to be conscious of how they make decisions on their life together in home, job, community, and congregation.

Virtues

Service to other human creatures is governed by the self-sacrificing model of *agape* love, which Christ enables us to give to others (1 John 4:7–12). This agape is different from a love that shares or seeks its own in loving. Agape is ready to sacrifice itself for the object of its love.[4] In this fullest sense of the word love is the highest of the virtues that God designed for human life (1 Cor. 13:13).

Virtues, the good or excellent attitudes and actions that fulfill the highest human potential in thought and deed, provide another category in which Christians have thought about the Christian life. Ancient pagan philosophers as well thought of the good life in terms of the practice of such skills as prudence, justice, courage, and temperance. To those "natural virtues" Christian theologians added the "theological virtues" of faith, hope, and love. The list may be broadened to include all those attitudes and actions commanded by God, which he designed for the practice of the good human life.[5]

Thinking of virtues in contrast to vices, the perversion of human attitude and action, can often help sharpen the believer's view of what is right and wrong (cf. Col. 3:5–17). Believers strive, under the Spirit's guidance, to put to death the vices that spring from their need to secure life on their own terms. They repent—are turned by the Holy Spirit—from vices to virtues as God uses them as his masks. They strive to practice those attitudes and actions that reflect the image of God's love, care, and concern into the lives of others. They do so in every situation of human life.

Spiritual Gifts

During this past century some Christians have organized certain biblical material into a category labeled "spiritual gifts." This term can be helpful in thinking through Christian service within the callings of the situation of the congregation. It dare not become the prime concept of Christian living since it pertains only to what the Holy Spirit does with his people in this one situation.

"Spiritual gifts" or "gifts of the Holy Spirit" are terms that are used in different ways in the Pauline epistles. In 1 Cor. 2:14 Paul clearly spoke of the ability to trust in Christ, whose cross is a stumbling block to the Jews and folly to the Gentiles, when he used the term (cf. the entire context from 1 Cor. 1:18 to 2:14). In 1 Cor. 12:1, only the adjective *spiritual* stands in the Greek text. Most English translations have referred the term there to the gifts discussed after verse 4. More likely it refers to "spiritual persons," for the immediate context speaks of those whom the Holy Spirit moves to trust in Jesus Christ and confess him as Lord (1 Cor. 12:2–3). But in 1 Cor. 14:1, the adjective clearly does refer to gifts that the Holy Spirit gives his people. Though viewed as gifts of God, these "gifts" become concrete in human actions that edify the body of Christ's people, or the believer who has the gift, or both.

In the technical sense the gifts of the Holy Spirit have their base in God's creative order. They have their base in the first article of the Creed. They are not magical. The gift of prophesy was apparently the gift to use the Word of God to convict people in their hearts through the Law and to bring them to the consolation of the Gospel (1 Cor. 14:22–25, 31, 39). That ability operates on the basis of the same psychological characteristics one might use in persuasive speech as a politician or sales representative. The gift of tongues apparently used nonrational (not irrational!) sounds, such as those lovers and sports fans put to effective use in communicating their feelings. As a spiritual gift, such use of sound praises God and prays to him. These sounds—which do not fall into commonly understood words, or propositional patterns with subjects and verbs—have been used in many cultures not only to express delight or fear but also religious sentiments.

The "first article" base, in the blessings of our nature as God fashioned it in Eden, does not yet make an ability or activity a spiritual gift. To it must be added the power of the Holy Spirit, the third article element, for a specific purpose. That purpose of the exercise of every spiritual gift is to point to Christ, the second article element of the spiritual gift. Thus, playing the piano Friday evening at a restaurant is a talent God has given to some believers as well as to some nonbelievers. When the Holy Spirit directs that believer to use such keyboard skills on Sunday morning to accompany hymns of praise to the Savior, that first article base has become a spiritual gift.

It dare not be ignored that the lists of spiritual gifts that are often cited from Paul's letters do not only focus on the talents of individual believers that the Holy Spirit uses to serve others. The list in Rom. 12:6–8 is indeed such a list. But the lists in Eph. 4:11 and 1 Cor. 12:28–30 enumerate the people who have these abilities and are using them as gifts under the direction and power of the Holy Spirit. Not only can my abilities become spiritual gifts; I, as a fellow believer, am the Spirit's gift to the whole body as I share God's Word with others or point to the love and presence of Christ with deeds of love that help and heal. Furthermore, the exercise of these ability-gifts takes place in specific situations. The opportunities for service are as much gifts of the Spirit as are the abilities to serve in specific ways.

Such gifts are a matter of the Holy Spirit's strategy for carrying out his plan for his people. They do not reflect on the one who "has" or is the gift at all. Therefore, we dare not make anything of the way in which the Holy Spirit works through us and uses us. Although he enriches us as individuals through his use of us as his tools, he does so to enrich others and bring the presence of Christ to them. Therefore, believers will use this concept of spiritual gifts with care and within its limits in the wider framework of the exercise of the Christian calling. God calls us not only to direct people to Christ with our verbal witness to his incarnation, death, and resurrection but also to serve within his design for human life in home, occupation, and community as well.

Making God-Pleasing Decisions

God did not inspire a computer, from which we could draw specific commands or advice for every situation. He created his human creatures as moral computers, who could make decisions over the course of life. The wiring in these moral computers has gotten crossed by our sinfulness, and therefore even believers sometimes have trouble seeing—and doing—what is right and best for themselves and others.

God has given moral guidance to his people in the Scriptures. Much of his inspired direction for human life there, however, comes in the form of regulations for the cultic, political, and moral life of his ancient people Israel, regulations that Paul rejected in the freedom of the Gospel (Col. 2:16–17). The church has even changed its judgment on issues that were regarded as moral precepts for centuries. Charging of interest on loans is an example of this. Throughout most of its history the church has regarded any charging of interest at all as a transgression against God's command to Israel, "Do not take interest of any kind from [your countryman] . . . you must not lend him money at interest or sell him food at a profit" (Lev. 25:36–37; cf. Ex. 22:25; Deut. 23:19). The advent of capitalistic methods in the last century has convinced most Christians that charging interest is not in itself a violation of God's command to love others. Even church bodies charge congregations interest on loans.

God's commands in Scripture do provide believers with moral guidance, but believers must still use God-given, sanctified wisdom to determine how specific biblical commands and prohibitions apply to life in this society. This involves determining what Saint Paul determined in his day: which of these commands God provided specifically to his people of old, and which embrace not only universal principles, which God has written into humanity itself, but also applications of those principles, which dare not be altered in any age (Col. 2:16–18). Christians will struggle in their own consciences and in good faith, with mutual support, together with fellow believers on such decisions.

Furthermore, the Scriptures do not speak directly to all the issues with which modern life confronts us. However, Christians do apply the general principles of the Ten Commandments and other biblical expressions of God's design for human life in our radically different cultural context. Therefore, they are continually making judgments regarding, for example, what "You shall not steal" says about duplication of copyrighted music for the church choir. In such decisions believers begin with Christ's fundamental command to love the Lord God and to love the neighbor as we love ourselves, or as we would want others to love us (Matt. 22:36–40). The application of this basic command or guideline for human living is worked out in specific instances within the framework that Scripture sets in place, with consideration for how God's will can best be accomplished in this specific instance. Christians reflect and convey God's kind of love, the agape that sets aside self and self's concerns in reaching out to embody the love and presence of God for the neighbor.

Christians also recognize that there is no one "correct" decision in every instance. The church has long recognized that some things are neither prohibited nor commanded by God. Within his design for human life more than one possibility may best meet human need and serve him. Actions neither commanded nor prohibited are called *adiaphora* [singular *adiaphoron*] from the Greek.

Human reason is able to make those kinds of decisions with some degree of accuracy even apart from the Gospel of Jesus Christ. Because the Gospel takes away the necessity of securing our own identity, security, and meaning through manipulation or exploitation of others, it enables believers to evaluate their own abilities and the needs of others more clearly than would otherwise be the case. God's concerns have become the concerns of believers. Reason taken captive by the Gospel makes decisions based on giving glory to God (1 Cor. 10:31). We render service within our callings to others "doing the will of God from [our] heart" (Eph. 6:6).

Believers also count on one another as they make decisions in Christian living. The Gospel frees them to be open with one another as they test assessments of situations and possible actions. The mutual conversation of believers with one another not only edifies the church with the Gospel and the forgiveness of sins. Such conversation also helps guide God's people as they make the decisions that confront them.

Conversation with God also helps vitally in the decision-making process. Turning to God in prayer will not magically provide some sure signal from heaven to guide or confirm our decisions. Prayer will help us summon God's help in the midst of making the decision. Praying will prepare us to turn to him for forgiveness if we later find that the decision did indeed lead us in the wrong direction.

Living the Crucified Life

The life believers live is a life that has been joined with Christ's death in Baptism (Rom. 6:4). Believers live a crucified life, the result of which is that Christ lives in them (Gal. 2:20). Therefore, they are in a constant struggle to "put to death, therefore, whatever belongs to [their] earthly nature: sexual immorality, impurity, lust, evil desires and greed . . . anger, rage, malice, slander, and filthy language," lying and other ungodly practices (Col. 3:5–10; cf. Gal. 5:24). "For the sinful nature desires what is contrary to the Spirit, and the Spirit what is contrary to the sinful nature. They are in conflict with each other, so that you do not do what you want" (Gal. 5:17).

The Struggle of Sanctification

The battle continues, but Paul puts it in perspective in Romans 7. There he admitted that he did not understand his own actions, for what he did not want to do, he did, and what he wanted to do, he did not do (7:15). He recognized that his "flesh" (RSV), that is, his old nature apart from his death to sin in Christ, had nothing good within it. It cut short his ability to do the right things that he wanted to do. It remained under the Law's condemnation. But as the newborn child of God Paul could say, "For in my inner being I delight in God's law; but I see another law at work in the members of my body, waging war against the law of my mind and making me a prisoner of the law of sin at work within my members." He conceded, "What a wretched man I am!" But he knew who would deliver him from this body of death. "Thanks be to God—through Jesus Christ our Lord!" he exclaimed (7:22–25).

Every believer repeats Paul's experience of the struggle against sin. The Law condemns daily; the Gospel renews the baptismal life each day as well. As they struggle with temptations, believers also have God's assurance—the assurance of the Gospel—that God will not permit them to slip from him. In the struggle he gives strength (1 Cor. 10:13).

Crosses in Christian Living

Not only do believers experience the Holy Spirit's continual crucifying of their sinful urges and planning, as through the Word in all its forms God turns his children in repentance back to him each day. Believers also bear the cross as it afflicts those around them into whose lives God reaches through their love, care, and concern. "If anyone would come after me, he must deny himself and take up his cross and follow me," Christ said (Mark 8:34).

Christians have defined the "crosses" of Christian living in various ways. The thorns of the flesh that come through bodily ailments or besetting sins that never seem completely conquered (2 Cor. 12:7–10) are probably not what Christ included in the crosses his followers naturally assume. Crosses come in the course of our callings, or at the edge of our callings, as we gather neighbors from further rather than nearer into the circle of our care and concern.

Christ bore the cross for others, to deliver them from death. His people bear the crosses of others, to give them support as evils fall upon them. Christ bore the cross to atone for his people. His people bear crosses to relieve the sufferings of their fellow human creatures. In home and on the job, in the community and the congregation, our callings bring us close to those who suffer. Christ calls us to stand next to those who suffer and help them bear their afflictions. We may be able to help them escape those afflictions. We may not be able to do so. We may simply hold their hands and give them comfort. Most believers do not mind doing that for a short time, particularly if we can "fix" the problem. Most believers find that their patience wears thin when Christ calls them simply to stand by another person, for a long time, with no fix for the neighbor's woe in sight. But Christ calls us to do just that.

Crosses seem to take life away; they deprive us of things and time we think we need. But in losing things and time for the welfare of those whom we are called to stand by and support, we are given life in its richness and fullness. All the things and time we could accumulate mean nothing if we forfeit life with the one who calls us to take up crosses. As we fall into the troubles of this world, under its crosses, we do so in full confidence that our Lord will never be ashamed of us (Mark 8:34–38). In the process, loving the needy around us will suppress and starve our own desires to do things our own way (1 Peter 4:1–2). Standing by those who need our love in their affliction will turn our attention toward God and build our faith and trust (1 Peter 1:6–7; 2 Cor. 4:16–18), as we throw ourselves upon him in prayer (Is. 26:16–19). As we die a little to all that we have been trying to hang onto for ourselves under these crosses of the horizontal realm, God gives an ever fuller appreciation of life as he wants it to be lived.

Believers never seek such crosses. Self-imposed crosses usually reflect a desire to earn our own salvation. Crosses fall upon us as we live in the callings of daily life.

No Offense

Part of the believer's life of caring for others involves consciously avoiding anything that would trip up those around us. Not only do Christians do everything of a positive nature possible to convey God's love, care, and concern to those around them, but at all costs believers avoid doing anything to cause others to fall or fail, particularly in regard to the vertical relationship with God. (Offense can include the believer's failure to bring the Law to someone who needs to hear it, for that, too, can separate another from God.) Jesus hardly ever expressed himself more strongly than when he said, "And if anyone causes one of these little ones who believe in me to sin, it would be better for him to be thrown into the sea with a large millstone tied around his neck" (Mark 9:42). Such playing with the faiths of others is called "causing to stumble" or "offense."

Some Christians like to think that "other people take offense; I don't give it." Neither Jesus nor Paul looked at the matter in this way. In 1 Corinthians 8 Paul discussed matters of *adiaphora*, which believers might do or not do in Christian liberty, but which might cause others to stumble. Knowing that something is not wrong, Paul stated, does not mean that believers are free to do it. Their love for the neighbor might prevent them from eating food from pagan temple butcher shops if that would cause others, with weak consciences, to stumble or fall in their faith. Liberty dare not harm others. Love sacrifices its own liberty so that others do not fall (1 Cor. 8:1–13).

There are instances in which believers must demonstrate their freedom in Christ to those who are fixed in false conceptions, particularly when such people try to impose their laws upon other believers. But even in those instances, the Christian strives to win the neighbor, to correct perceptions and build faith rather than simply to flaunt liberty and to prove one's own point. Sinning against fellow believers and wounding their weak consciences is sinning against Christ. At all costs, believers avoid causing others who are joined with them in Christ's body to fall (1 Cor. 8:12–13).

The Holy Spirit has sanctified us so that we might live the mature

255

Christian life. That life lives out of God's mercy and favor, doing the good works that serve those around us, reflecting in every one of our callings the fullness of Christ's love (Eph. 2:8–10; 2 Tim. 3:15–17; Eph. 4:11–16).

Notes for Chapter XV

1. On the New Testament concept of holiness and sanctification, see Otto Procksch and Karl Georg Kuhn, *"hagios,"* *Theological Dictionary of the New Testament,* vol. 1, ed. Gerhard Kittel, trans. and ed. Geoffrey W. Bromiley (Grand Rapids: Eerdmans, 1964), 88–115.
2. Apology of the Augsburg Confession, IV, 125, 189, *The Book of Concord,* trans. and ed. Theodore G. Tappert (Philadelphia: Fortress, 1959), 124, 133.
3. See ch. III, pp. 48–72.
4. See Anders Nygren, *Agape and Eros,* trans. Philip S. Watson (London: SPCK, 1953).
5. Gilbert C. Meilaender, Jr., *The Theory and Practice of Virtue* (Notre Dame: University of Notre Dame Press, 1984).

Chapter XVI

The Church

God creates the church. Its members belong to it because he has brought them into this body, which Christ claims as his own body (1 Cor. 12:12–26; Col. 1:18; Eph. 4:15; Rom. 12:4–5). God has made individuals who were "not a people" his own people. They had lived apart from his mercy, but he has brought them together as the people who live in his mercy and live to tell about it. He has chosen them as his own kind of people. He has made them a royal priesthood and a holy nation, so that they might "declare the praises of him who called you out of darkness into his wonderful light," the light of Jesus Christ (1 Peter 2:9–10).

The Royal Priesthood

Just as God created the universe out of nothing, so he took those who had no standing before him and were alienated from the commonwealth of Israel and strangers to the covenants of promise, having no hope and without God in the world. But God has brought both Jew and Gentile near to himself through Christ's blood. Christ has become the peace that reconciles those who had been hostile toward each other and toward God. That peace rests in the cross. The people of the cross, drawn together into Christ's own body, are now fellow citizens, saints and members of God's family. The Word of the Lord, as it came through apostles and prophets, constructed this household, the temple of God's people, upon the foundation of Jesus Christ (Eph. 2:11–22). The church, as God's new Israel, lives in the power and for the purposes of its Creator, who has called it into existence through his Word.

Thus, the church is not a voluntary association, which people join and leave at will. God's re-creative power, as it comes through baptism or some other form of the Word, incorporates sinners into the church. They are made God's people, and God's people they remain, even when they try to stray. They may turn their backs on God and his people, but God and his people will pursue them, striving to reclaim them so that they might live the life God gives to those whom he chooses to be his own.

Priests not only have free access to God on behalf of God's people (Heb. 5:1). Priests also return with the Word of the Lord to others. Priests pray for others and carry their needs before the Father in heaven. One of the Latin words for priest, *pontifex*, as noted in chapter VIII, means "bridge-builder." Believers build bridges to God not only for themselves but also for others. God has instituted the royal priesthood so that his priests might declare the wonderful deeds of him who called them out of darkness into his wonderful light (1 Peter 2:9–10).

God has called his people to be his people, his priests, in their Baptisms. There he has incorporated them into the body of Christ, which his church is, through Baptism. There Jews and Greeks, slaves and free, have been joined together (1 Cor. 12:12–13). There the baptized are not regarded according to their status in the horizontal realm; they are neither Jew nor Greek, neither slave nor free, neither male nor female. They are all one in Christ Jesus, Abraham's off-spring in the new Israel, and heirs of Christ's promise (Gal. 3:27–29). The church is the assembly of all those whom God has chosen to be his own, all those who trust in him. The church is thus, at its root, a matter of the vertical relationship. Yet, because God joins us to his family as well as to himself, it becomes immediately a matter of the horizontal relationship as well. The royal priesthood describes the vertical relationship that the believer has with God. It also involves the horizontal calling to share his word with others and live together with fellow believers in mutual love.

Lambs Hearing the Shepherd

Luther defined the church as holy believers and lambs who are listening to the voice of the shepherd.[1] Melanchthon identified the church as the gathering of all believers, among whom the Gospel is correctly proclaimed and taught and the sacraments are correctly administered.[2] God's rule extends itself through his re-creative Word, and by that Word it forms the church. God's rule, or the kingdom of God, is thus distinct from the church. The kingdom of

God creates the church. The kingdom is God's power to put his chosen people to death as sinners, and raise them to new life, gathering them into his family, the church.

The "Invisible" Church and the "Visible" Church

Christians have often distinguished the church in its vertical dimension, the gathering of individuals whom God has made his children, from the church in its horizontal dimension, the gathering as it fleshes itself out in the forms of daily life in the world. They have sometimes called the former the "invisible church" and the latter the "visible church." The chief function of this distinction is to recognize that hypocrites and unbelievers do gather among the people of God around Word and sacrament. Luther and Melanchthon treated this fact without using the distinction between "visible" and "invisible" churches. They did not focus on the people in the visible church as they admitted that "false Christians, hypocrites, and even open sinners" are to be found in it. They focused instead upon the power of the Word, which remains at work whether pastors (and by implication people) are faithful children of God or not.[3]

The distinction between invisible and visible churches has sometimes left Christians in doubt as to whether they truly were members of the invisible church. If the concept of the invisible church is severed from the biblical understanding of the means of grace, then God's people will be driven to speculate about their membership in the family of God. They will never be able to know for sure if God has gathered them into the invisible church or whether they are simply among the weeds and chaff that lie alongside God's grain in the granary of the visible church.

On the other hand, if the biblical understanding of grace and the means of grace prevails, then believers can assure other members of the visible church that God will not go back on his baptismal promise. If God has pledged his salvation to another person in Baptism and absolution, in the Lord's Supper and the sermon, then *for all practical purposes* I can assure that person of forgiveness and life forever in Christ. Indeed, if I concentrate on the person, I cannot speculate or probe the depths of the Hidden God's resolve over against that person. I am not called on to do so. I am called by God to deliver the Word to my acquaintances. The Gospel they have already received from the sacraments and the proclaimed Word, as well as from their reading of Scripture, has established their relationship with Jesus Christ. I can only reiterate his Word of assurance to them that nothing can separate them from him (Rom. 8:28–39).

The Church Hidden and Revealed

Yet we dare not ignore the distinction between true believers gathered around Word and sacrament and those who mingle with them for other reasons than a faith in Christ. God both hides and reveals his people as he hides and reveals his presence around and through Word and sacrament. Therefore, a more precise contrast may be made by using the terms "the hidden church" and "the revealed church." God's chosen children are in one sense truly hidden from other human creatures since we cannot plumb the depths of the hearts of those around us to perceive and confirm whether their faith is "true" or not. The body of those who have been joined to Christ in death and resurrection remains an object of faith, to be sure. The church is hidden from human eyes in one sense.

At the same time God reveals the church as the place of his presence, where his family gathers. There the Word is proclaimed and shared in written and sacramental form among those whom the Holy Spirit gathers through and around it. God reveals that these people are his own as his rule and kingdom alter their lives through death and resurrection in Christ.[4] Distinguishing between the hidden church and the revealed church helps keep our focus on God.

Rather than using the terms *visible* and *invisible*, we might also employ the terms *audible* or *tangible* or *tastable* for the revealed church, since its presence is revealed as the Word is heard, and the baptismal water that frames the Word of death and life touches us, and the bread-body and wine-blood feed our faith.

The church takes form as a human institution, with the need for rules and regulations and the activities of God's Law in the administration of its daily life. It is not exactly the same kind of institution, however, as those institutions that take shape in the situations of home, occupation, and society. God has designed it for other purposes. Although the home also has assignments in the vertical realm (Deut. 6:4–7; Eph. 6:4), the situations of occupation and society do not. The church will inevitably be involved in works of love in the horizontal realm, not only among its own people, but also in behalf of the world around it (Gal. 6:10). But its prime purpose is to declare the wonderful deeds of God, who has called us out of darkness into his marvelous light. For that purpose God has instituted the church. Therefore, Augustine could write that outside the church there is no salvation. The church has been given the means of grace, the only means whereby salvation is given to sinners.[5]

In Response to the Word

The church serves as the channel for God's kingdom to be extended into the lives of his children, as it brings them to faith in his holy Word and leads them to live a godly life here in time and beyond in eternity. God's people respond individually and as the body of Christ to God's Word in all its forms as this Word raises them out of their death in sin to new life in Christ. These functions and activities of God's people begin as they are assembled together to hear the Word and receive it also in its sacramental form.

The Church Worships

When the life of God's people beyond the earthly realm is pictured in Revelation, the picture reveals them at worship. There the saints together sing their praise of their Lord and God; there they exult and give him glory with their songs of praise (Rev. 19:6–8). God has made them his own kingdom and his own priests. In anticipation of this eschatological worship of God, and to give him thanks and to acknowledge his greatness on this day, his children gather together in worship. They do so to praise him for all that he has done for them. As they assemble to listen to his Word and receive life from it, his people cannot contain themselves. They burst forth with their praise, as well as their petitions for his continued presence and blessing.

In their worship as a congregation, God's children express their own unity and fellowship with one another. They come together in obedience to God's command to assemble (Heb. 10:25) and in adherence to the pattern of the early church (Acts 2:42). Those who neglect or forsake coming together to confess their faith to others in the public assembly of God's people cheat themselves and others as well as God. Their failure to use this opportunity to stir one another up to love and good works deprives their family of an important form of service, which God calls them to give to him and to their fellow believers. It subverts God's plan for the use of his Word and the practice of the faith when those who are able to make their way to public worship services with other believers do not, but rather substitute worship in front of a television set or radio (Heb. 10:23–25).

Human response to God's Word must take form. Human responses of all kinds fall into normal forms, which are designed to heighten and sharpen meaning through ritual repetition. The church's common worship takes form in the liturgy. The western church has developed a common liturgical structure for its worship, and certain fundamentals of this form convey meaning the world around, through the ages. This liturgical structure binds believers together and expresses something of the oneness that the Lord prayed that his flock would share (John 17:20–23). At the same time, the outline of this common liturgy gives each Christian community ample room to adapt the ritual of the whole church for use in its particular cultural setting. The liturgy does not restrict. It binds us together with others, and it frees us to express the common faith within a common structure while we respond to God's Word in forms meaningful for our own setting.

Often North Americans, particularly the young, dismiss liturgy as confining in form and meaningless in content. Those who do so ignore fundamental facts about the way in which God has shaped his human creatures. Variety may be the spice of life, but routine is its sustenance. God's human creatures need and are always inventing ritual for their lives. Rituals embody values and reinforce habits of mind and heart. God uses human rituals to impress upon his people the message of his Word and to form their praise of him. Ritual plays an important role in faith, for it supplies subconscious support to the work of the Word. Our liturgies offer words to us when words fail, in crisis, illness, or old age. Therefore, believers sensitively work hard on liturgy. They frame their worship services around Christ and the proclamation of his Word. They structure their responses in such a way that he is glorified and their attention is turned to him, and not to themselves.

Worship in the congregation leads to worship outside it. Christ's people praise him and pray to him individually, in their own private mediation or devotions. They praise him and pray to him with family members or with friends. They also worship and praise him as they carry out his will in all of their callings, in home, job, community, and congregation. Congregational worship orients believers for their life of praise in these other situations. The Word they receive there strengthens their faith. Furthermore, the practice of perceiving God in all his world and praising him for his loving presence there begins in congregational worship.

Worship does lead us out of the standards and values and practices of daily activity in the other situations of human life. Worship therefore should not only connect with the world outside. It should also impress upon believers that they are a people set apart, a holy people, who have their own songs of praise, their own calendar, their own message and understanding of life. This worship binds believers together in one family, so that they sense the solidarity of God with his people, and his people with one another through the worship service.

The Church Witnesses

The Word of death and life proclaimed in the congregation's worship opens the door for all people to come into this family. Believers carry that Word there proclaimed to others whom they meet in other situations of life throughout the week. That is the church's mission of salvation. The church is a light to the world, and salt to preserve and sustain and to flavor the lives of its people (Matt. 5:13–16). Believers usually begin their witness through their deeds, Jesus noted, but unbelievers must hear the specific Word of Jesus Christ if they are truly to become acquainted with him—and thus become a child of God.

Believers live as missionaries at all times. Jesus set the tone of the entire life of the church and its individual members when he sent his disciples forth to make disciples through baptizing and teaching the word of Christ to people all over the world (Matt. 28:18–20). The Holy Spirit not only empowers the witness of those who had experienced Jesus' career on earth, but also of those who have witnessed the word of prophets and apostles made more certain in the inspired Scriptures (Acts 1:8). Christ sends all his disciples to fix his judgment on those who reject him so that they might repent. He sends all believers to announce his peace as they forgive the sins of the repentant in his name (John 20:19–23). Through the church he continues to open believers' minds to the scriptures so that they may share the message of his suffering and resurrection. As they do so, their words become the instrument through which he effects repentance and the forgiveness of sins in the lives of those who hear (Luke 24:44–48).

The Church Edifies Its Own Members

The members of Christ's body not only speak his Word to those outside the church, drawing them into the circle of the saved. They also speak the Word to one another. God has given the responsibility of the public proclamation of his word of life to those whom he calls to lead the church. In Ephesians 4 Paul listed apostles, prophets, evangelists, pastors and teachers as God's gifts to the church. They equip the saints, who along with their leaders carry out all the callings of service that God gives to his people. Together the congregation of Christ's body builds itself up as its members bring the Word of repentance and the forgiveness of sins to one another (Luke 24:46–47). This mutual edification aims at bringing the family of God into an ever fuller unity in its faith and knowledge of Christ. Such faith signals maturity in us. The restoration of the practice of our humanity, measured against Christ's image of that humanity, anchors life. Immature faith can be tossed to and fro, carried about by all sorts of breezes that flow through our culture. Human cunning devises the best systems it can for charting how to find identity, security, and meaning. All such systems deceive their adherents. Only in Christ can the truth about the ultimate source of our identity, security, and meaning be found. So believers gather together to share Christ's truth as they practice Christ's love, growing up in every way into Christ, the head of the body. Christ knits us together, and the Holy Spirit helps each part to work properly. As a result the body of Christ in the congregation and in church bodies grows and upbuilds itself in his love (Eph. 4:11–16).

Therefore, believers live together in their churches, suffering with one another and rejoicing with one another because they are bound together in Christ's body (1 Cor. 12:12–27).

The Church Disciplines Its Own Members

The edification of the church involves the practice of both Law and Gospel. Believers are called to discipline one another as well as to encourage and comfort one another. Christians cannot let fellow believers live in a lie that carries them away from God into eternal condemnation. Therefore, Paul urged the Corinthians to deal with one of their company who was living apart from Christ with all the weight of the Law. The congregation, which was assembled under the power of the Lord Jesus, was to "hand this man over to Satan, so that the sinful nature may be destroyed." This action of the congregation was designed to destroy his desire to live "in his flesh," that is, outside God's rule. It was further designed to restore him so that "his spirit [may be] saved on the day of the Lord" (1 Cor. 5:5).

The church has practiced this discipline for the most part under the guidance found in Matt. 18:15–18. There Jesus set forth four steps for dealing with those who are victims of Satan's and their own deceit, believing that they are living as children of God when they are actually living as children of darkness. (In each case we hope that the stage under discussion is the last stage necessary to bring the wayward to repentance.) First, an individual should approach such a person and show that person his or her fault. If this admonition does not regain the fellow member of the church, the individual should take a small number of others along to repeat the admonition. If this, too, fails, the congregation itself, in whatever form it acts as a congregation, should admonish the sinner. If this admonition fails to elicit repentance, the congregation takes the fourth step and confronts this person with the truth: his or her lifestyle offends God and the congregation of his people. No more deception: this person is cast out from the family of God. Congregations can, of course, err in their judgments, and their word cannot be effective against God's Word and will. But acting as God's instrument and agent, the church and its members bind and loose sins as they exercise God's call to bring sinners into death and to raise them up as the newborn children of God in Christ (Matt. 18:18).

As it exercises discipline, Christ's church must never forget that it does not do so to purify itself. Like the individual believer, the church is both righteous and sinful at the same time. This is true in two senses. First, the church gathers the broken and weary into its midst. It collects people who are sinners and who are struggling with their sinfulness. It recognizes that its Lord was interested not in those who thought themselves whole—those who "had it all together"—but rather in those whose battered lives cried out for mercy (Matt. 9:12–13). The church welcomes sinners; it constitutes "Sinners Anonymous."

Second, the church is both righteous and sinful at the same time because its people as a group are engaged in the struggle against sin. Therefore, the Word that constitutes it as the people of God proclaims the righteousness of all its members. At the same time they err as they live together as believers. They together make wrong decisions and carry them out. Together they stand in the continuing need of God's forgiveness, not only as individuals but also as human institutions made up of many people.

The Church Provides Love in the Horizontal Realm

God provides for the temporal needs of believers and unbelievers alike in all sorts of ways (Matt. 5:45). God draws his people into acts of love for each other and for those outside the household of faith as well. Almost immediately, the Holy Spirit directed the church to take care of human need in daily life by setting up an office of deacon to distribute food to widows and to administer other temporal acts of love (Acts 6:1–6). In reaching out to those in temporal need the church continues the feeding and healing functions of Jesus' ministry, expressions of the Messianic expectation (Matt. 11:5; Luke 4:17–21). Inevitably, the church will be drawn into acts of temporal love toward its own members and those outside the church. In addition, societies have often drafted the church to administer its own activities, particularly in education and in treatment of the sick and dying.

The Church Suffers and Is Tempted

Alongside these characteristic functions and activities of the church are two characteristics that describe what happens to it apart from that which the Holy Spirit plans for its program. It suffers, and it is tempted.

The church does not suffer vicariously, to save its members. But it does share the suffering of the societies in which it is located when their disobedience to God's plan for human life wreaks havoc for its people. And it suffers because the world opposes it and tries to suffocate its voice. The church does not focus on its suffering, nor does it indulge in self-pity as it encounters the frustrations of persecution or harassment. As it submits to suffering, it serves.

The church is also continually confronted with a variety of temptations. It is tempted to cling to divine virtues and to use its association with God as a club, to protect or advance itself at the expense of others. The church is tempted to forget that God's strength is made perfect in weakness, his own and the church's (2 Cor. 12:9). Furthermore, it is tempted to accommodate itself and its message to the culture in which it is called to proclaim and serve. As the Word of the Lord is brought to human cultures, it must be applied in language understandable in that cultural context. The attempt to do so inevitably creates the temptation to accommodate the Gospel to the standards of the world in this particular society. Finally, the church constantly struggles against the temptation to make itself an idol, a primary source of identity, security, and meaning for its members.

Only the Gospel can combat these temptations. There is no way to secure the holiness or safety of the church except through the power God has put in the Word. Therefore, the whole life of the church in all its forms, congregation, church body, ecumenical organization, is a life of repentance.

Marks of the Church

Christians have defined the church by noting its "marks," those signs that characterize its nature. The adjectives *one, holy, catholic,* and *apostolic,* used to describe the church in the Nicene Creed, have often been used to designate the essential elements of the church, without which it does not exist. The church is one; all believers are gathered into the hidden church through their vertical relationship with the triune God. The church is holy; the Holy Spirit has cleansed it through the re-creative Word, which forgives the sins of all its members. The church is catholic; it has spread to the ends of the earth and has continued to exist in all periods of human history since Pentecost. The church is apostolic; it is bound to the inspired Word of God in the apostolic writings, and from them it receives its life and its life-giving power.

Martin Luther informally suggested other lists of marks of the church. In 1539 he composed a list stating that the church always has the preaching of the Gospel, Baptism, the Sacrament of the Altar, the Office of Keys or formal confession and absolution, called pastoral leadership, public prayer, praise, and thanksgiving. Furthermore, the church will always suffer under the cross of misfortune and persecution. Finally, although this does not distinguish it from upright groups of unbelievers, the church is marked by its practice of love, in good works of all kinds.[6] Two years later he constructed a similar list, this time enumerating Baptism, the Lord's Supper, confession and absolution, the public ministry of preaching, the Apostles' Creed, the Lord's Prayer, respect for temporal political powers and for marriage and family life, suffering and persecution, and the rejection of physical force against its enemies.[7] Other Christians have suggested that the church cannot exist without the exercise of discipline, of excommunication. Lutherans have never accepted the practice of excommunication as a mark of the church, apart from its proper exercise within the Office of the Keys.

The Lutheran confessions stipulate that the church is simply marked by God's Word, in oral and sacramental forms. The church exists where the Gospel is rightly proclaimed and the sacraments are rightly administered, or the church is holy believers, lambs who are listening to the voice of the Shepherd.[8] However believers describe and delimit the church, that much must be remembered. It is nothing other than Christ's holy people, whose holiness depends on the continuing action of the re-creating Word among them.

Church Government and Organization

As God's church reveals itself through its use of the Word, it takes on structures for regulating its life, as an institution of the horizontal sphere. It assumes forms for governing itself. These forms have often reflected the political forms of the society in which it was set at the time.

Forms of Polity

In the early church monarchical forms developed quite quickly, reflecting the habits of organization of Roman society, under the imperial form of government. Bishops headed the church and cared for its people. The church calls this form of government *episcopal,* from the Greek word for "bishop" or "overseer."

In the aristocratic municipal setting of Geneva, in the sixteenth century, John Calvin developed a form of government for the church labeled *presbyterian,* for elders, comparable to city fathers, governed the church (the Greek word for "elder" is *presbyteros*).

Particularly in England, as more democratic concepts from ancient Germanic tribal law were being revived, some groups of Christians developed congregational forms of church government, reflecting the democratic idea. As modern Western governments rely increasingly on bureaucratic agencies, church bodies have increasingly found that the exercise of regulatory power and leadership within them has shifted toward paid staffs.

Scripture prescribes no one form of church government. Each of these forms has served the Gospel, and sinners within the church have used each form to subvert the Gospel. Only the Gospel guarantees the Gospel. No form of church government can in and of itself provide insurance against the accommodation of God's Word to cultural norms. No ecclesiastical polity can prevent the devil's deceit from misleading the church and perverting its message.

Finally, in any form of church polity, Christ remains Lord of the church. The church invites his judgment when—under any form of government—it misrepresents his Word. It serves him faithfully when it uses any of these forms to promote the proclamation of his Law and Gospel as he has given them to the church in the Scriptures.

Sociological Analyses of the Church

Because the revealed church exists not only as the expression of the kingdom of God, which exercises its rule through the Word, but also as a human institution in the horizontal realm, it takes institutional forms. These forms can be analyzed sociologically. That fact is no more or no less than evidence that God is comfortable in his creation and works in and through it.

Ernst Troeltsch's Analysis. A predominant sociological analysis of the church arose in the early twentieth century out of the work of a German churchman and sociologist, Ernst Troeltsch (1865–1923). Troeltsch's categories provided a somewhat useful sociological analysis of the German church scene of his time. They help little in analyzing contemporary North American church life. Troeltsch distinguished churches from sects, and both groups from spiritualistic individuals, who remain outside organized gatherings of Christians. Churches open their doors to all people in a given area; admission to their rolls is easy if not automatic, reflecting the practice of European "state churches" of Troeltsch's period. They symbolize this openness in the practice of infant Baptism, often combined with some kind of penitential system for dealing with guilt. In Troeltsch's day churches were called "confessions" because their life was organized around specific doctrinal confessions, such as Lutheran, Roman Catholic, Reformed, or Anglican. Churches, according to Troeltsch's definition, cooperate with and condone the actions of the society in which they exist. Sects, on the other hand, are fiercely exclusive, not comprehensive. Their high entrance standards, in regard to both belief and conduct, are symbolized by "believer's baptism," and they strictly enforce their standards through excommunication. They usually separate themselves from society to a greater or lesser extent and refuse to participate in certain aspects of society.[9]

North American Denominationalism

Troeltsch's analysis is losing its applicability in Europe. It never gave an apt description of American church life. In North America Christians have organized themselves according to denominations. These denominations have found their origin in a number of factors. Indeed, they trace their roots back to European groups that were organized around specific doctrinal confessions of faith, whether "churches" such as Lutheran, Roman Catholic, Calvinist, or Anglican of the Troeltsch type, or "sects," such as Baptists and Methodists in his typology. These denominations also took into account differing national origins and languages. Thus, among Lutherans synods developed for Germans, Norwegians, Swedes, Danes, Finns, and Slovaks. They also developed out of differing doctrinal and practical concerns, some leaning more toward German or Scandinavian Pietism, others influenced by the revival of confessional Lutheran theology in the mother countries of Europe. Furthermore, there were German Baptists, German Methodists, German Congregationalists, etc.

Many American Protestant denominations were racked by internal strife as the nineteenth century closed, and the battles launched then between "Fundamentalists" and "Liberals" or "Modernists" have evolved but not ended in the intervening century. The result is that often the heirs of "Fundamentalism," for example, the "Evangelicals," will have more in common with other "Evangelicals" in other denominations than with the "mainline" heirs of nineteenth-century "Liberalism" or "Modernism" of their own denomination. Lutherans largely stood apart from the Modernist-Fundamentalist battles. They have not avoided the influences of the North American religious currents around them, but the Lutheran confessions have provided a different focus and agenda for North American Lutherans than those of other church bodies. Nonetheless, Lutherans have not been immune from the confusion in the church's expression of itself and of God's Word that tempts and plagues believers in this era, as in every other period of the church's history.

Therefore, members of a church body should commit themselves to a common confession of the teachings of the Scriptures. They should live in harmony as they walk together in their confession of the faith. They should give a united witness to God's Word and will for his chosen people. When they do not, it is difficult for them and for those outside the church to take their message as seriously as God's Word should be taken. It is God's will that the church's confession be clear, and that for the sake of this clear confession believers draw lines between themselves and those who deny God's truth, especially when they try to cause divisions among those who are confessing the Gospel of Jesus Christ (1 John 4:1–6; Titus 1:9; 3:10–11; 1 Tim. 1:3–7; 6:3–5.

271

"Para-Church" Organizations

Alongside "denominations" on the current North American ecclesiastical scene so-called "para-church" organizations and "non-" or "cross-denominational" groups play an ever larger role. *Para* is the Greek word for "alongside of." There can, of course, be no group of Christians alongside the church, for the people of God are created by God's re-creating presence in the Word. They all stand in the one relationship of faith that unites believers, whether they share a common confession of faith or not (Eph. 4:3–6). Believers may find such groups useful as they pursue certain interests, in the political arena, for instance, or in certain locations together with those with whom they share a common Lord but not a common understanding of how he works in this world. But such groups dare never become the central focus of the believer's life. God calls his people into congregations where life centers on his coming to them in Word and sacrament.

Ecumenical Christianity

God's hidden church is one, united by a common Lord and a common faith and hope and Baptism (Eph. 4:4–6), even if its members disagree seriously on specific elements of the confession of that faith. God's revealed church is divided, and it has been from its earliest appearance as its members interpret God's Word and will in different ways (Acts 15:1–2; Gal. 1:6–10). This division does not reflect God's plan or desire for his church; he wants his children to be united in the same mind and the same judgment (1 Cor. 1:10). Christ prayed for such unity among God's people (John 17:20–26).

Nonetheless, Jesus also warned against those who would deceive his people and divert them from a faithful understanding of his message (Matt. 7:15–16). Admonition to return to the faithful teaching of the biblical message does not make an enemy of those who are admonished. Such admonition must be conducted in a spirit of love and concern (2 Thess. 3:14–15), but that love and concern compels believers to call those who are teaching falsely to repentance (James 5:19–20; 2 Tim. 4:1–3).

Believers are always engaged in the difficult task of building bridges between God's Word in Scripture and the culture in which

God calls them to make that Word clear to people. The very nature of this task provides constant temptation to accommodate the Word to cultural ideas which pervert it. Thus, in the world in which Satan the deceiver is always working, believers should recognize that the admonition to turn away from false teaching is always necessary for all Christians. Both the temptation to refashion the faith into a cultural Christianity and the temptation to defend oneself individually through false teaching will always plague the church. Disputes between Christians can break out as some defend their false perceptions of the faith. That does not remove the necessity of these admonitions.

Ecclesiastical Fellowship

Since its earliest period the church has institutionalized these admonitions in the form of altar and pulpit fellowship.[10] God calls Christians to fellowship, to communion, to visible expressions of unity with one another. The common faith in Jesus Christ demands that all believers call one another fellow children of God, brothers and sisters in Christ. This common faith permits all to pray with one another. But the church universal has at the same time limited preaching and communing in its midst to those who agree upon the teaching of the faith. Only in those periods and areas where the pure preaching of the Word has been taken less seriously have believers failed to limit preaching and communing in their midst to those with whom they shared a common confession of the church's teaching. These limitations are not designed, in the final analysis, to exclude. They are designed to call those within the fellowship and those outside it to a common realization of what God's Word says on specific issues of teaching.

Christians have not always practiced these limitations of pulpit and altar fellowship in a loving manner. This fact does not remove the necessity of this means of carrying out God's commands to teach his Word properly. It does help explain why in the twentieth century the ecumenical movement arose to tear down barriers between Christian churches.

The Ecumenical Movement

Particularly those who were engaged in work among youth and in "foreign mission" work felt compelled to join together with believers outside their own denominations to further their witness of the faith. To too large an extent, however, the ecumenical movement has tried to solve problems of Christian disunity institutionally and organizationally, rather than through repentance for false teaching. Differing interpretations of God's Word are too often permitted through approaches that set aside the necessity of doctrinal agreement for external expressions of Christian unity. Some organizations, such as the World Council of Churches, bring together any groups that claim a Christian heritage into their organizations. Others operate on the principle of "reconciled diversity," which acknowledges a common core of confession of the biblical message and diverse interpretations on many significant issues, thus blurring the clear confession of God's truth.

External, institutional, organizational unity of the church is certainly a worthy goal. However, such ecclesiastical institutions are subject to all the temptations to which all human institutions can fall victim. In the church, as in every other human organization, power corrupts. Even in "democratically run" church organizations, the power of the institution as an institution can divert the gaze of its leaders and its members from the power of God's Word, in all its weakness, to institutional power. Therefore, believers will recognize that they will always be the tiny flock of God (Luke 12:32), the remnant of his people, in whom he reveals his power made perfect in weakness. They will seek the unity of the faith he has commanded ardently and urgently. They will never sacrifice the proclamation of his Word for external expressions of that unity of faith, which the Word gives.

God's people live from the Word. The Word calls the church into being. When it strays from this Word of his, the church begins to die. Only in the Word of the Lord and in its proclamation and teaching does the church find purpose and life.

Notes for Chapter XVI

1. Smalcald Articles, III:XII, 2, *The Book of Concord*, trans. and ed. Theodore G. Tappert (Philadelphia: Fortress, 1959), 315.
2. Augsburg Confession VII, 1, ibid., 32.
3. Augsburg Confession VIII, 1, ibid., 33.

4. Gerhard O. Forde, *Theology Is for Proclamation* (Minneapolis: Fortress, 1990), 188–90.

5. For a more complete summary of Augustine's understanding of the church, see Bengt Hägglund, *History of Theology,* trans. Gene J. Lund (Saint Louis: Concordia, 1968), 128–30.

6. Martin Luther, "On the Councils and the Church, 1539," *Church and Ministry: III,* Luther's Works, vol. 41 (Philadelphia: Fortress, 1966), 148–67.

7. "Against Hanswurst," ibid., 41:194–98.

8. Smalcald Articles, III:XII, 2, *The Book of Concord,* 315.

9. Ernst Troeltsch, *The Social History of the Christian Churches* (New York: Macmillan, 1911).

10. Werner Elert, *Eucharist and Church Fellowship in the First Four Centuries,* trans. Norman E. Nagel (Saint Louis: Concordia, 1966).

Chapter XVII

The Public Ministry

God fashioned human nature. He knows what his human creatures need, as individuals and as groups. All groups of human beings have structures by which they are organized and led. God designed the public ministry as an office or structure within his church for the public dispensing of his means of grace. The public ministry provides public leadership for the priests, who constitute the church.

The Public Ministry
and the Royal Priesthood of Believers

God has called all believers to approach him and to serve him as his priests (1 Peter 2:5, 9; Rev. 1:6; 5:10; Rom. 12:1). This relationship is anchored first of all in the realm of the vertical. Above all, it involves being the child of God, in his presence—although it also involves worshiping and witnessing alongside other believers in the horizontal realm, in the church, where God's people are gathered by the Word in oral and sacramental forms. The public ministry, on the other hand, is firmly anchored in the horizontal realm, as a calling of service to other believers. It brings the power of God in his Word, the instrument of God's kingdom, to his priests. Thus, this calling of the horizontal realm is God's public instrument for establishing and sustaining the vertical relationship of the members of Christ's body.

Those who hold the office of the public ministry do not, by virtue of their office, have a vertical relationship that is different from other members of the congregation. They differ only in the horizontal calling God has given them in the church. God calls the public ministers of the church to serve him by serving their fellow believers with the public application of God's Word to their lives.

The Necessity of the Public Ministry

Sociologically, human institutions are always structured to provide leadership. They do not function without the designation of responsibilities to various people within them. Among these responsibilities the obligations of leadership fall upon people with abilities appropriate to the needs of the institution. Every team has a captain. Apart from the smallest of groups, pure democracy does not exist among human creatures, and certainly not in the church. The kingdom of God provides not only the church's power but also something of a model for its life.

Furthermore, order is necessary for freedom. Anarchy or chaos, not freedom, is the opposite of order. If God's people are to be free to live together in love, if they are to be free to carry out their own responsibilities, they must have leadership. God is a God of peace, not of confusion, and he wants everything to be done decently and in order in his church (1 Cor. 14:33, 40). Therefore, he has freed his people for performing their various functions by providing them with the leadership of the public ministry.

Far more important than any sociological reasons for the public ministry—but not disconnected from them—is God's command to his church to establish and maintain the public ministry. God gave the gift of this public leadership to the church as the Holy Spirit caused the Word of the Lord to grow in the church's first days. Paul appointed elders as leaders in every church (Acts 14:23). Titus was given the charge to appoint elders for the believers in every town on Crete (Titus 1:5). The church of Jerusalem added to the ministry of the Word a formal ministry of service as one of its first organizational actions (Acts 6:1–6).

The precise institutional shape of the public ministry in the New Testament era eludes us as we read the texts. Precisely where function and formal office meet behind the titles of *apostle, prophet, pastor, teacher,* and *evangelist* (Eph. 4:11) is unclear. The terms *bishop* and *elder* can be used interchangeably for the pastoral leadership of the early Christian congregation (cf. Acts 20:17, 28; Titus 1:5, 7). Nonetheless, at every point in which the epistles of the New Testament turn to glimpse the organization and structure of the church, it is clear that God had instituted formal, public leadership for his people as they gathered together in the institution of the church.

The public ministry centers around the public proclamation of the Word, the unique function of the church. The public ministry is therefore vested in the person whom God calls to exercise responsibility for the public action of his Word. The care of God's people through the Word has most often been compared to the gentle care of the Good Shepherd, and so this office has most often been called the *pastoral* office. Although the Scriptures never provide a complete job description for the pastor, the functions of this office center upon the public proclamation of the Word.

But the church has often created offices that exercise certain functions of public ministry to aid the pastor in this proclamation. In the early church teachers and evangelists apparently joined deacons rather quickly to provide specific kinds of service to God's people in conjunction with the pastoral care provided through the calling of the pastor. What distinguishes the pastoral office from the responsibilities of the teacher or the evangelist or the deacon is its responsibility for the total public ministry of the church. The church may order and arrange its public life with a variety of callings, so long as this design serves the Word and the needs of Christ's people and places ultimate responsibility for the public service of the Word in the pastor.

Nonetheless, those who offer leadership to the church through ministries that specialize in teaching, evangelism, service to a variety of temporal needs, or leadership in music serve God and his people as fully as any others do. The congregation of God's children should treasure and respect and sustain them in their service to the church.

Ministry Serves

The term *ministry* is derived from the Latin word *ministerium,* which means "service." "The ministry" became the designation for the service of bringing God's Word to his people in the public arena early in the church's history. By the time of the Reformation "the ministry" had become a formal office within the church, the office of pastor or priest. The Wittenberg reformers recognized that the office of the ministry exists to perform the functions of a particular kind of service, the service of the Word, and for no other reason.

Ministry is a verbal noun.[1] It speaks of a formal, institutionalized calling within the church, but God instituted and sustains that calling only for the service of the members of Christ's body. When those who hold the public ministry no longer function as the servants of God's people, they have betrayed their calling. God's servants must serve.

God has called all believers to serve as priests and deliver his Word to others. Those Bible passages that speak of the activities of the Word apply to the whole people of God. They commission all his children for his mission of making disciples (Matt. 28:18–20) and for the condemnation of sin and the sharing of the forgiveness of sins (Matt. 16:19; 18:18; Luke 24:47–48; John 20:23). But God also has given the calling of public minister to the church as a gift for its edification (Eph. 4:11–12).

The biblical writers use the term *ministry* in a variety of ways. The term can refer to all kinds of service and to the service of the Word as exercised individually by all members of the body of Christ. The public ministry, however, is a term the church has used to designate the calling of those who have specific duties, responsibilities, and accountability as they function in behalf of the congregation in the public arena. This does not mean that all acts of the public ministry are public acts. It does mean that those whom the church calls as its publicly designated servants are acting in behalf of the other members of the church when they carry out functions that bring God's Word to others.

Although the Scriptures do not prescribe what functions must or may be exercised by those who hold the "office of the public ministry," this calling or office is responsible for the public representation and action of the church in the dispensing of the means of grace. Throughout its history the church has attached other duties and responsibilities to its public ministers. These have included various tasks of service and administration within the congregation of Christ's people. Churches may indeed add and subtract such responsibilities. The public ministry itself, however, must hold responsibility for public teaching and preaching and administration of the sacraments.

This calling is described as one of shepherding (Acts 20:28), following the example of the Lord himself, who cares for his people like a shepherd, ready to sacrifice his life for his sheep, always

279

striving to bring them together into his fold (John 10:7–18; 1 Peter 2:25). Peter also calls Jesus a "Guardian" or "Overseer" of his people; this word is *episkopos* in Greek (1 Peter 2:25). It is often translated *bishop*. Ancient groups used the term for leaders who indeed did oversee the activities of their followers. Particularly in the framework of biblical thought, the obligations of an overseer embraced functions of guarding and protecting, of serving in general. God exercises his dominion by serving; his dominion is performed "under" his people as he lifts them up. Thus, the public servants of his Word "oversee" by protecting and serving.

The "Power" of Ministry

Particularly in the democratic societies of the last two centuries debates have arisen about the division of power between church and public ministry, between God's people as a whole and their public leaders. This debate reflects a presupposition that there is only so much power to go around and thus this power must be divided rightly. It ignores the biblical presupposition that power in God's church resides in the Word, not in the priests or the pastors. It ignores the biblical presupposition that both people and pastors serve God first of all, and not themselves. God has called them to serve one another, and their relationships to each other are governed by their calling to be his servants as they relate to each other.

Pastors and people do not divide power between them. They share the power of the Word. Pastors who are "strong" strengthen their people in exercising the common callings of worshiping the Lord in all areas of life and in witnessing to the Word of God wherever and whenever they have the opportunity to do so. "Strong" congregations support their public ministers in all their activities, with admonition, when necessary, as well as encouragement and cooperation. Both pastor and congregation support one another modestly and humbly. Working together in the Lord's callings, pastors and people do not worry about dividing "power" between them. They focus their concern on bringing the power of the Gospel to all who need to hear it, inside and outside the congregation.

Thus, pastors care for their people as the beloved children of God. Their care focuses always on the welfare of their people as children of God. They serve their people selflessly, as Christ shepherded his people, laying aside the desire to hang onto his prerogatives as well as his human life (Phil. 2:6–8). People, therefore, respect and care for their overseers in the Lord as they receive from them the service of leadership and the service of the Word. They do not endow their pastors with special powers, as if they were some shamans or holy men who have special powers of their own. They love them because they are gifts from God who come with his Word.

The Service of the Word, or the Office of the Keys

The specific kind of service that God's called overseers or shepherds perform for his people involves the application of his Word to their lives. It is the ministry of reconciliation whereby God draws his fallen and straying human creatures back to himself (2 Cor. 5:18–21). It is the service that brings those who were estranged from God and hostile to him to the hope of the Gospel of Jesus Christ (Col. 1:21–23). The church has called this ministry the public exercise of the Office of the Keys because Jesus gave Peter, as the representative of the whole church,[2] "the keys of the kingdom of heaven" (Matt. 16:19). These "keys" enable the church to preach the Law, which locks people out of a relationship with God, and to preach the Gospel, which opens this relationship for them. Thus, "the primary paradigm for ministry is absolution—concrete, present-tense, I-to-you declaration in Word and sacrament authorized by the triune God."[3]

In preaching and Baptism, in confession and absolution as well as the Lord's Supper, pastors publicly exercise this calling for God's people. They do indeed serve as God's hit men as they proclaim the Law and lock the door to the kingdom of God as a call for repentance. They fulfill God's plan for them as they serve as his midwives, bringing fallen sinners to new life in Christ, opening up the fullness of God's gift of our humanity to his people once again.

The use of these keys of God's Word, the key to life with him or the key to death under his condemnation, involves life and death. Those who bring the Word to others do not simply share information with them. They bring the presence and power of Christ's death and resurrection into the middle of other people's lives. They announce the plan God fashioned for his people before the world was created (Eph. 1:3–23). They pronounce upon God's people the forgiveness of sins and the restoration of life through Jesus Christ. God accomplishes his saving will through their words.

As they function with God's keys to the kingdom, pastors function as prophetic proclaimers of his Word and as priestly intermediaries for his people in the public arena, as public representatives of the church to which God has entrusted the prophetic proclamation of the Word and priestly mediation for his people. They bring the Word to others, in their sermons and in private confession and absolution, in the sacraments, in pastoral counseling and common conversation. They bring the pleas of their people to God in public prayer and praise and in their private praying for their people.

The "holiness" of the "holy ministry" consists therefore in the holiness of God's Word, for the public ministry is totally bound up with that Word and inseparable from it. The office carries with it no special merit independent of the Word, no ontological blessing that works apart from the Word.

Aspiring to the Office of Public Ministry

God has carefully designed the structures of human life. He has given different people different gifts, talents, and opportunities, to serve him in home, occupation, community, and congregation. He wants to fit the right people for the right tasks. He has described the characteristics and abilities that make for proper pastoral leadership in 1 Tim. 3:1–7 and Titus 1:5–9. Pastors should be above reproach. Their family life must be an example for their people, and they must display temperance, common sense, dignity, hospitality, gentleness, and self-control. They must be able to teach effectively and to refute those who oppose the faith. Their lives dare not be marred by drunkenness and violence of temper or fist. They must not be greedy and preoccupied with money. They should not be recent converts, lest they seek the office for other reasons than service. They must be respected in the community.

In two passages Paul indicated that it is contrary to God's will for women to fill the pastoral office (1 Cor. 14:34–35; 1 Tim. 2:11–12). It is clear that Paul did not object to women praying and prophesying in public (1 Cor. 11:5), but he commanded their silence in the public worship service. In some Protestant churches within the context of Western culture in the past century and a half, some have argued that Paul's restriction of the pastoral office to men was culturally conditioned and therefore no longer applicable to the contemporary church. Few disagree on the intention of the texts in 1 Corinthians and 1 Timothy; they disagree only with the continued application of this command in a different cultural context. The cultural argument cuts both ways. If only cultural conditions determined Paul's prohibition in the first century, it is just as possible that only contemporary cultural conditions obscure the view of modern Christians from seeing God's order in this distinction in his arrangement for the pastoral office.

Ordination and Call

The church has found pastors and other called ministers for its congregations and other institutions within it in various ways. The apostles and their colleagues appointed leaders for the church themselves (Titus 1:5). Episcopal, presbyterian, and congregational forms of church government have created various means for placing leaders in called positions. The earliest Lutherans followed medieval custom and altered it little. Local nobles or town councils often nominated pastors, who were examined by neighboring pastors and the congregation, and then the single candidate was ratified by the congregation. The Scriptures command no particular form for choosing the servants called to the public ministry of the church.

Congregational calling of pastors and others who assist them in the public ministry has the advantage of placing this responsibility among the people whom they will serve. Congregations—or other agencies within the organized church—call fellow members of Christ's body to the pastoral office or to other offices within the church. They extend such calls as servants of God. God calls through the church. Thus, the congregation or other institution of the church does not "hire"—nor "fire"—its servants. God gives the church these public servants through the call. Therefore, the public ministers of the Word owe their responsibility to God. Their responsibility is defined by his call, and it is defined as service to God's people, serving up the Word for their salvation.

When the public ministers of the church fail to do that well, the people of God are called to admonish them and to help them repent and correct their failures. When the people of God fail to live as his children, God calls upon the public ministers whom he has given to the church for its edification to call his children to repentance. The Word remains the Lord's; the calling remains the Lord's. Neither the Word nor the calling dare ever become subject to the whim of the people or of the pastor. Both Word and calling are gifts from God to his people. The people of the congregation may abuse the responsibility of calling their own pastors by filling the public ministry with those who tickle their ears rather than serve the Word of the Lord to them effectively. Nonetheless, God can and does work through congregations to insure the effective proclamation of his Word. The call process does not work by magic. God guides congregations and other calling agencies within the church through more and better information just as effectively as he might guide them without such information about candidates for the church's call.

God calls individuals into every responsibility of human life. He also calls people into the public ministry. There is no magical process by which he does so. As Lord of his creation, he works through natural means to interest individuals in serving the church and him through an office in the public ministry. He aids certain believers in perceiving that his will for their lives can be fulfilled through public service in the church. This "personal call" brings with it both a sense of the burden of proclaiming God's Word and the exhilaration and joy that such service brings with it. This personal call is distinct from the public calling of the church. The church's call confirms the personal call.

Since apostolic times the church has "ordained" its pastors. Fellow pastors "laid hands" upon candidates for the public ministry to give them the gift of their calling to serve the Word to the church (1 Tim. 4:14; 5:22). No command from God instituted ordination. It serves as a means by which the church publicly designates those whom it has called as its public servants.

This rite orders the public ministry in two senses. God orders— or calls—the pastor to the tasks of proclaiming the Word and administering the sacraments, along with attendant responsibilities. In a decently ordered fashion the rites of ordination and of commissioning and installation make it clear that God takes special care of the proclamation of his saving Word in his people's midst. In this rite God reasserts his claim on the office. He is giving it to the church. It and its exercise belong to him. With this public rite God makes it clear that pastors are responsible to him, to serve his people for him. This public rite also reminds pastor and people that the public ministry operates in public, before the world. The church does not hide its message from the world but shares it gladly and freely.[4]

Ordination carries God's priests into a public responsibility. It marks those whom he has called into this responsibility before the church and the world as specially designated servants of the Lord and his church. God risks all sorts of human abuse of his Word as he places it into our hands, as priests but particularly as public ministers of his mysteries. His ministers have frequently used their public office for their own ends and not for his. Nonetheless, he has taken the risk. He refuses to operate his church without the public ministry. In the rite of ordination he confirms that for the church in regard to the individual being ordained and in regard to the public office itself.

Believers have argued over the nature of the public ministry. Some have argued that it is simply a public exercise of the functions all Christians are given, so things may be done decently and in order. This "functionalism" fails to recognize sufficiently that God has given the public office of the ministry of the Word to the church as a special gift for dispensing his Word. Without this gift the Word can easily disappear into a swamp of cultural relativism (although only the Gospel itself, not even the public ministry, can guarantee the continued faithful use of the Gospel). Other believers have viewed the public ministry from an "ontological" point of view, as if ordination bestows upon pastors an "indelible character," or as if the office itself, once conferred, carries some status before God apart from its function. This point of view fails to recognize that God's kingdom comes not through some magical bestowal of power upon persons but only through the power of the Word itself, as it is conveyed in oral, written, and sacramental form in the midst of God's people.

When believers are asked how important the pastor really is, they will ask why the question is being posed. If the person asking is seeking some magical security in a holy priest figure, then the focus of our answer must be on the Word of God and upon the Lord himself. Yet the believer's pastor is of great importance. The pastor formally conveys the forgiveness of sins (which all can convey in behalf of the Lord and the congregation). That ministry is a particularly precious gift of God.

Therefore, the Word, which God gives to both pastors and people, rules in his church. The Word determines what is right and proper in the life of the church. The whim or will of neither congregation nor public ministers does so. From this Word both pastors and people receive life and calling, as God's priests and, for some, as his public ministers. And the Word of the Lord shall remain forever.

Notes for Chapter XVII

1. Peter Fraenkel, "Revelation and Tradition: Notes on Some Aspects of Doctrinal Continuity in the Theology of Philip Melanchthon," *Studia Theologica* XIII (1959):97–113.
2. Oscar Cullman, *Peter: Disciple, Apostle, Martyr,* trans. Floyd V. Filson (Cleveland: World, 1953), 223–38.
3. Gerhard O. Forde, *Theology Is for Proclamation* (Minneapolis: Fortress, 1990), 179.
4. Ibid., 180–83.

Chapter XVIII
Last Things and the New Beginning

The wages of sin is death, but the free gift of God is eternal life in Christ Jesus our Lord (Rom. 6:23). The Christian faith takes note of beginnings and ends and new beginnings.

Most human beings want to avoid thoughts of death. Sociologist Ernest Becker has asserted that North American society strives above all else to deny death, for death casts its shadow across all human endeavors.[1] To speak of beginnings also limits human life. Therefore, much of modern Western society has tried to obscure thoughts about human origins, in order to deny the implications of the fact that there was a time when we were not.[2]

The Greek word for "last" has given the church the topic "eschatology," or last things. Traditionally, outlines of Christian teaching have concluded with the topic eschatology. Eschatology treats death and resurrection, God's judgment—and his liberation of his own chosen children from bondage to death.

Dying and Rising

The whole life of a Christian is a life of dying and rising, of repentance.[3] Luther's conviction that repentance permeates human life on this earth reflected his understanding of God's killing and making alive in Baptism. Paul stated that the wages of sin is death in the context of discussing the burial of sinners and their sins in Christ's tomb through Baptism. The apostle gloried in God's gift of eternal life as he discussed the implications of Baptism for daily life since through the sacrament God raises up his people to newness of life in Christ (Rom. 6:3–11).

Baptism is a rehearsal for Judgment Day. In Baptism God "preenacts" his judgment upon sinners, and the judgment is executed as they are joined to Christ's death. Baptism is a repetition of the Sixth Day. In Baptism God reenacts his original creation of human creatures living in faithful harmony with him; by being joined to Christ's resurrection the new creatures are raised up to live with him, to live his style of living.

God is the Author of Life. Turning our backs on God causes death. He had made that clear from the beginning (Gen. 2:17; 3:19). Death entered the world through sin (Rom. 5:12). God did not let loose an uncontrollable enemy when death entered human existence; he remains Lord over death even though he is the Lord of life (2 Kings 20:1–6; Ps. 90:3; Job 14:5; Heb. 9:27). God does not, however, want his human creatures to die. Death remains the enemy of God and his human creatures. Sin pays its wages to those who have tried to live apart from the Author of Life (Rom. 6:23; 5:12; 1 Cor. 15:56).

In his goodness and mercy God has turned this final enemy into the pathway to life. Baptismal death has led to baptismal life in Christ (Rom. 6:3–11; Col. 2:11–15). Earthly death leads to completed life with God in heaven (1 Cor. 15:51–57; Phil. 1:23), for Christ has cleared the way for his people through the tomb into life that never ends (Heb. 2:14–15; 1 Cor. 15:20–26; Heb. 2:8–11; 12:2).

The Day of the Lord:
The Day of Judgment and Liberation

Human History Is Linear

The final dying and rising of God's children will take place when death is done to death for this realm of existence as Christ returns to judge sinners and to liberate his people. This Day of Judgment and Liberation will end this sphere of existence.

Human cultures have held various views of how human history takes its course. Some ancient cultures saw in the revolution of the sun and the turning and returning of the seasons a pattern for all human history. They defined the course of human history as cyclical. It had no—meaningful—beginning, for some belief systems no beginning at all. Matter was viewed as eternal, and human history as revolving in a circle without beginning or end. The evolutionary dogma of much of contemporary Western culture senses only vague beginnings and limitless futures for human development.

In the beginning God created the heavens and the earth. At the end he shall consummate his creation by gathering all things under his final control as he defeats every rule, authority, and power (1 Cor. 15:20–28). The biblical view of history defines it as linear.[4] Human history began when God created the human creature, Adam and Eve. Human history shall end when Christ returns to judge and to liberate (Matt. 25:31–46). He shall close this age or realm of existence by judging those who have not been brought to faith in him—and thus not been given true human life in him—and by liberating those whom he has made his own people. Those whose lives did not reflect his love will go away into eternal punishment; those whose lives did reflect this love will be taken into eternal life (Matt. 25:46).

Life after Death

Hell exists. There can be no doubt that there is a continued existence apart from the Author of Life after Judgment. Christ described this as weeping and wailing and gnashing of teeth (e.g., Matt. 13:41–42; 25:30); and as never-ending fire or wrathful destruction (Matt. 5:22; 18:8; 25:46; Mark 9:43; cf. Jude 13; Rev. 14:11); it is hell. God will inflict judgment upon those who do not know him and who have not listened to the Gospel of Jesus (John 3:18, 36). They will suffer the punishment of eternal destruction and exclusion from the presence of the Lord and the glory of his might (2 Thess. 1:5–10). There is but one name through which people come to the Father, and those who do not trust in Jesus Christ, the name through which God has revealed himself in crib and cross and crypt, do not have access to God (Acts 4:12; John 14:6).

Heaven is beyond description even though John tried (Rev. 19–21); it fulfills our humanity because there our relationship with God is restored to Edenic fullness and perfection. Yet care should be taken that heaven not be overemphasized. "Heaven" can be an essentially selfish concern, the expression of a desire for self-gratification. "Heaven" is not the important matter for God's children. God is.

Life with God begins, perhaps a bit tattered and torn in our experience, when he claims us for life in Baptism. Heaven would not be heaven without God. We must focus our faith and attention on our Lord. At the same time we dare not underemphasize heaven. Life at best in the earthly realm of existence is tattered and torn, at worst much worse than merely tattered and torn. People plagued by evil need to hear the promise of life beyond its pale shadow under sin.

Most people, even in the midst of sin, do believe that heaven can wait. They fear the unknown on the other side of death—with good reason when they face it apart from faith in Christ, of course. The practical, day-to-day religious concerns of Christians and non-Christians alike focus much more on what God can do for them in the midst of daily life rather than his promises for life after death. But ultimately life apart from those promises does not make sense. God is the center of the biblical message; heaven is not. The Scriptures discuss life with God on every page; they relatively seldom mention life after death. Nonetheless, heaven is the destination which God promises to his people. It dare not be ignored in Christian teaching.

As they think about death, and life eternal, even believers often experience fear and dread. That happens for several reasons. We hate to leave our loved ones. We love God's gracious presence and rich blessings in this life. We sense how unnatural and wrong death is, perhaps more clearly than those who do not have a biblical understanding of the potential for good human living. Among the saddest expressions sin has forced upon us is that which claims, "What a blessing she could die!" Death can be called a "blessing" only because life has been so wrecked and ruined. Death remains a curse even when it frees from sorrow and pain. Furthermore, believers will fear death because they do not like the pain we often associate with it. They will also be plagued with doubts, particularly as Satan focuses their attention on their own sins in those moments of reviewing their lives as death approaches. Therefore, even believers need consolation and support from fellow believers as death approaches and heaven looms on the horizon.

Realized Eschatology and Future Eschatology

Christians have debated what the biblical concept of "the Day of the Lord" or the End Times means. Some have proposed that the

End Time is that Judgment and Liberation Day that will come as the last moment of this age and realm of existence, the end of earthly time. Others have insisted that the Day of the Lord began with the incarnation of our God, with Christ's passion, death, and resurrection, with Pentecost. The former view is called "future eschatology," the latter "realized eschatology." There is biblical material to support both views, and the two can be complementary.

Realized eschatology. Realized eschatology celebrates God's fulfilling of Old Testament eschatological hopes through the defeat of all that threatens his people, above all death, in Jesus Christ (Col. 2:11–15; 1 Cor. 15:55–57; 1 John 3:8). God's rule has been established through Christ's death and resurrection. Believers receive new life decisively as a result of his death and resurrection in their Baptisms (Rom. 6:3–11; Col. 2:11–15; Titus 3:3–6). When God's creative and re-creative Word expressed itself in Jesus, he had said it all (Acts 4:12; 1 Cor. 2:2; Heb. 1:1–4). As the Holy Spirit fell upon the disciples at Pentecost, Peter acknowledged that the Day of the Lord, of which Joel had spoken (2:28–32), had begun (Acts 2:16–36). From now on, God is only mopping up after the victory has been insured.[5] Christ's presence has established God's rule in the midst of his people (Luke 17:20–21; Col. 1:13–14). The day of salvation is already at hand (2 Cor. 6:1–2). The end of this age has come (1 Cor. 10:11).

And yet, even though God's rule has established itself *already,* it is *not yet* complete and full for his children who still live with sinful selves in the midst of a sinful world. The "already" of realized eschatology requires the complement of the "not yet" of future eschatology. There is more to come.

Future eschatology. Future eschatology focuses on the final day of Christ's coming. A Greek word for "coming," *parousia,* is sometimes used as a term for his return to conclude this earthly sphere of existence. God has fixed such a day for this Parousia (Acts 17:31). Jesus Christ will appear to execute his final acts of judgment and liberation. He shall appear again to save those who are eagerly waiting for him (Heb. 9:28; cf. Matt. 24:29–31; Acts 1:11; 1 Thess. 4:16–18). Because this day of termination for earthly existence is unknown (Mark 13:32; 1 Thess. 5:1–6)—and because the hour of our own death is not known—believers always live in anticipation of the Lord's return and of his call to us personally (Matt. 24:36–51; Acts 1:11). He will come in glory as he comes to judge and liberate

(Matt. 24:30–31; 25:31–46; John 5:25–29; Acts 10:42; Rom. 2:16).

Apocalyptic Literature. Signs point to his coming, Jesus also promised. Jews had become accustomed to thinking of God's judgment upon their enemies and his liberation of his own people in terms described by a specific literary genre. This genre, called "apocalyptic," used pictures and metaphors to rehearse God's power and might exercised against his people's foes in their behalf.[6] These pictures drew all of the created order and all political forces into their orbit. Jesus used this kind of language to which his contemporaries were accustomed in describing his ongoing and his final triumph over all those hostile to his own people. His disciples asked him what sort of sign would point them to "the close of the age." Jesus' answer was more ambiguous than most Christians have since recognized.

Without asking them why they wanted to know, Jesus directed his disciples to what is really important, no matter how close the Final Day of the Lord is. "Watch out that no one deceives you" (Matt. 24:3–4). He noted that wars and rumors of war may seem to point to the End, "such things must happen, but the end is still to come" (Matt. 24:6). Nations rising against nation, famines, earthquakes, and the like are "but the beginning of birth pains" (Matt. 24:8). There will be persecutions throughout the days in which the Gospel extends itself into the corners of the world. But no sign should command the attention of Christ's people; he should (Luke 17:22–37). Finally, in the midst of such persecution of God's people, the only sign that matters will appear: the Son of Man will return (Matt. 24:30). He is the only sign to which we should pay attention. Repent today, do not speculate about tomorrow. That is his message for those who want to know where the world is going and when it will end.

The Antichrist. Among the most important signs of God's approaching termination of this realm of existence for Lutherans has been the appearance and activity of "the Antichrist." John spoke of "many antichrists" who had arisen in his own day. He defined their doctrine as the denial of Jesus' messianic nature and the denial of the Father and the Son (1 John 2:18, 22–24), or simply the failure to confess Jesus (1 John 4:3). Medieval Christians anticipated an Antichrist, occasionally identifying this figure with a particular pope.

Because the papacy as an institution persecuted the Gospel and claimed to be the authoritative representative or vicar of Christ on earth, Lutherans identified the institution—though not its individual occupants—as the "man of sin" spoken of in 2 Thess. 2:3–12. Thus, they labeled the papacy "the Antichrist." The papacy had claimed by divine right supremacy over all Christendom, as Christ's vicar; it claimed by divine right to be obliged to regulate all secular affairs on earth; it claimed that salvation depended upon the believer's acknowledging the papacy as the vicar of Christ. The early Lutherans believed that this was that self-exaltation, that claim to be God, of which Paul had spoken (2 Thess. 2:4).[7] The continued accuracy of this assessment of the papacy depends on whether the characteristics of the institutional papacy correspond to the description given in this passage.

Millennialism

Speculation about our future always allures. We seek security in pinning down the final Day of the Lord. Particularly at times of crisis in society or church, some Christians have indulged in trying to chart the details of the future, when Christ will liberate his people and give their enemies what is coming to them.[8]

Premillennialism arose already in the early church. Its adherents taught that Christ would return after a period of "tribulation," in which believers would experience severe persecution, such as the early Christians often experienced. Christ would come, they believed, to convert all Jews in an instantaneous display of his power; he would kill the Antichrist, bind the devil, and establish his own kingdom on earth for a thousand years. In that kingdom dead believers would be raised to rule with Christ upon the earth. At the end of the thousand years a final battle against Satan would take place. Following his defeat dead unbelievers would be raised, and all humankind would be judged.

Postmillennialism arose in the Enlightenment, when some Christians fashioned a similar belief that Christ would appear after a thousand-year period, in which his indirect rule would bring prosperity and peace. Postmillennialists believe that evil will beat a slower retreat than is envisioned by premillennialists, but that Christian values will reign in the world for a thousand years before the end.

Dispensational premillennialism has commanded much attention in the nineteenth and twentieth centuries. The product of an English preacher, John Nelson Darby, it has taken several forms as its interpreters have tried to chart the last times as precisely as they find possible. Most "Dispensationalists" teach that God has divided his interaction with his human creatures into seven "dispensations" as his revelation of himself and his mode of governing his people moves from the Innocence of the Garden of Eden through periods of Promise and Law and Church. The Millennial Kingdom lies before us, according to their understanding. Dispensationalists disagree on how the Millennial Kingdom will be inaugurated. They do teach that God will take the most faithful of his people away from the "time of tribulation" through a "rapture," or sudden, direct removal from this earth. They will remain with him in heaven during this time of "great tribulation" and will return with him to establish a thousand-year kingdom on earth. Because some of those who are converted at Christ's return will have unbelieving descendants, there will be one last "little season" for Satan to stage his last revolt against God before the final judgment.

Millennial doctrine is without biblical foundation in spite of the massive biblical citation that often backs its claims. It misinterprets biblical words such as *rapture* and concepts such as the thousand-year reign of Christ. It attempts to interpret literally what the biblical writers expressed in a nonliteral genre, the genre of *apocalyptic.* In doing so millennial interpreters actually tear the biblical word from its intended meaning in the context in which it was used by writers from Ezekiel through Daniel to John in his book of Revelation (Apocalypse). These writers used this genre, as did a host of other Jewish authors during the intertestamental period. All apocalyptic writings—biblical and nonbiblical—are typified by a complex network of symbols that represent forces in the struggle between God and Satan, as Satan oppresses the people of God. The purpose of such writing was always to announce the hope of God's people for the final triumph of God over every evil.

When modern readers try to impose a literal interpretation on Daniel's visions or the book of Revelation, its mysterious code language inevitably confuses and distracts them. To read these books accurately and with profit, we must learn the nature of this literary genre. This genre vanished at the time of the early church, and practiced interpreters of it vanished with the passing of its common use.

God keeps his secret regarding his governance of history and his plans for the End Time. Satan sends believers on wild goose chases when they approach Daniel or John without having the tools necessary to study this kind of literature. To interpret apocalyptic sections of the gospels or Ezekiel, or the books of Daniel and Revelation, literally is comparable to a person in the twenty-second century picking up J. R. R. Tolkien's stories of hobbits and believing that hobbits once actually existed. We know that Tolkien used another literary form than historical reporting. In a similar way Ezekiel and Daniel, Jesus and John were using another form of discourse than literal description when they used this genre that was so familiar to the Jews of their time and so unfamiliar to modern Western people. We do know enough about the way in which apocalyptic writers used symbols to determine what these apocalyptic texts meant for their day and what they can mean for ours. We are not left to the speculation of our contemporaries who want to twist biblical words to their own fancies if we are willing to invest in the study of the text itself.

Two attendant dangers of millennial doctrine should be noted even though not all millennialists fall into these traps. Throughout the history of the church some have been tempted to abandon the exercise of callings for the care of those around them when they believed the Parousia was near. This problem recurs when people focus on waiting for the Lord by looking to the heavens. We wait for the Lord in the midst of our callings to daily service to his world and his people, not by laying these callings aside.

Furthermore, millennialism can slip into a theology of glory, which delights in vengeance upon enemies rather than rejoices in the deliverance God gives to his own children. On this earth Christ has promised a cross to his followers (Matt. 16:24), not some kind of temporal triumph. The triumph of the resurrection gives us new life in the midst of tribulation, not in escape from it, until the final Day of the Lord when we are raised beyond death for the full life of peace with God.

The Resurrection of the Body and the Life Everlasting

In a moment, in the twinkling of an eye, at the last trumpet the dead will be raised and never perish again. We shall be changed (1 Cor. 15:52). Paul conveyed God's promise that the victory over death—and over the sin that created death—belongs to those who are joined together with the Lord Jesus Christ (1 Cor. 15:57).

Belief in the resurrection of the human body and life everlasting as a human creature was a rare commodity in Paul's time—and in most periods of human history. Neoplatonic systems of thought taught a life after death, but on a radically different basis than Paul presented, above all, in 1 Corinthians 15. Neoplatonists believed in the immortality of the soul. Many of them believed that the soul is immortal because it is a piece of the eternal Spirit. That meant that the individual human soul had an absolute right to its own existence; it was indestructible by right and nature. Many Gnostic systems of thought at the time of Paul also believed that the salvation or completion of the soul's existence would take place in its return to the essential unity of the one Spirit. That meant a contempt for individuality. Alongside this deprecation of individuality these Gnostics taught that the material was evil, and that the human body would have to be sloughed off to regain perfection. To be saved in such systems of thought meant to lose one's individuality as well as one's material baggage.

The Old Testament writers all believed that the "spirit" or "being" [the Hebrew word *nephesh* is often translated "soul"] that God created by breathing into the dust (Gen. 2:7) is a creature of God. The biblical writers could not conceive of this spirit or soul apart from its body. They did not believe that the soul had no beginning, nor was it for them a part of an eternal Spirit. It is the product of God's creative breath and Word. Ezekiel, for instance, also knew that this *nephesh*—soul or spirit or being—could die because of sin (Ezek. 18:4). The biblical writers treasured the integrity of the individual human creature (although none of them could conceive of an individual human creature apart from community with God and with other human creatures [Gen. 2:18]). The biblical writers recognized that human creatures were fashioned for communion with God as human creatures. No higher aspirations could be possible for the crown of God's creation.

Against the contempt for the material aspect of our humanity and our integrity as particular, individual creatures of God Paul wrote 1 Corinthians 15. He defined eternal life for God's human creatures in terms of the resurrection of the human body of each individual believer. He staked the promise of life without end upon Christ's resurrection from the dead. It makes no sense to speak of Christ's resurrection if we abandon hope of our own resurrection, just as we have no hope of our own resurrection if Christ did not rise (1 Cor. 15:12–19). Christ retraced the steps of sinners into the grave so that he might become the firstfruits of God's re-creation of human life through his resurrection. The victory of his resurrection has placed not only death but also all other enemies of God under him (1 Cor. 15:20–28).

How did Christ attain the victory? Paul compared the principle to the planting and sprouting of a seed. A seed must be buried to come alive and fulfill its potential. Likewise, the sinful person must be buried to be given new life (1 Cor. 15:35–50). Paul struggled to express the mystery of the transformation from a perishable body to an imperishable body, a mortal body to a body that death can touch never again. He spoke of the contrast between a physical body and a spiritual body (a contradiction in terms if interpreted literally). Throughout he insisted on two fundamental points, in his opposition to Gnosticism. We remain bodies. Our humanity, expressed in our physical bodies, shall be transformed but shall remain bodily and thus human. Second, we shall therefore remain individuals. Salvation is not absorption of our souls into an "ultimate soul" or spirit in which individual identity and integrity vanishes as we lose our bodies. Salvation is the resurrection of our own body, for life with God forever. In this way death is swallowed up in victory (1 Cor. 15:54–57).

The Lord Jesus Christ will transform the tattered and torn body, with all its signs of the oppression of sin and disease, into the glorious body in which we will live forever with Christ (Phil. 3:21). All that means, Paul concluded, is that on a daily basis believers should be going about the work of the Lord in a steadfast, unshakable way. The resurrection of the body calls forth service in vocation today.

The heavenly realm is different from the creation as we experience it, but the biblical writers do describe it in terms that affirm the goodness of the material order. It is a new creation (2 Peter 3:13; Rev. 21:1), but also the liberation or restoration of this order of existence (Rom. 8:19–23), as God had originally designed it.

Indeed, the day has already come when God's children can say, "I will praise you, O Lord. Although you were angry with me, your anger has turned away and you have comforted me. Surely God is my salvation; I will trust and not be afraid. For the Lord, the Lord, is my strength and my song; he has become my salvation." With joy we draw upon the baptismal water that is the well of our salvation, and we give thanks to the Lord. We call upon his name. We make known his deeds among the peoples of the earth, and we proclaim his exalted name. We shout and sing for joy because the Lord who has done wondrous things is with us (Is. 12:1–6).

We continue to be his people, and he continues to be our God, in the life that began with our baptismal death as sinners and in our baptismal resurrection to new life in Christ. In this life we shall live, finding our identity, security, and meaning through trust in God alone, who has come near to us in Jesus Christ and remains with us forever.

Notes for Chapter XVIII

1. Ernest Becker, *The Denial of Death* (New York: Free Press, 1973).
2. Dietrich Bonhoeffer, *Creation and Fall: A Theological Interpretation of Genesis 1–3, Temptation* (New York: Macmillan, 1959), 13.
3. Martin Luther, "Ninety-Five Theses, or Disputation on the Power and Efficacy of Indulgences, 1517," *Career of the Reformer: I,* Luther's Works, vol. 31, (Philadelphia: Fortress, 1957), 25.
4. Oscar Cullmann, *Christ and Time: The Primitive Christian Conception of Time and History,* trans. Floyd V. Filson (London: SCM, 1962); and *Salvation in History* (New York: Harper & Row, 1967) summarizes this viewpoint.
5. Cullmann, *Christ and Time,* xix, 39–40, 141–45.
6. D. S. Russell, *The Method and Message of Jewish Apocalyptic* (London: SCM Press, 1964).
7. Treatise on the Power and Primacy of the Pope, *The Book of Concord,* trans. and ed. Theodore G. Tappert (Philadelphia: Fortress, 1959), 320–35.
8. Summaries of the basic approaches to millennialism are offered in Robert G. Clouse, ed., *The Meaning of the Millennium: Four Views* (Downers Grove: InterVarsity, 1977).